FrontPage® 2002

in an *instant*

Visual™

From
maranGraphics®

&

Hungry Minds™

Best-Selling Books • Digital Downloads • e-books • Answer Networks •
e-Newsletters • Branded Web Sites • e-learning

New York, NY ♦ Cleveland, OH ♦ Indianapolis, IN

FrontPage® 2002 In an Instant

Published by
Hungry Minds, Inc.
909 Third Avenue
New York, NY 10022
www.hungryminds.com

Copyright© 2001 by maranGraphics Inc.
5755 Coopers Avenue
Mississauga, Ontario, Canada
L4Z 1R9

Library of Congress Control Number: 2001091976

ISBN: 0-7645-3626-5

Printed in the United States of America

10 9 8 7 6 5 4 3 2 1

1B/QS/QY/QR/MG

Distributed in the United States by Hungry Minds, Inc.
Distributed by CDG Books Canada Inc. for Canada; by Transworld Publishers Limited in the United Kingdom; by IDG Norge Books for Norway; by IDG Sweden Books for Sweden; by IDG Books Australia Publishing Corporation Pty. Ltd. for Australia and New Zealand; by TransQuest Publishers Pte Ltd. for Singapore, Malaysia, Thailand, Indonesia, and Hong Kong; by Gotop Information Inc. for Taiwan; by ICG Muse, Inc. for Japan; by Intersoft for South Africa; by Eyrolles for France; by International Thomson Publishing for Germany, Austria and Switzerland; by Distribuidora Cuspide for Argentina; by LR International for Brazil; by Galileo Libros for Chile; by Ediciones ZETA S.C.R. Ltda. for Peru; by WS Computer Publishing Corporation, Inc. for the Philippines; by Contemporanea de Ediciones for Venezuela; by Express Computer Distributors for the Caribbean and West Indies; by Micronesia Media Distributor, Inc. for Micronesia; by Chips Computadoras S.A. de C.V. for Mexico; by Editorial Norma de Panama S.A. for Panama; by American Bookshops for Finland.
For corporate orders, please call maranGraphics at 800-469-6616 or fax 905-890-9434.
For general information on Hungry Minds' products and services, please contact our Customer Care Department within the U.S. at 800-762-2974, outside the U.S. at 317-572-3993 or fax 317-572-4002.
For sales inquiries and reseller information, including discounts, premium and bulk quantity sales, and foreign-language translations, please contact our Customer Care Department at 800-434-3422, fax 317-572-4002, or write to Hungry Minds, Inc., Attn: Customer Care Department, 10475 Crosspoint Boulevard, Indianapolis, IN 46256.
For information on licensing foreign or domestic rights, please contact our Sub-Rights Customer Care Department at 212-844-5000.
For information on using Hungry Minds' products and services in the classroom or for ordering examination copies, please contact our Educational Sales Department at 800-434-2086 or fax 317-572-4005.
For press review copies, author interviews, or other publicity information, please contact our Public Relations department at 317-572-3168 or fax 317-572-4168.
For authorization to photocopy items for corporate, personal, or educational use, please contact Copyright Clearance Center, 222 Rosewood Drive, Danvers, MA 01923, or fax 978-750-4470.

Trademark Acknowledgments

Permissions

Hungry Minds™ is a trademark of Hungry Minds, Inc.

U.S. Corporate Sales	**U.S. Trade Sales**
Contact maranGraphics at (800) 469-6616 or fax (905) 890-9434.	Contact Hungry Minds at (800) 434-3422 or fax (317) 572-4002.

Some comments from our readers...

"I have to praise you and your company on the fine products you turn out. I have twelve of the *Teach Yourself VISUALLY* and *Simplified* books in my house. They were instrumental in helping me pass a difficult computer course. Thank you for creating books that are easy to follow."
—*Gordon Justin (Brielle, NJ)*

"I commend your efforts and your success. I teach in an outreach program for the Dr. Eugene Clark Library in Lockhart, TX. Your *Teach Yourself VISUALLY* books are incredible and I use them in my computer classes. All my students love them!"
—*Michele Schalin (Lockhart, TX)*

"Thank you so much for helping people like me learn about computers. The Maran family is just what the doctor ordered. Thank you, thank you, thank you."
—*Carol Moten (New Kensington, PA)*

"I would like to take this time to compliment maranGraphics on creating such great books. Thank you for making it clear. Keep up the good work."
—*Kirk Santoro (Burbank, CA)*

"I write to extend my thanks and appreciation for your books. They are clear, easy to follow, and straight to the point. Keep up the good work!"
—*Seward Kollie (Dakar, Senegal)*

"What fantastic teaching books you have produced! Congratulations to you and your staff. You deserve the Nobel prize in Education in the Software category. Thanks for helping me to understand computers."
—*Bruno Tonon (Melbourne, Australia)*

"Over time, I have bought a number of your 'Read Less, Learn More' books. For me, they are THE way to learn anything easily."
—*José A. Mazón (Cuba, NY)*

"I was introduced to maranGraphics about four years ago and YOU ARE THE GREATEST THING THAT EVER HAPPENED TO INTRODUCTORY COMPUTER BOOKS!"
—*Glenn Nettleton (Huntsville, AL)*

"Compliments To The Chef!! Your books are extraordinary! Or, simply put, Extra-Ordinary, meaning way above the rest! THANK YOU THANK YOU THANK YOU! for creating these."
—*Christine J. Manfrin (Castle Rock, CO)*

"I'm a grandma who was pushed by an 11-year-old grandson to join the computer age. I found myself hopelessly confused and frustrated until I discovered the Visual series. I'm no expert by any means now, but I'm a lot further along than I would have been otherwise. Thank you!"
—*Carol Louthain (Logansport, IN)*

"Thank you, thank you, thank you...for making it so easy for me to break into this high-tech world. I now own four of your books. I recommend them to anyone who is a beginner like myself. Now... if you could just do one for programming VCRs, it would make my day!"
—*Gay O'Donnell (Calgary, Alberta, Canada)*

"You're marvelous! I am greatly in your debt."
—*Patrick Baird (Lacey, WA)*

maranGraphics is a family-run business
located near Toronto, Canada.

At *maranGraphics*, we believe in producing great computer books—one book at a time.

Each maranGraphics book uses the award-winning communication process that we have been developing over the last 25 years. Using this process, we organize screen shots and text in a way that makes it easy for you to learn new concepts and tasks.

We spend hours deciding the best way to perform each task, so you don't have to!

Our clear, easy-to-follow screen shots and instructions walk you through each task from beginning to end.

We want to thank you for purchasing what we feel are the best computer books money can buy. We hope you enjoy using this book as much as we enjoyed creating it!

Sincerely,

The Maran Family

Please visit us on the Web at:
www.maran.com

CREDITS

Author:
Ruth Maran

Copy Editors:
Roxanne Van Damme
Stacey Morrison

Project Manager:
Judy Maran

Editing & Screen Captures:
Teri Lynn Pinsent
Luis Lee
Norm Schumacher
Faiza Jagot

Layout & Screen Artists:
Sean Johannesen
Paul Baker
Treena Lees

Indexer:
Stacey Morrison

Permissions Coordinator:
Jennifer Amaral

**Senior Vice President and
Publisher, Hungry Minds
Technology Publishing Group:**
Richard Swadley

**Publishing Director,
Hungry Minds Technology
Publishing Group:**
Barry Pruett

**Editorial Support,
Hungry Minds Technology
Publishing Group:**
Jennifer Dorsey
Sandy Rodrigues
Lindsay Sandman

Post Production:
Robert Maran

ACKNOWLEDGMENTS

Thanks to the dedicated staff of maranGraphics, including
Jennifer Amaral, Roderick Anatalio, Paul Baker, Cathy Benn,
Joel Desamero, Faiza Jagot, Kelleigh Johnson,
Wanda Lawrie, Luis Lee, Treena Lees, Jill Maran, Judy Maran,
Robert Maran, Ruth Maran, Russ Marini, Suzana G. Miokovic,
Stacey Morrison, Teri Lynn Pinsent, Steven Schaerer,
Norm Schumacher, Raquel Scott, Natalie Tweedie,
Roxanne Van Damme and Paul Whitehead.

Finally, to Richard Maran who originated the easy-to-use
graphic format of this guide. Thank you for your
inspiration and guidance.

TABLE OF CONTENTS

TABLE OF CONTENTS

FrontPage allows you to create, edit and format your Web pages. You can also use FrontPage to manage the Web pages in your Web site. When you finish creating your Web pages, FrontPage helps you transfer the pages to a Web server to make the pages available on the Web.

EDIT AND FORMAT TEXT

FrontPage offers many features to help you edit and format text on your Web pages. You can add, delete and re-arrange text as well as check your Web pages for spelling errors. You can enhance information by using various fonts, sizes, styles and colors and apply a theme to instantly give your Web pages a professional look.

ADD IMAGES

You can add images to your Web pages to illustrate concepts or enhance the appearance of your pages. FrontPage includes a large selection of ready-made clip art images, simple shapes and text effects that you can add to your Web pages. FrontPage also offers many ways to customize images, such as adding borders and cropping images.

CREATE LINKS

You can create links to connect a word, phrase or image on a Web page to another Web page. You can also create links that visitors can select to send you an e-mail message. FrontPage can check all the links in your Web site to determine if the links are working properly.

CREATE TABLES

You can create a table to neatly display information on a Web page. Tables are also useful for controlling the placement of text and images on a Web page. FrontPage offers many ready-to-use designs that can instantly enhance the appearance of a table you create.

WORK WITH NAVIGATIONAL STRUCTURE

You can work with the navigational structure of your Web site to define how the pages in your site are related. Once you set up the navigational structure of your Web site, you can add navigation buttons to your Web pages. Navigation buttons are links visitors can select to easily move through the pages in your Web site.

CREATE FRAMES

You can create frames to divide a Web browser window into sections. Each section will display a different Web page. Frames allow you to keep information such as an advertisement or navigational tools on the screen while visitors browse through your Web pages.

CREATE FORMS

Forms allow you to gather information from visitors who view your Web pages. You can create forms that allow visitors to send you questions or comments about your Web pages. You can also create forms that allow visitors to purchase your products and services on the Web.

PUBLISH WEB PAGES

When you finish creating your Web pages, FrontPage helps you transfer the pages to a Web server to make the pages available on the Web. Once your Web pages are stored on a Web server, you can notify friends, family, colleagues and people on the Web about your Web pages.

The World Wide Web is part of the Internet and consists of a huge collection of documents stored on computers around the world. You can obtain a vast amount of information and meet people with similar interests on the World Wide Web. The World Wide Web is commonly known as the Web.

WEB PAGE

A Web page is a document on the Web. Web pages can include text, images, sound and video.

HOME PAGE

A home page is the main Web page in a Web site and is usually the first page people see when they visit a Web site. A home page is usually named index.htm.

WEB SITE

A Web site is a collection of Web pages created and maintained by a college, university, government agency, company, organization or individual.

WEB SERVER

A Web server is a computer that stores Web pages and makes the pages available on the Web for other people to view.

URL

Each Web page has a unique address, called a Uniform Resource Locator (URL). You can display any Web page if you know its URL.

LINKS

Web pages contain links, which are highlighted text or images on a Web page that connect to other pages on the Web. You can select a link to display a Web page located on the same computer or on a computer across the city, country or world. Links allow you to easily navigate through a vast amount of information by jumping from one Web page to another. Links are also known as hyperlinks.

WEB BROWSERS

A Web browser is a program that allows you to view and explore information on the Web. Microsoft Internet Explorer is a popular Web browser that comes with the latest versions of Windows. You can also obtain Internet Explorer at the www.microsoft.com/windows/ie Web page. Netscape Navigator is another popular Web browser that you can obtain at the www.netscape.com Web site or at computer stores.

HTML

HyperText Markup Language (HTML) is a computer language used to create Web pages. Web pages are HTML documents that consist of text and special instructions called tags. A Web browser interprets the tags in an HTML document to determine how to display the Web page. When you create a Web page in FrontPage, the HTML tags are hidden from view.

START FRONTPAGE

You can start FrontPage to create Web pages that you can publish on the Web. FrontPage offers all the features you need to create, edit, manage and publish your Web pages. When you start FrontPage, the last Web site you worked with will open.

START FRONTPAGE

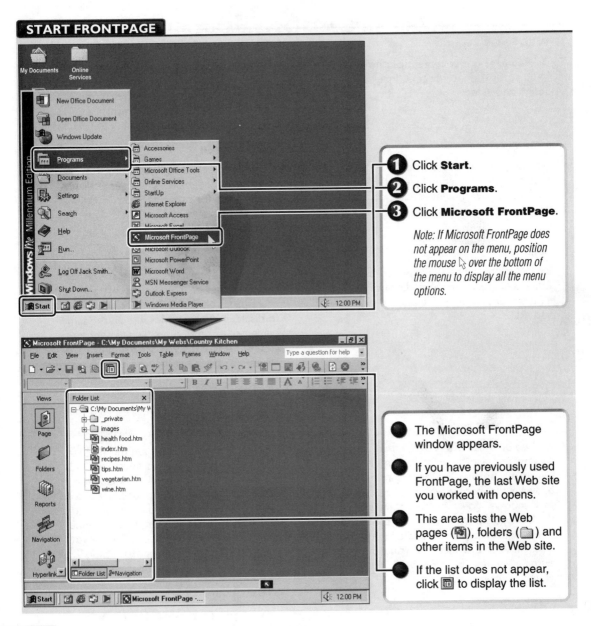

1 Click **Start**.

2 Click **Programs**.

3 Click **Microsoft FrontPage**.

Note: If Microsoft FrontPage does not appear on the menu, position the mouse over the bottom of the menu to display all the menu options.

● The Microsoft FrontPage window appears.

● If you have previously used FrontPage, the last Web site you worked with opens.

● This area lists the Web pages (), folders () and other items in the Web site.

● If the list does not appear, click to display the list.

The FrontPage window displays many items you can use to create and work with your Web site, such as menus, toolbars and scroll bars.

Standard Toolbar

Contains buttons you can use to select common commands, such as Save and Print.

Menu Bar

Provides access to lists of commands available in FrontPage and displays an area where you can type a question to get help information.

Title Bar

Shows the location and name of the displayed Web site.

Web Page Tabs

Each tab displays the file name of an open Web page. The displayed Web page has a white tab.

Formatting Toolbar

Contains buttons you can use to select common formatting commands, such as Bold and Italic.

Views Bar

Provides access to six different views of your Web site.

Folder List

Lists the folders, Web pages and other items in your Web site.

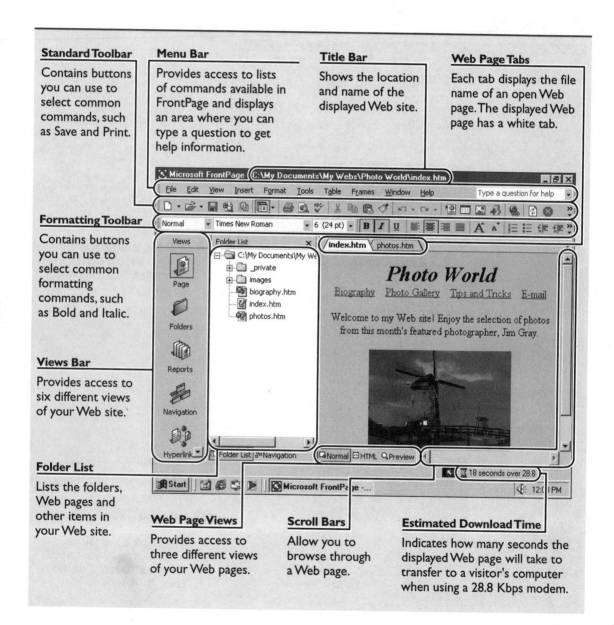

Web Page Views

Provides access to three different views of your Web pages.

Scroll Bars

Allow you to browse through a Web page.

Estimated Download Time

Indicates how many seconds the displayed Web page will take to transfer to a visitor's computer when using a 28.8 Kbps modem.

5

GETTING HELP

If you do not know how to perform a task in FrontPage, you can search for help information on the task. After you specify a task you want to get help information on, FrontPage displays a list of related help topics. You can select a topic of interest to display help information on the topic.

GETTING HELP

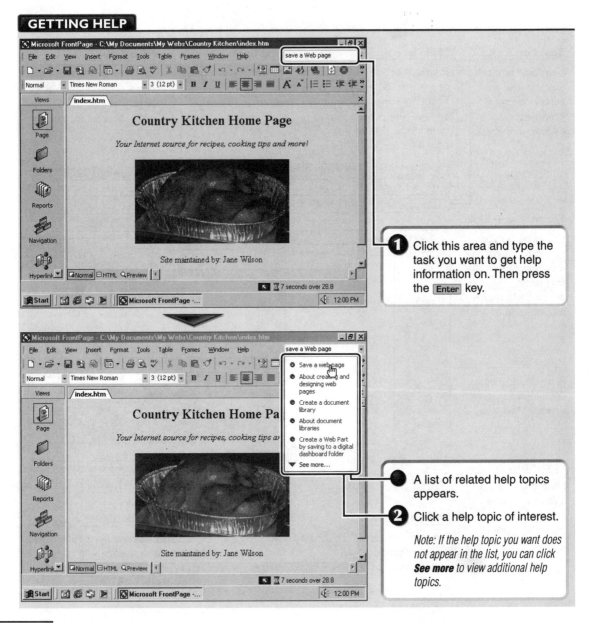

1 Click this area and type the task you want to get help information on. Then press the `Enter` key.

A list of related help topics appears.

2 Click a help topic of interest.

*Note: If the help topic you want does not appear in the list, you can click **See more** to view additional help topics.*

in an instant

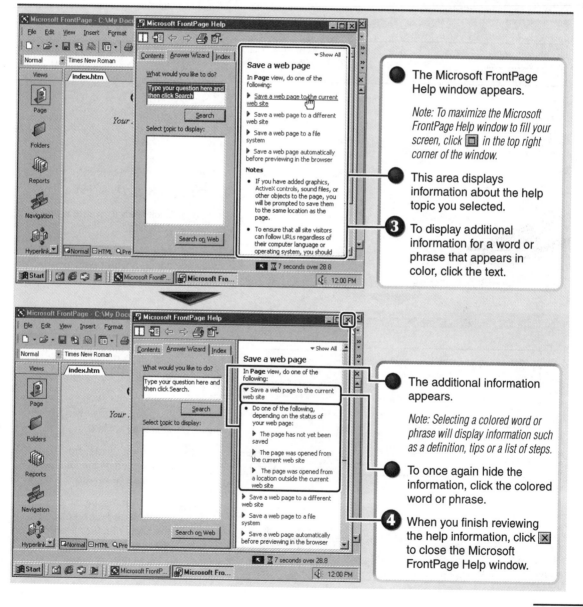

The Microsoft FrontPage Help window appears.

Note: To maximize the Microsoft FrontPage Help window to fill your screen, click □ in the top right corner of the window.

This area displays information about the help topic you selected.

3 To display additional information for a word or phrase that appears in color, click the text.

The additional information appears.

Note: Selecting a colored word or phrase will display information such as a definition, tips or a list of steps.

To once again hide the information, click the colored word or phrase.

4 When you finish reviewing the help information, click ☒ to close the Microsoft FrontPage Help window.

CREATE A NEW WEB SITE

You can use a template or wizard to create a new Web site. A template provides the layout, design and sample text for the Web pages in a Web site. A wizard asks you a series of questions and then uses your answers to create a customized Web site.

CREATE A NEW WEB SITE

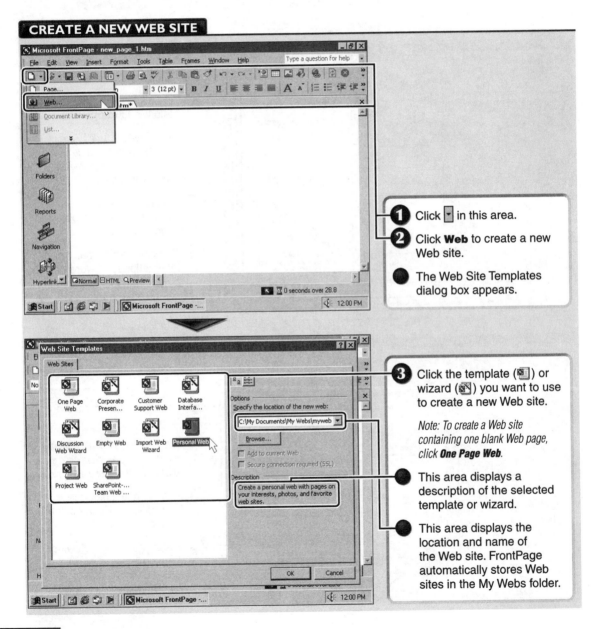

1 Click ▼ in this area.

2 Click **Web** to create a new Web site.

● The Web Site Templates dialog box appears.

3 Click the template (▣) or wizard (▣) you want to use to create a new Web site.

*Note: To create a Web site containing one blank Web page, click **One Page Web**.*

● This area displays a description of the selected template or wizard.

● This area displays the location and name of the Web site. FrontPage automatically stores Web sites in the My Webs folder.

in an instant

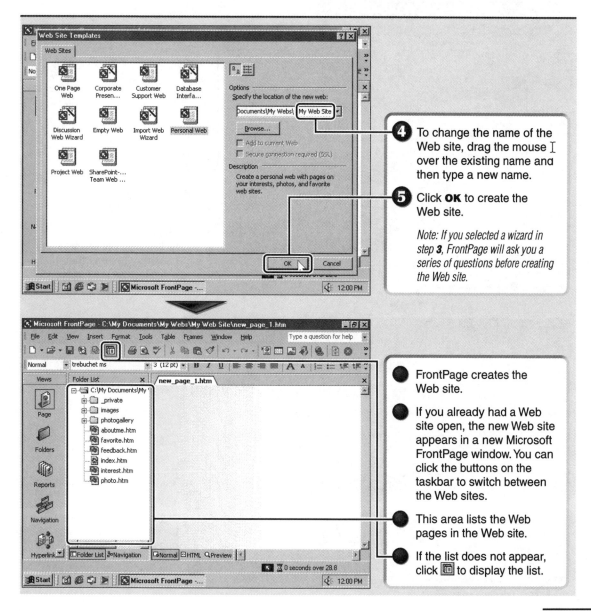

4 To change the name of the Web site, drag the mouse I over the existing name and then type a new name.

5 Click **OK** to create the Web site.

Note: If you selected a wizard in step 3, FrontPage will ask you a series of questions before creating the Web site.

● FrontPage creates the Web site.

● If you already had a Web site open, the new Web site appears in a new Microsoft FrontPage window. You can click the buttons on the taskbar to switch between the Web sites.

● This area lists the Web pages in the Web site.

● If the list does not appear, click 🖻 to display the list.

DISPLAY OR HIDE THE FOLDER LIST

You can display or hide the Folder List, which lists all the Web pages, folders and other items in your Web site. Displaying the Folder List allows you to easily browse through your Web pages. Hiding the Folder List gives you a larger and less cluttered working area.

DISPLAY OR HIDE THE FOLDER LIST

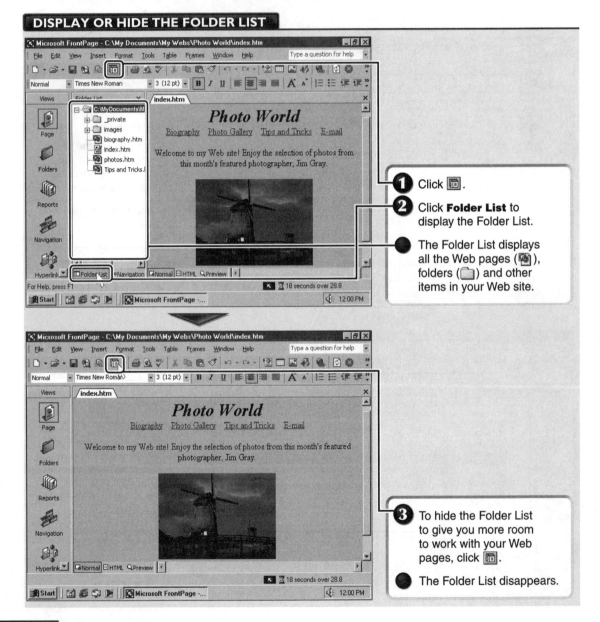

1 Click 🔲.

2 Click **Folder List** to display the Folder List.

● The Folder List displays all the Web pages (📄), folders (📁) and other items in your Web site.

3 To hide the Folder List to give you more room to work with your Web pages, click 🔲.

● The Folder List disappears.

You can display or hide the Navigation pane, which shows the navigational structure of your Web site. The navigational structure of your Web site defines how the Web pages in your Web site are related. For information on working with the navigational structure of your Web site, see pages 138 to 147.

DISPLAY OR HIDE THE NAVIGATION PANE

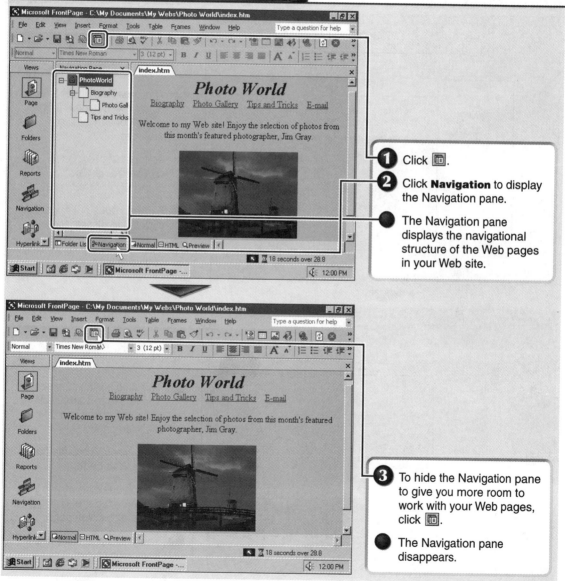

① Click 🖽.

② Click **Navigation** to display the Navigation pane.

● The Navigation pane displays the navigational structure of the Web pages in your Web site.

③ To hide the Navigation pane to give you more room to work with your Web pages, click 🖽.

● The Navigation pane disappears.

OPEN A WEB PAGE

You can open a Web page to view the page on your screen. Opening a Web page allows you to review and make changes to the page. You can have several Web pages in your Web site open at once.

OPEN A WEB PAGE

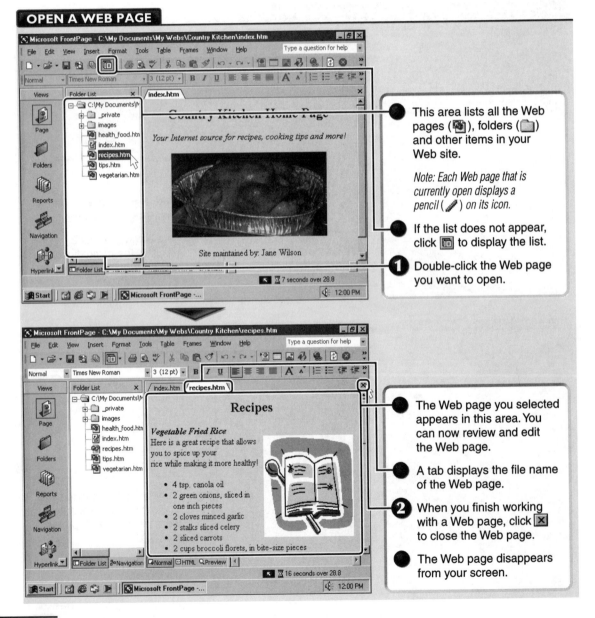

This area lists all the Web pages (), folders () and other items in your Web site.

Note: Each Web page that is currently open displays a pencil (✐) on its icon.

If the list does not appear, click 🗔 to display the list.

1 Double-click the Web page you want to open.

The Web page you selected appears in this area. You can now review and edit the Web page.

A tab displays the file name of the Web page.

2 When you finish working with a Web page, click ☒ to close the Web page.

The Web page disappears from your screen.

You can have several Web pages in your Web site open at once. FrontPage allows you to easily switch from one open Web page to another. Switching between Web pages is useful when you are working on several related Web pages.

SWITCH BETWEEN WEB PAGES

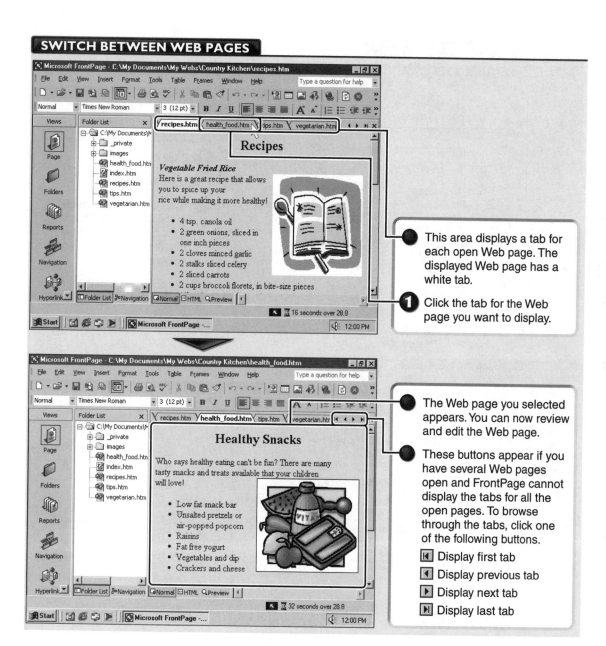

● This area displays a tab for each open Web page. The displayed Web page has a white tab.

1 Click the tab for the Web page you want to display.

● The Web page you selected appears. You can now review and edit the Web page.

● These buttons appear if you have several Web pages open and FrontPage cannot display the tabs for all the open pages. To browse through the tabs, click one of the following buttons.

◄ Display first tab
◄ Display previous tab
► Display next tab
►| Display last tab

DISPLAY OR HIDE A TOOLBAR

FrontPage offers several toolbars that you can display or hide at any time. Toolbars contain buttons that you can select to quickly perform common tasks. When you first start FrontPage, the Standard and Formatting toolbars appear on your screen.

DISPLAY OR HIDE A TOOLBAR

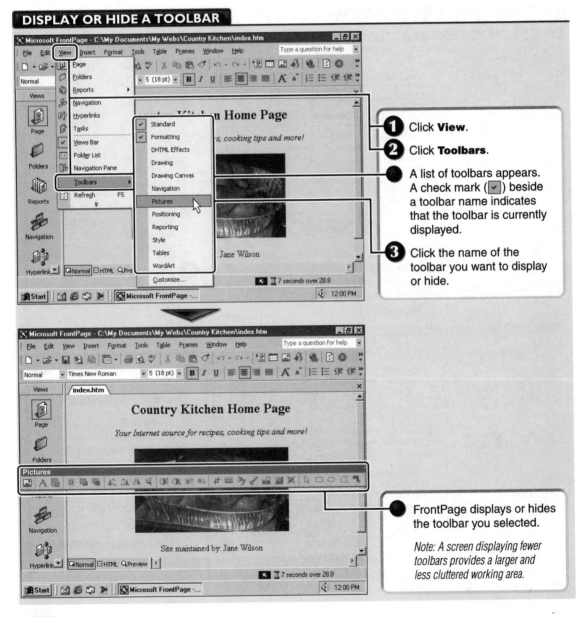

1 Click **View**.

2 Click **Toolbars**.

A list of toolbars appears. A check mark ( ) beside a toolbar name indicates that the toolbar is currently displayed.

3 Click the name of the toolbar you want to display or hide.

FrontPage displays or hides the toolbar you selected.

Note: A screen displaying fewer toolbars provides a larger and less cluttered working area.

You can add a blank Web page to your Web site to provide information about a new topic. FrontPage gives each new Web page a temporary name, such as new_page_1.htm. You can immediately start adding information to a blank Web page that you create.

CREATE A BLANK WEB PAGE

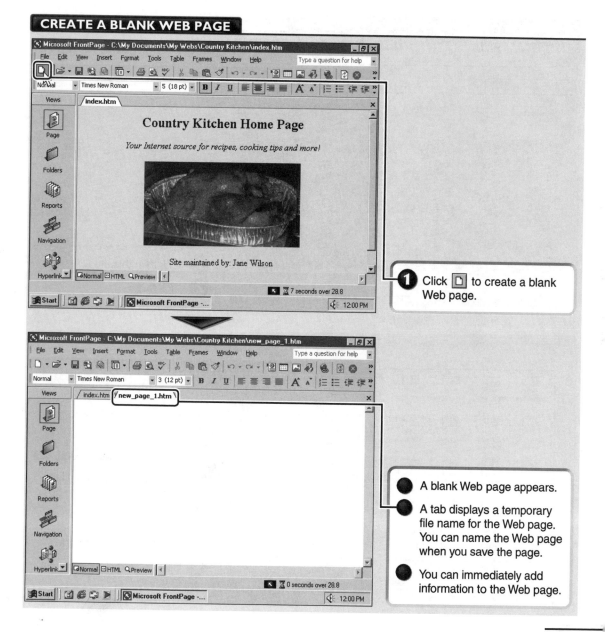

1 Click 🗋 to create a blank Web page.

● A blank Web page appears.

● A tab displays a temporary file name for the Web page. You can name the Web page when you save the page.

● You can immediately add information to the Web page.

CREATE A WEB PAGE USING A TEMPLATE

FrontPage provides several ready-to-use templates that you can choose from to quickly create a new Web page. Templates provide a good starting point for the layout and design of your Web pages. The sample text that templates provide can help you determine what text you should include on a Web page.

CREATE A WEB PAGE USING A TEMPLATE

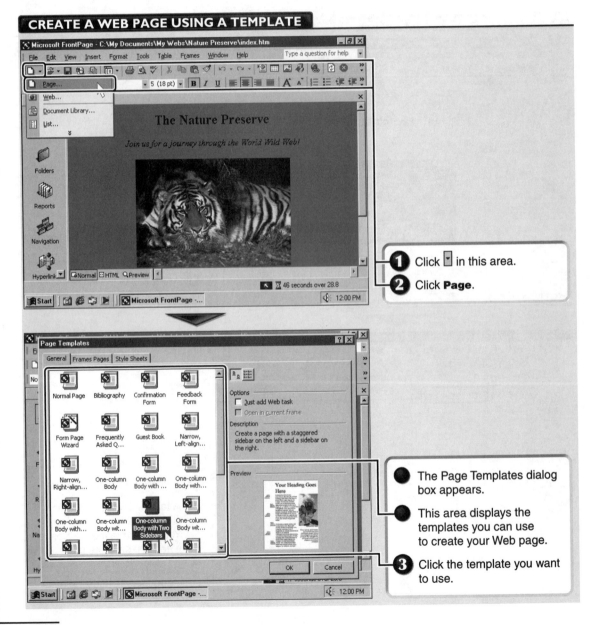

1 Click ▾ in this area.

2 Click **Page**.

● The Page Templates dialog box appears.

● This area displays the templates you can use to create your Web page.

3 Click the template you want to use.

in an *Instant*

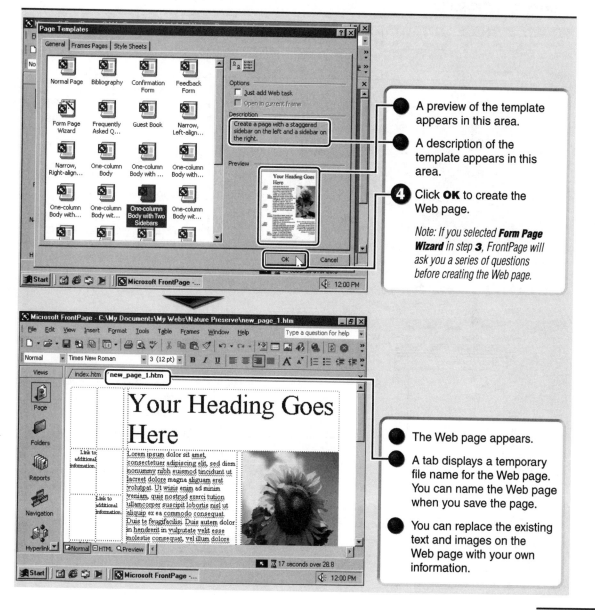

A preview of the template appears in this area.

A description of the template appears in this area.

4 Click **OK** to create the Web page.

*Note: If you selected **Form Page Wizard** in step **3**, FrontPage will ask you a series of questions before creating the Web page.*

The Web page appears.

A tab displays a temporary file name for the Web page. You can name the Web page when you save the page.

You can replace the existing text and images on the Web page with your own information.

SAVE A WEB PAGE

You should save a Web page to store the page for future use. Saving a Web page allows you to later review and edit the page. You should regularly save changes you make to a Web page to avoid losing your work.

SAVE A WEB PAGE

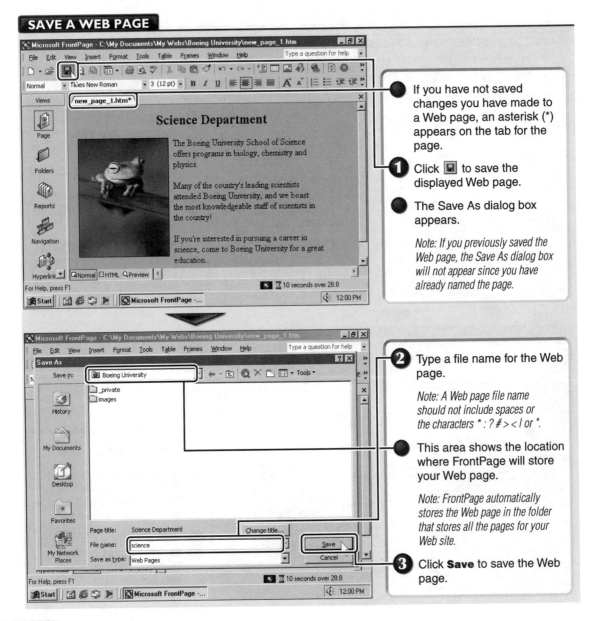

● If you have not saved changes you have made to a Web page, an asterisk (*) appears on the tab for the page.

① Click 🖫 to save the displayed Web page.

● The Save As dialog box appears.

Note: If you previously saved the Web page, the Save As dialog box will not appear since you have already named the page.

② Type a file name for the Web page.

*Note: A Web page file name should not include spaces or the characters * : ? # > < l or ".*

● This area shows the location where FrontPage will store your Web page.

Note: FrontPage automatically stores the Web page in the folder that stores all the pages for your Web site.

③ Click **Save** to save the Web page.

in an instant

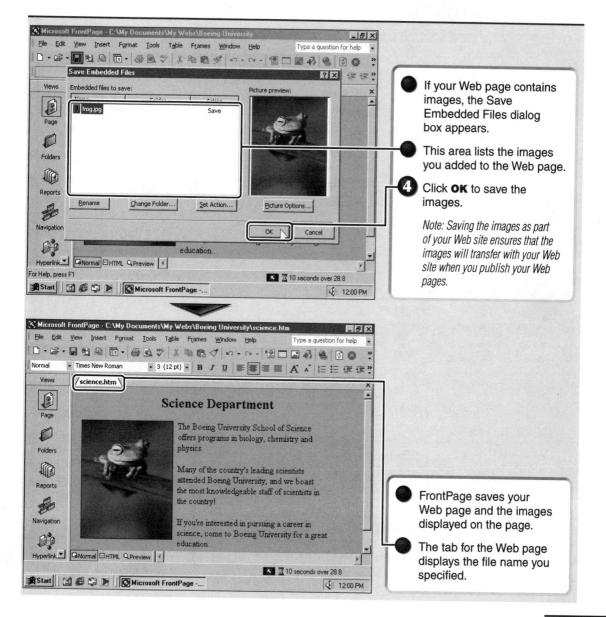

If your Web page contains images, the Save Embedded Files dialog box appears.

This area lists the images you added to the Web page.

4 Click **OK** to save the images.

Note: Saving the images as part of your Web site ensures that the images will transfer with your Web site when you publish your Web pages.

FrontPage saves your Web page and the images displayed on the page.

The tab for the Web page displays the file name you specified.

FrontPage offers three task panes that allow you to perform common tasks. The New Page or Web task pane allows you to quickly open or create a Web page or Web site. The Clipboard task pane displays each item you have selected to move or copy. The Search task pane allows you to search for files.

USING THE TASK PANE

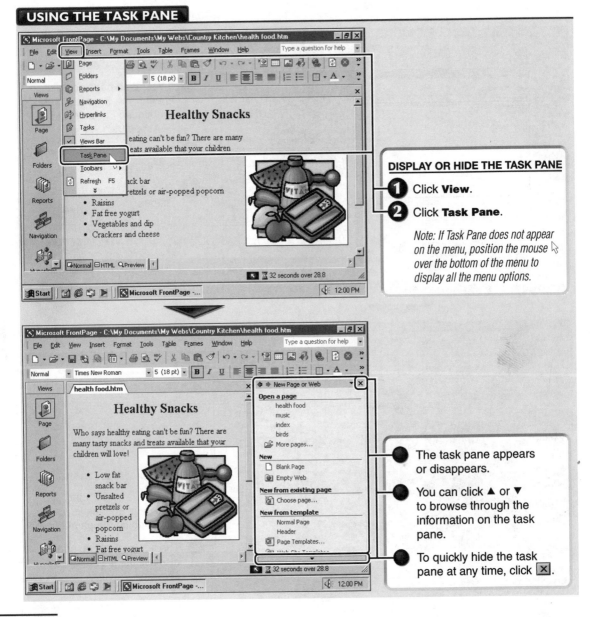

DISPLAY OR HIDE THE TASK PANE

1 Click **View**.

2 Click **Task Pane**.

Note: If Task Pane does not appear on the menu, position the mouse over the bottom of the menu to display all the menu options.

● The task pane appears or disappears.

● You can click ▲ or ▼ to browse through the information on the task pane.

● To quickly hide the task pane at any time, click ⊠.

in an instant

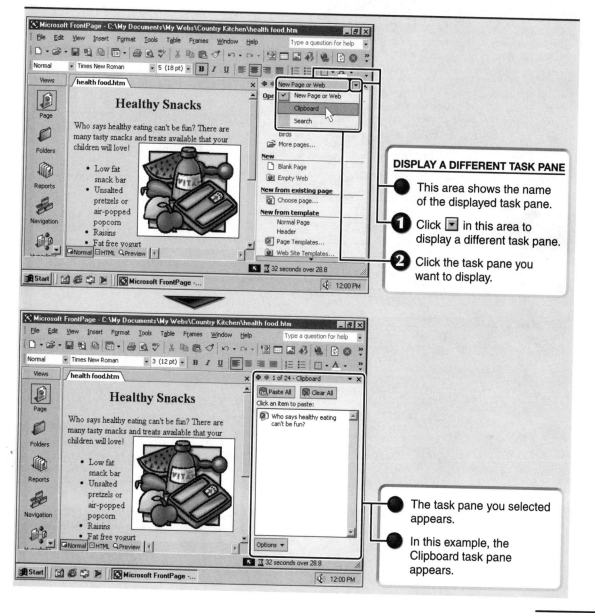

DISPLAY A DIFFERENT TASK PANE

This area shows the name of the displayed task pane.

1 Click ▾ in this area to display a different task pane.

2 Click the task pane you want to display.

The task pane you selected appears.

In this example, the Clipboard task pane appears.

CHANGE THE VIEW OF A WEB SITE

FrontPage offers six different views of your Web site that you can use to create and work with your Web pages. Each view is useful for performing specific tasks. For example, you can use the Hyperlinks view to display the links that connect the Web pages in your Web site.

CHANGE THE VIEW OF A WEB SITE

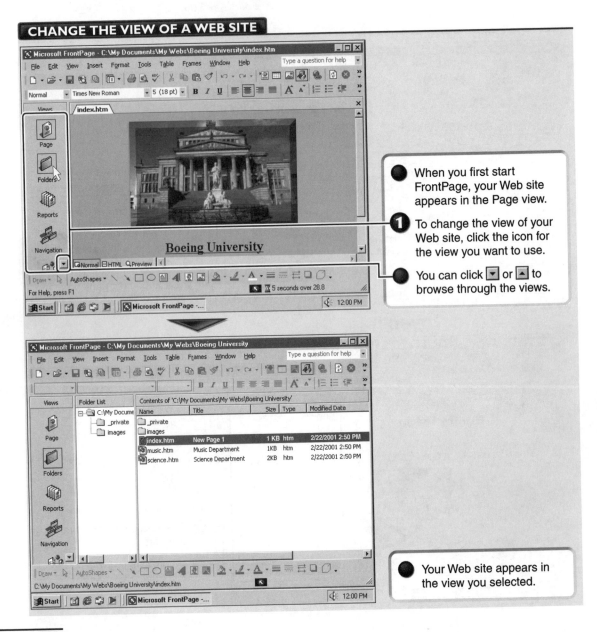

● When you first start FrontPage, your Web site appears in the Page view.

1 To change the view of your Web site, click the icon for the view you want to use.

● You can click ▼ or ▲ to browse through the views.

● Your Web site appears in the view you selected.

in an *instant*

THE WEB SITE VIEWS

Page

The Page view allows you to enter, edit and format the information on your Web pages.

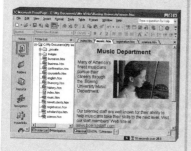

Folders

The Folders view displays the organization of the folders in your Web site and lists information about the Web pages, images and other items in your Web site.

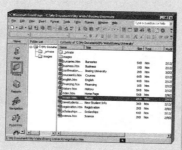

Reports

The Reports view allows you to display various reports that analyze and summarize information about your Web site.

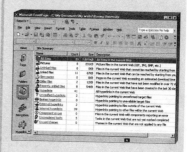

Navigation

The Navigation view allows you to view and work with the navigational structure of the Web pages in your Web site.

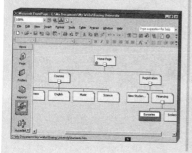

Hyperlinks

The Hyperlinks view allows you to view the links that connect the Web pages in your Web site.

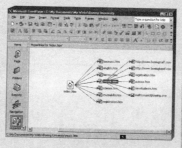

Tasks

The Tasks view allows you to create a to-do list to keep track of tasks you need to accomplish to complete your Web site.

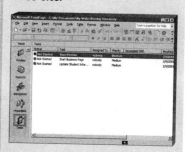

OPEN A WEB SITE

You can open a Web site to review and make changes to the Web pages and other items in the site. FrontPage automatically stores your Web sites in the My Webs folder. You can have more than one Web site open at a time.

OPEN A WEB SITE

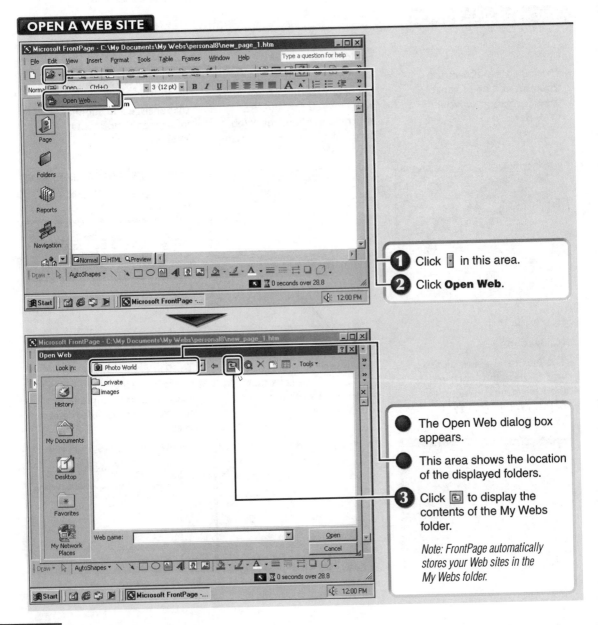

1 Click ⬒ in this area.

2 Click **Open Web**.

● The Open Web dialog box appears.

● This area shows the location of the displayed folders.

3 Click ⬚ to display the contents of the My Webs folder.

Note: FrontPage automatically stores your Web sites in the My Webs folder.

in an instant

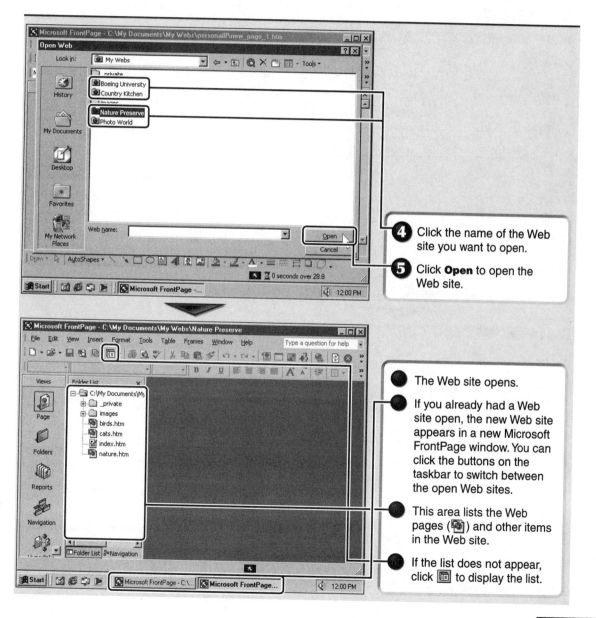

4 Click the name of the Web site you want to open.

5 Click **Open** to open the Web site.

● The Web site opens.

● If you already had a Web site open, the new Web site appears in a new Microsoft FrontPage window. You can click the buttons on the taskbar to switch between the open Web sites.

● This area lists the Web pages (🖼) and other items in the Web site.

● If the list does not appear, click 🖽 to display the list.

You can easily add text to a Web page. When adding text, you can start a new paragraph or a new line at any time. Starting a new paragraph adds a blank line between lines of text. Starting a new line does not add a blank line between lines of text, which is useful when entering information such as an address.

ENTER TEXT

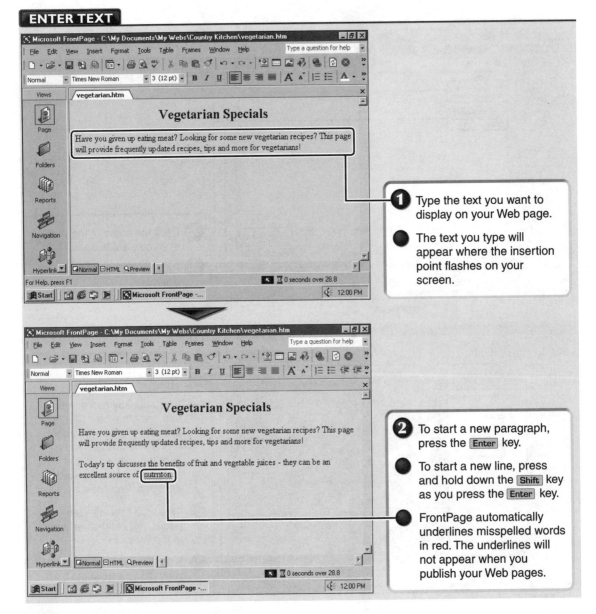

1 Type the text you want to display on your Web page.

● The text you type will appear where the insertion point flashes on your screen.

2 To start a new paragraph, press the Enter key.

● To start a new line, press and hold down the Shift key as you press the Enter key.

● FrontPage automatically underlines misspelled words in red. The underlines will not appear when you publish your Web pages.

You can remove text you no longer need from a Web page. You can remove any amount of text, such as a word, sentence or paragraph. When you remove text from a Web page, the remaining text in the line or paragraph will move to fill the empty space.

DELETE TEXT

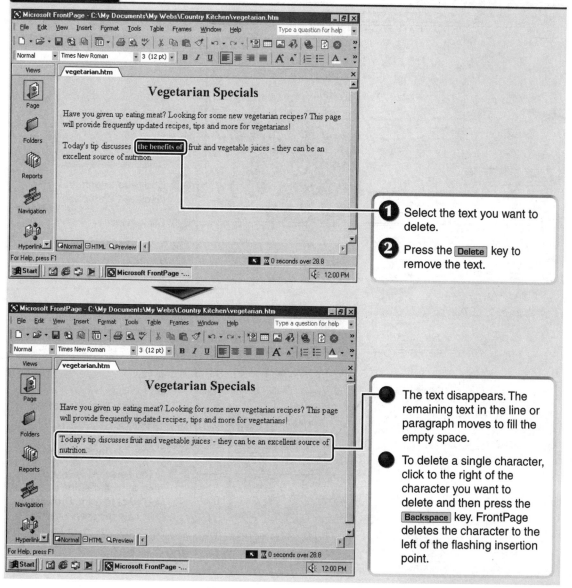

1 Select the text you want to delete.

2 Press the `Delete` key to remove the text.

■ The text disappears. The remaining text in the line or paragraph moves to fill the empty space.

■ To delete a single character, click to the right of the character you want to delete and then press the `Backspace` key. FrontPage deletes the character to the left of the flashing insertion point.

PRINT A WEB PAGE

You can produce a paper copy of the Web page displayed on your screen. This is useful if you want to review and edit the Web page. Before printing a Web page, make sure your printer is turned on and contains paper.

PRINT A WEB PAGE

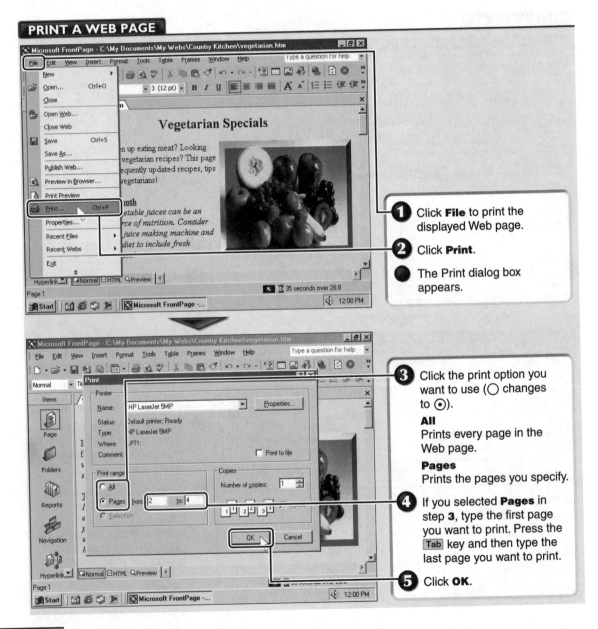

1 Click **File** to print the displayed Web page.

2 Click **Print**.

● The Print dialog box appears.

3 Click the print option you want to use (○ changes to ⊙).

All
Prints every page in the Web page.

Pages
Prints the pages you specify.

4 If you selected **Pages** in step **3**, type the first page you want to print. Press the Tab key and then type the last page you want to print.

5 Click **OK**.

DISPLAY WEB PAGE DOWNLOAD TIME

FrontPage displays the estimated amount of time a Web page will take to transfer to a visitor's computer. You can display the estimated download time for various types of connections, such as a 28.8 or 56 Kbps modem. Faster types of connections will download a Web page more quickly.

DISPLAY WEB PAGE DOWNLOAD TIME

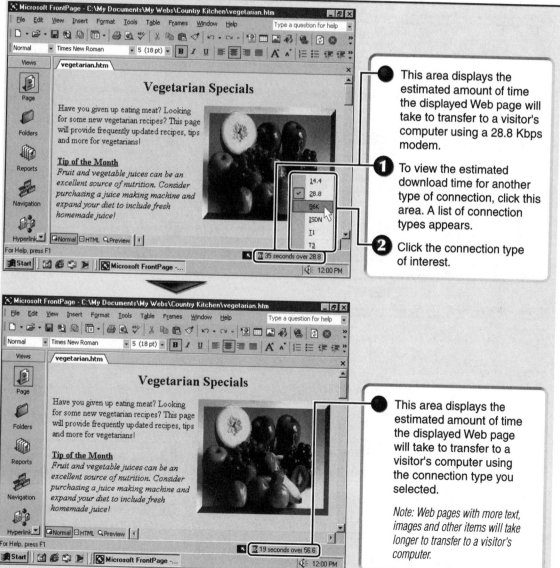

● This area displays the estimated amount of time the displayed Web page will take to transfer to a visitor's computer using a 28.8 Kbps modem.

1 To view the estimated download time for another type of connection, click this area. A list of connection types appears.

2 Click the connection type of interest.

● This area displays the estimated amount of time the displayed Web page will take to transfer to a visitor's computer using the connection type you selected.

Note: Web pages with more text, images and other items will take longer to transfer to a visitor's computer.

CHANGE THE VIEW OF A WEB PAGE

FrontPage offers three different ways you can view your Web pages. You will usually work in the Normal view to create, edit and format your Web pages. You can use the Preview view to see how your Web pages will appear on the Web. The HTML view displays the HTML code for your Web pages.

CHANGE THE VIEW OF A WEB PAGE

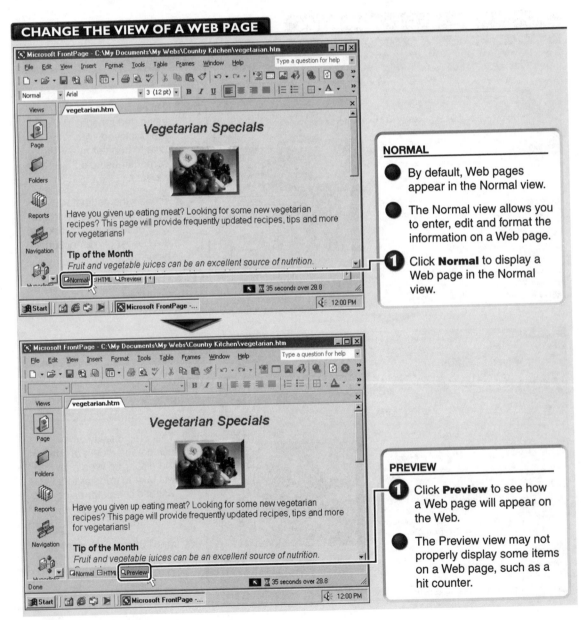

NORMAL

● By default, Web pages appear in the Normal view.

● The Normal view allows you to enter, edit and format the information on a Web page.

1 Click **Normal** to display a Web page in the Normal view.

PREVIEW

1 Click **Preview** to see how a Web page will appear on the Web.

● The Preview view may not properly display some items on a Web page, such as a hit counter.

in an *instant*

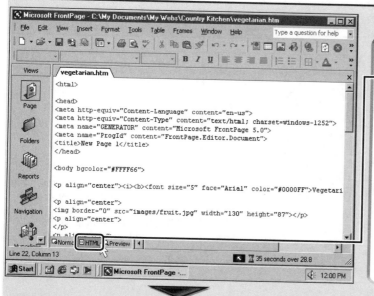

HTML

1 Click HTML to view the HTML code used to create a Web page.

● As you enter information in the Normal view, FrontPage automatically creates the HTML code for the Web page.

● HTML code consists of text and special instructions called tags that tell a Web browser how to display a Web page.

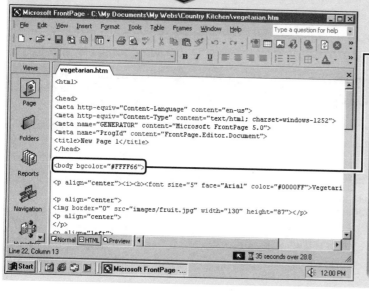

● Each tag is shown in blue and is surrounded by angle brackets < >.

● Most tags have an opening tag and a closing tag that affect the text between the tags. The closing tag has a forward slash (/). Some tags only have an opening tag. Here are some common tags:

\<b> Bolds text

\<i> Italicizes text

\<p> Starts a new paragraph

31

DISPLAY A WEB PAGE IN A WEB BROWSER

You can display a Web page in a Web browser to see how the page will appear on the Web. The most popular Web browsers are Microsoft Internet Explorer and Netscape Navigator. Make sure you display and test your Web pages in several Web browsers to ensure the pages will look and work the way you planned.

DISPLAY A WEB PAGE IN A WEB BROWSER

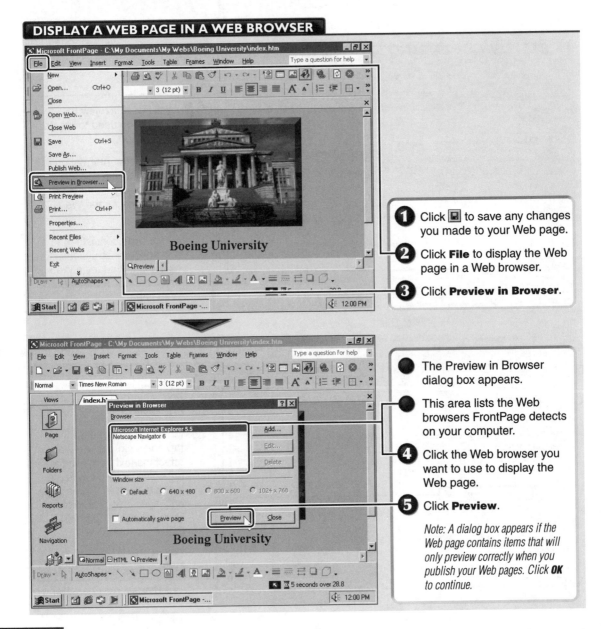

1 Click 🖫 to save any changes you made to your Web page.

2 Click **File** to display the Web page in a Web browser.

3 Click **Preview in Browser**.

■ The Preview in Browser dialog box appears.

■ This area lists the Web browsers FrontPage detects on your computer.

4 Click the Web browser you want to use to display the Web page.

5 Click **Preview**.

*Note: A dialog box appears if the Web page contains items that will only preview correctly when you publish your Web pages. Click **OK** to continue.*

in an *Instant*

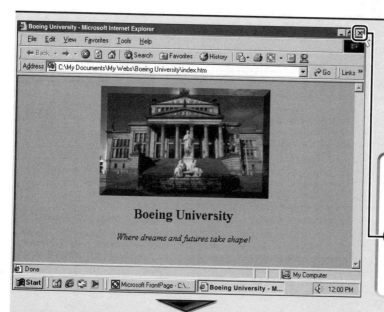

● The Web browser opens and displays the Web page. You can now review the Web page.

6 When you finish reviewing the Web page, click ☒ to close the Web browser window.

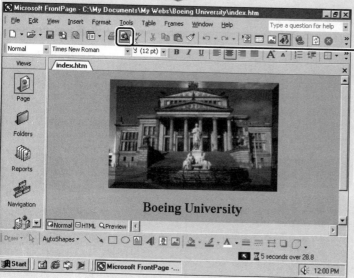

QUICKLY DISPLAY A WEB PAGE IN A WEB BROWSER

1 Click 🔍 to quickly view the displayed Web page in a Web browser.

● The Web page will appear in the Web browser you last used to display a Web page.

USING THE FOLDERS VIEW

You can use the Folders view to display information about the Web pages, images and other items in your Web site. You can view information such as the name, size and type of each file in a folder.

USING THE FOLDERS VIEW

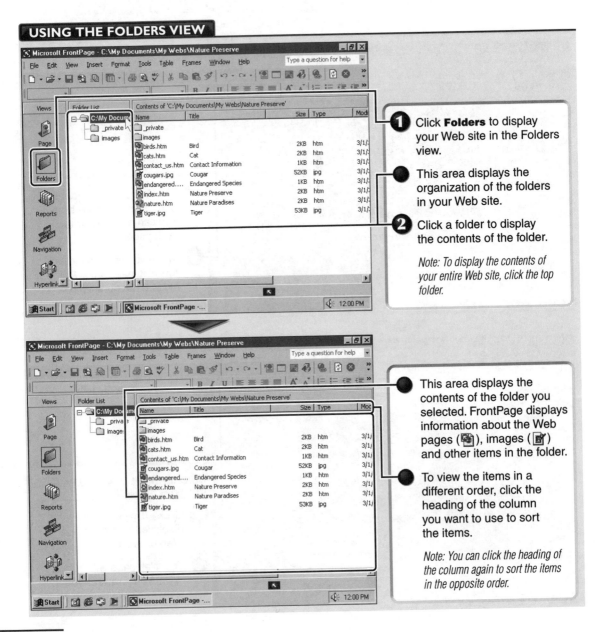

1 Click **Folders** to display your Web site in the Folders view.

● This area displays the organization of the folders in your Web site.

2 Click a folder to display the contents of the folder.

Note: To display the contents of your entire Web site, click the top folder.

● This area displays the contents of the folder you selected. FrontPage displays information about the Web pages (🖳), images (🖼) and other items in the folder.

● To view the items in a different order, click the heading of the column you want to use to sort the items.

Note: You can click the heading of the column again to sort the items in the opposite order.

You can give a Web page a descriptive title. The title
appears at the top of a Web browser window when a
visitor views the Web page. If you do not specify a title,
FrontPage will use the phrase "New Page" or the first
line of text on the Web page as the title.

CHANGE A WEB PAGE TITLE

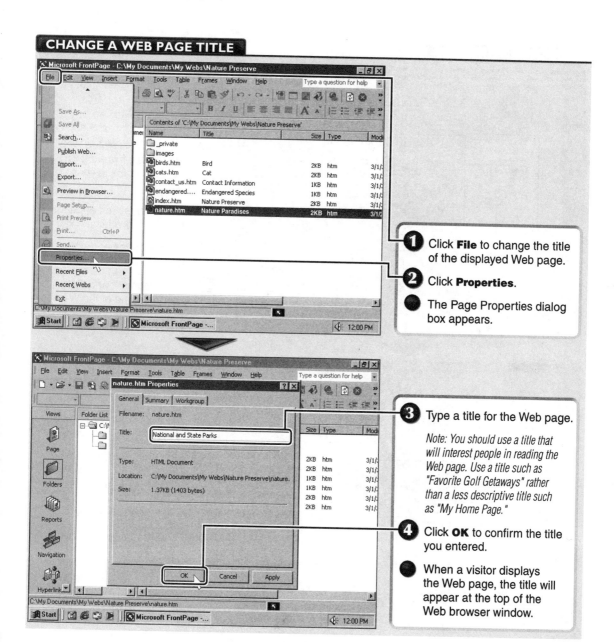

1 Click **File** to change the title of the displayed Web page.

2 Click **Properties**.

● The Page Properties dialog box appears.

3 Type a title for the Web page.

Note: You should use a title that will interest people in reading the Web page. Use a title such as "Favorite Golf Getaways" rather than a less descriptive title such as "My Home Page."

4 Click **OK** to confirm the title you entered.

● When a visitor displays the Web page, the title will appear at the top of the Web browser window.

RENAME A WEB PAGE

You can rename a Web page to better describe the contents of the page. You should not rename the Web page named index.htm since this is your home page. If you rename this Web page, visitors may get an error message when they visit your Web site.

RENAME A WEB PAGE

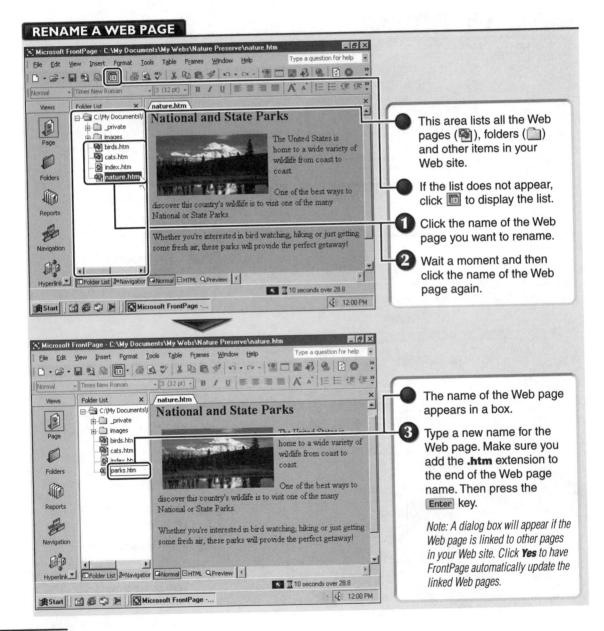

This area lists all the Web pages (📄), folders (📁) and other items in your Web site.

If the list does not appear, click 🔲 to display the list.

1 Click the name of the Web page you want to rename.

2 Wait a moment and then click the name of the Web page again.

The name of the Web page appears in a box.

3 Type a new name for the Web page. Make sure you add the **.htm** extension to the end of the Web page name. Then press the **Enter** key.

Note: A dialog box will appear if the Web page is linked to other pages in your Web site. Click **Yes** to have FrontPage automatically update the linked Web pages.

You can delete a Web page you no longer want to include in your Web site. You should not delete the Web page named index.htm since this is your home page. If you delete this Web page, visitors may get an error message when they visit your Web site.

DELETE A WEB PAGE

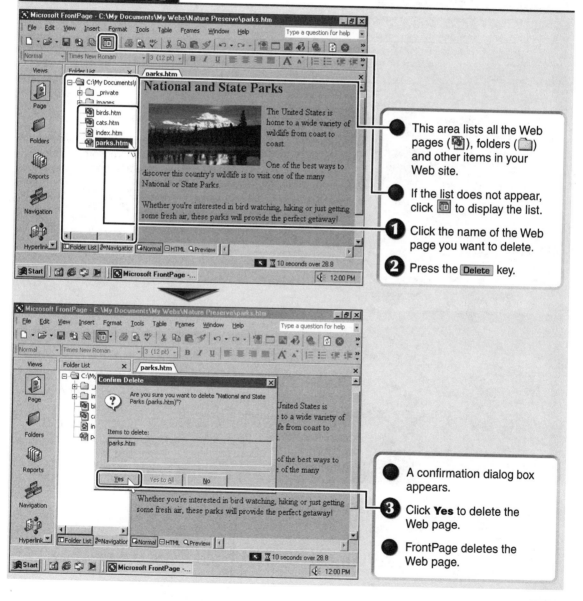

This area lists all the Web pages (📄), folders (📁) and other items in your Web site.

If the list does not appear, click 🔲 to display the list.

1 Click the name of the Web page you want to delete.

2 Press the Delete key.

A confirmation dialog box appears.

3 Click **Yes** to delete the Web page.

FrontPage deletes the Web page.

SEARCH FOR A WEB PAGE

If you cannot remember the name or location of a Web page you want to work with, you can search for the Web page on your computer. You will need to specify the words you want to search for. FrontPage will search the contents and file names of Web pages for the words you specify.

SEARCH FOR A WEB PAGE

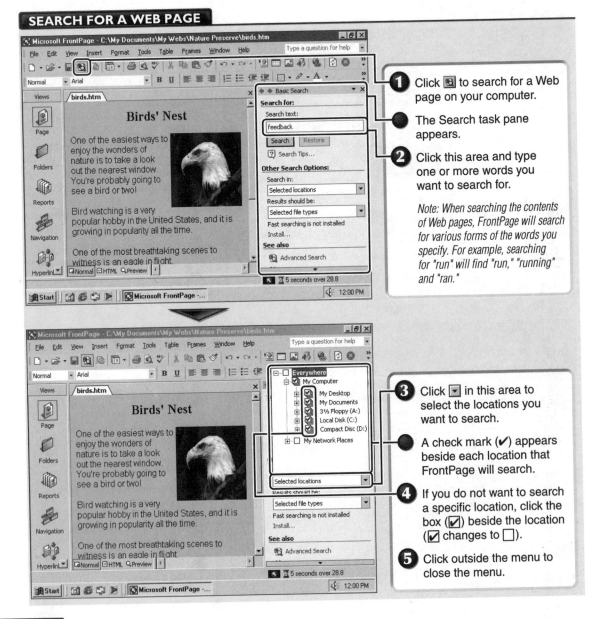

1 Click 🔍 to search for a Web page on your computer.

● The Search task pane appears.

2 Click this area and type one or more words you want to search for.

Note: When searching the contents of Web pages, FrontPage will search for various forms of the words you specify. For example, searching for "run" will find "run," "running" and "ran."

3 Click ▾ in this area to select the locations you want to search.

● A check mark (✔) appears beside each location that FrontPage will search.

4 If you do not want to search a specific location, click the box (☑) beside the location (☑ changes to ☐).

5 Click outside the menu to close the menu.

in an *Instant*

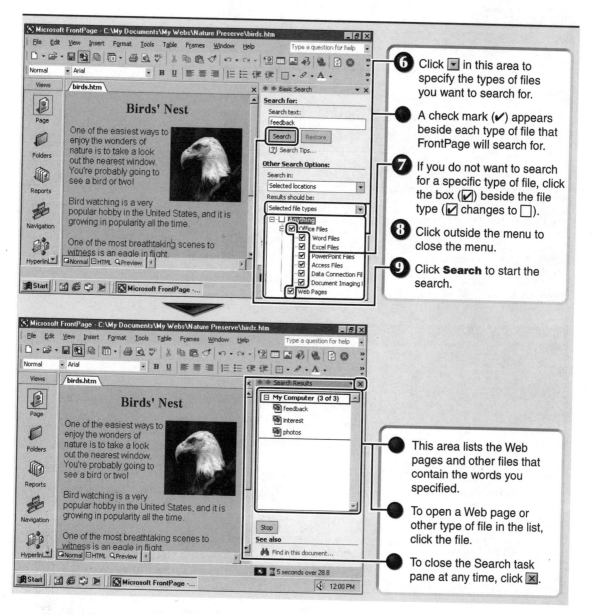

6 Click ▼ in this area to specify the types of files you want to search for.

● A check mark (✔) appears beside each type of file that FrontPage will search for.

7 If you do not want to search for a specific type of file, click the box (☑) beside the file type (☑ changes to ☐).

8 Click outside the menu to close the menu.

9 Click **Search** to start the search.

● This area lists the Web pages and other files that contain the words you specified.

● To open a Web page or other type of file in the list, click the file.

● To close the Search task pane at any time, click ☒.

Before performing many tasks in FrontPage, you must select the text you want to work with. You can select a word, sentence, paragraph or all the text on a Web page. Selected text appears highlighted on your screen.

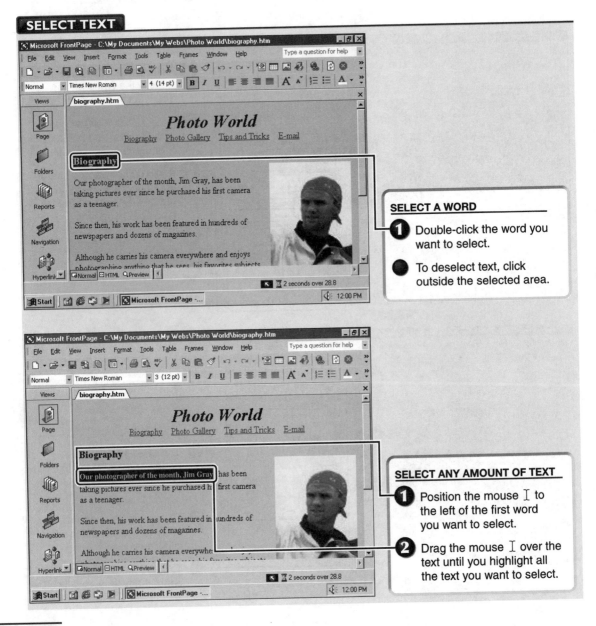

SELECT A WORD

1. Double-click the word you want to select.

● To deselect text, click outside the selected area.

SELECT ANY AMOUNT OF TEXT

1. Position the mouse I to the left of the first word you want to select.

2. Drag the mouse I over the text until you highlight all the text you want to select.

FrontPage remembers the last changes you made to your Web pages. If you regret these changes, you can cancel them by using the Undo feature. The Undo feature can cancel up to 30 of your last editing and formatting changes.

UNDO CHANGES

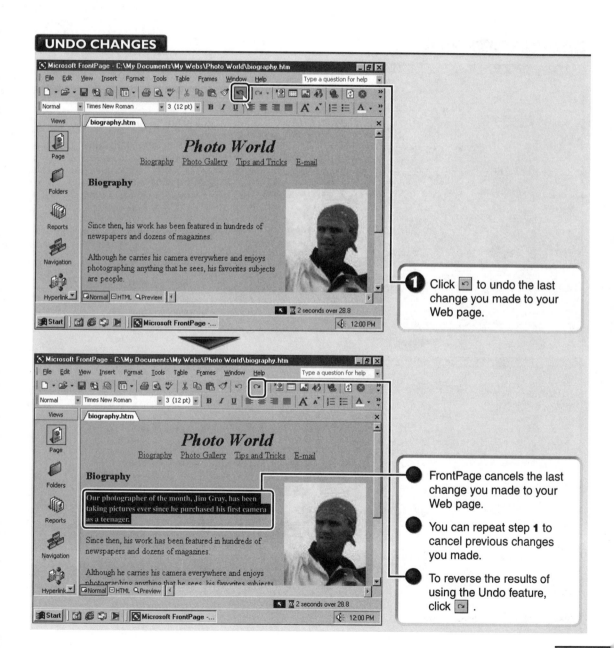

1 Click 🖺 to undo the last change you made to your Web page.

FrontPage cancels the last change you made to your Web page.

You can repeat step **1** to cancel previous changes you made.

To reverse the results of using the Undo feature, click 🖺 .

MOVE OR COPY TEXT

You can move or copy text to a new location on a Web page. Moving text allows you to re-arrange text on a Web page. Copying text allows you to repeat information on a Web page without having to retype the text.

MOVE OR COPY TEXT

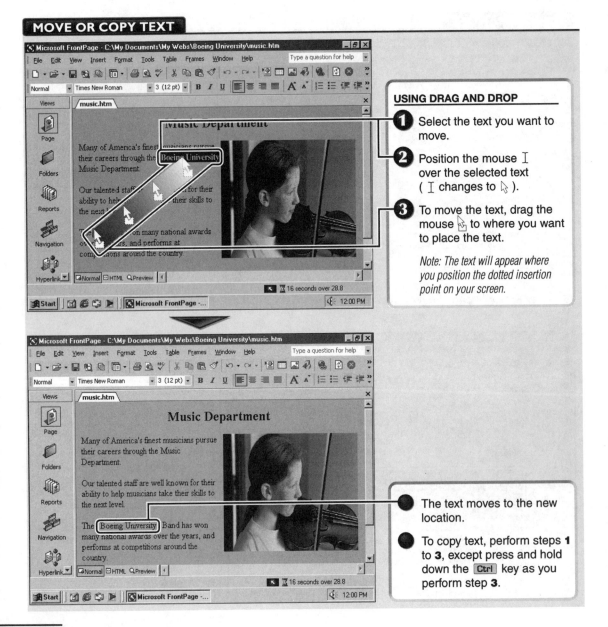

USING DRAG AND DROP

① Select the text you want to move.

② Position the mouse I over the selected text (I changes to ⇘).

③ To move the text, drag the mouse ⇘ to where you want to place the text.

Note: The text will appear where you position the dotted insertion point on your screen.

● The text moves to the new location.

● To copy text, perform steps **1** to **3**, except press and hold down the `Ctrl` key as you perform step **3**.

in an *instant*

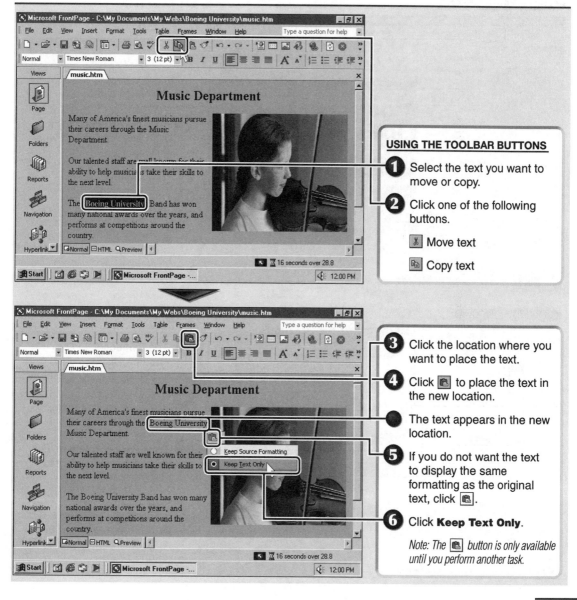

USING THE TOOLBAR BUTTONS

1 Select the text you want to move or copy.

2 Click one of the following buttons.

✂ Move text

📋 Copy text

3 Click the location where you want to place the text.

4 Click 📋 to place the text in the new location.

● The text appears in the new location.

5 If you do not want the text to display the same formatting as the original text, click 📋.

6 Click **Keep Text Only**.

Note: The 📋 button is only available until you perform another task.

43

ADD SYMBOLS

You can add symbols or special characters that do not appear on your keyboard to your Web pages. Symbols you can add include accented letters, the copyright (©) and registered (®) signs, arrows and fractions such as ½.

ADD SYMBOLS

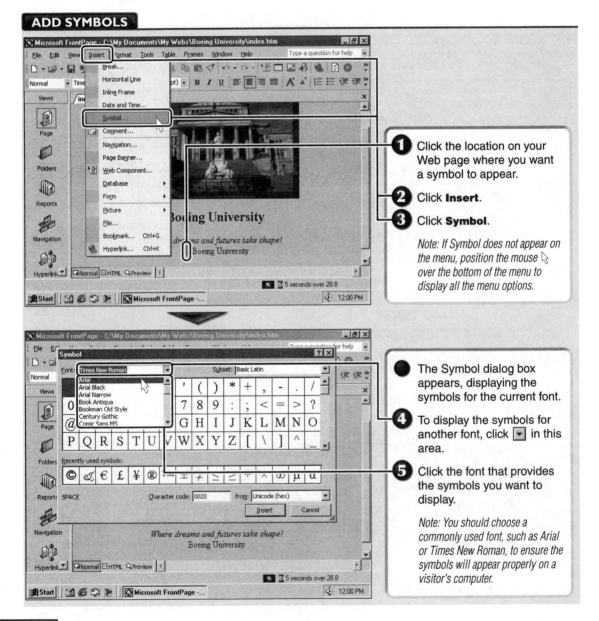

1 Click the location on your Web page where you want a symbol to appear.

2 Click **Insert**.

3 Click **Symbol**.

Note: If Symbol does not appear on the menu, position the mouse over the bottom of the menu to display all the menu options.

● The Symbol dialog box appears, displaying the symbols for the current font.

4 To display the symbols for another font, click ▼ in this area.

5 Click the font that provides the symbols you want to display.

Note: You should choose a commonly used font, such as Arial or Times New Roman, to ensure the symbols will appear properly on a visitor's computer.

in an instant

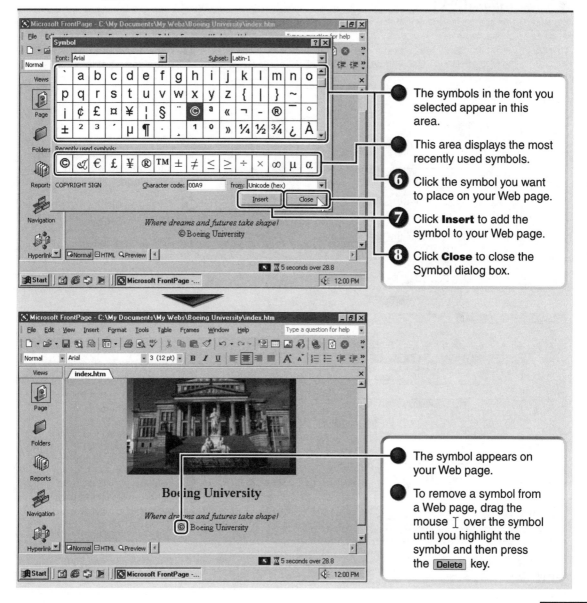

The symbols in the font you selected appear in this area.

This area displays the most recently used symbols.

6 Click the symbol you want to place on your Web page.

7 Click **Insert** to add the symbol to your Web page.

8 Click **Close** to close the Symbol dialog box.

The symbol appears on your Web page.

To remove a symbol from a Web page, drag the mouse I over the symbol until you highlight the symbol and then press the Delete key.

CHECK SPELLING

You can quickly find and correct all the spelling errors on a Web page. FrontPage automatically checks your Web pages for spelling errors as you type. Misspelled words display a wavy red underline. The underlines will not appear when you publish your Web pages.

CHECK SPELLING

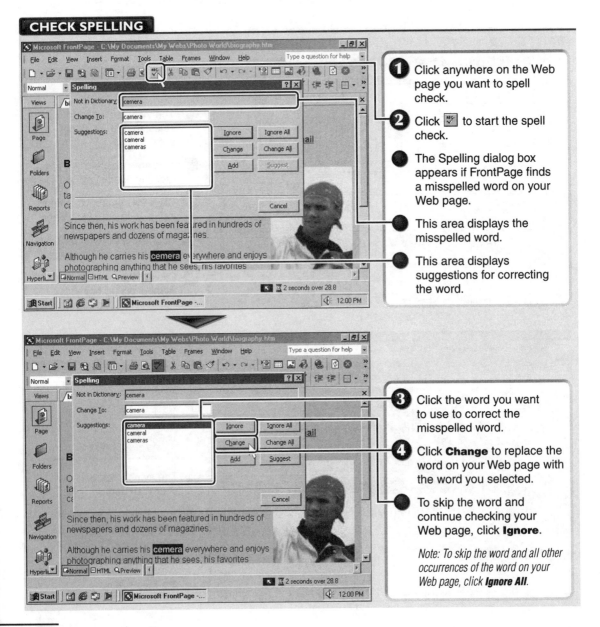

1 Click anywhere on the Web page you want to spell check.

2 Click 🦃 to start the spell check.

● The Spelling dialog box appears if FrontPage finds a misspelled word on your Web page.

● This area displays the misspelled word.

● This area displays suggestions for correcting the word.

3 Click the word you want to use to correct the misspelled word.

4 Click **Change** to replace the word on your Web page with the word you selected.

● To skip the word and continue checking your Web page, click **Ignore**.

*Note: To skip the word and all other occurrences of the word on your Web page, click **Ignore All**.*

in an *instant*

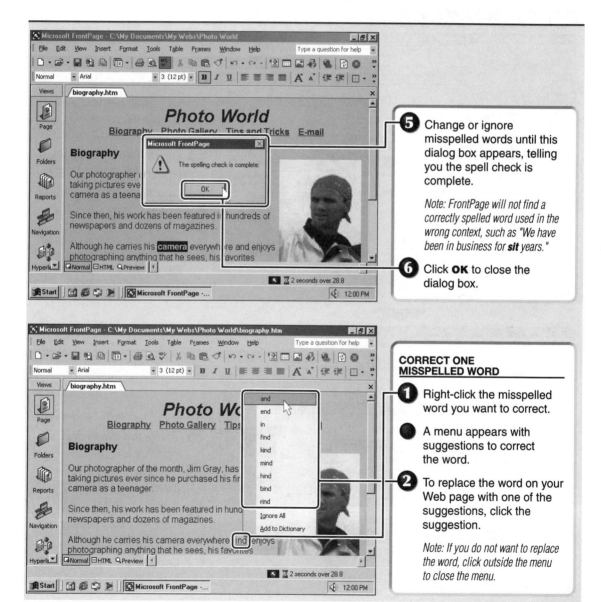

5 Change or ignore misspelled words until this dialog box appears, telling you the spell check is complete.

*Note: FrontPage will not find a correctly spelled word used in the wrong context, such as "We have been in business for **sit** years."*

6 Click **OK** to close the dialog box.

CORRECT ONE MISSPELLED WORD

1 Right-click the misspelled word you want to correct.

● A menu appears with suggestions to correct the word.

2 To replace the word on your Web page with one of the suggestions, click the suggestion.

Note: If you do not want to replace the word, click outside the menu to close the menu.

USING THE THESAURUS

You can use the thesaurus to replace a word on your Web page with a more suitable word. The thesaurus can help you replace repeated words on a Web page to add variety to your writing. You may also want to use the thesaurus to find a word that more clearly explains a concept.

USING THE THESAURUS

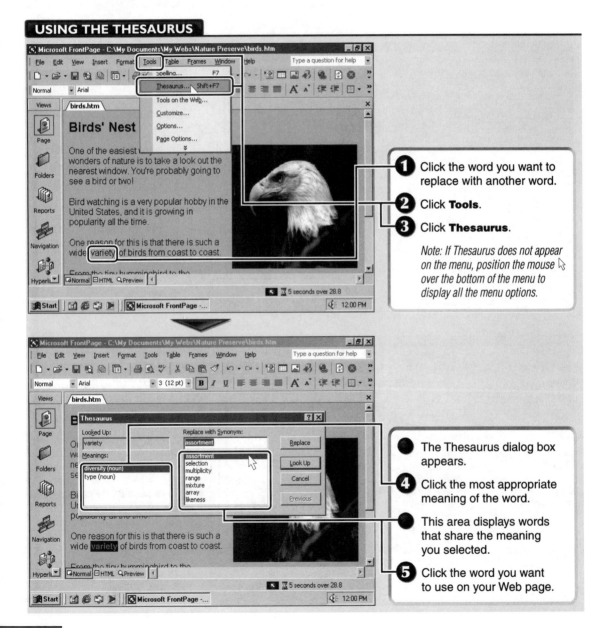

1 Click the word you want to replace with another word.

2 Click **Tools**.

3 Click **Thesaurus**.

Note: If Thesaurus does not appear on the menu, position the mouse over the bottom of the menu to display all the menu options.

■ The Thesaurus dialog box appears.

4 Click the most appropriate meaning of the word.

■ This area displays words that share the meaning you selected.

5 Click the word you want to use on your Web page.

in an *instant*

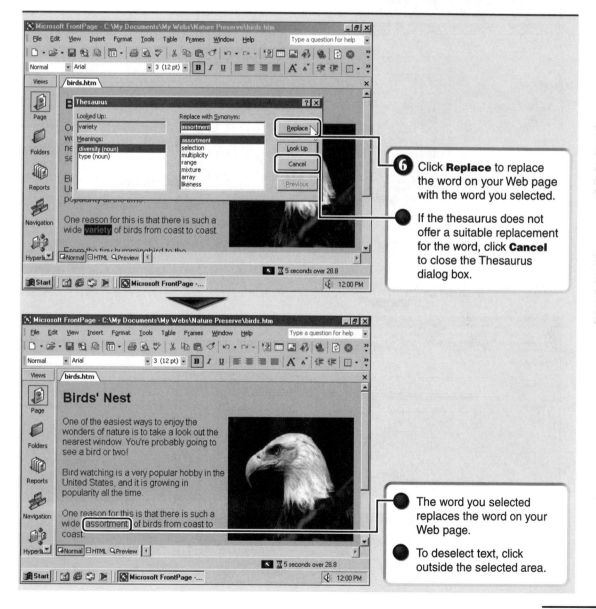

6 Click **Replace** to replace the word on your Web page with the word you selected.

● If the thesaurus does not offer a suitable replacement for the word, click **Cancel** to close the Thesaurus dialog box.

● The word you selected replaces the word on your Web page.

● To deselect text, click outside the selected area.

FIND AND REPLACE TEXT

You can find and replace every occurrence of a word or phrase on a Web page. This is useful if you have frequently misspelled a name. You can choose to replace specific occurrences of a word on a Web page or all occurrences of a word at once.

FIND AND REPLACE TEXT

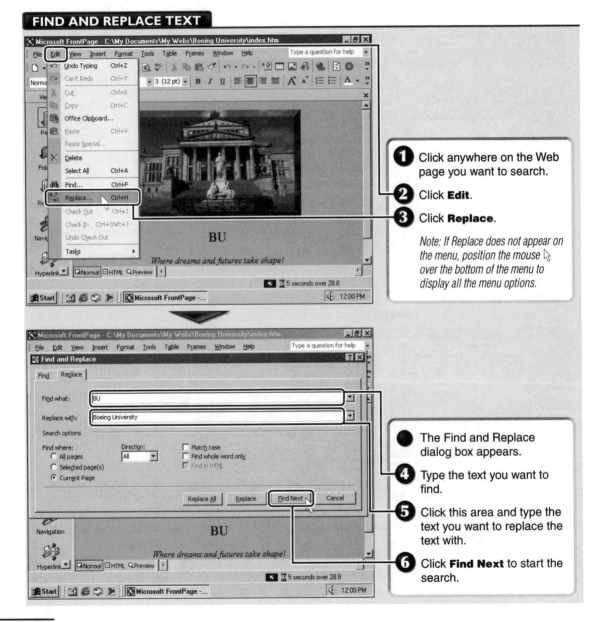

1 Click anywhere on the Web page you want to search.

2 Click **Edit**.

3 Click **Replace**.

Note: If Replace does not appear on the menu, position the mouse over the bottom of the menu to display all the menu options.

■ The Find and Replace dialog box appears.

4 Type the text you want to find.

5 Click this area and type the text you want to replace the text with.

6 Click **Find Next** to start the search.

in an *instant*

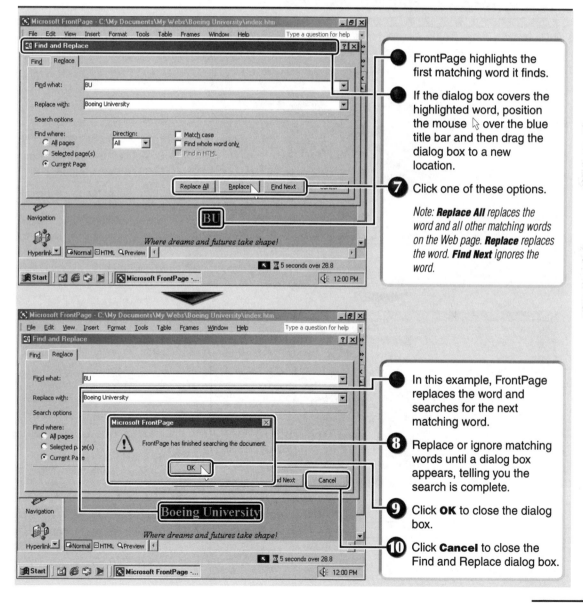

FrontPage highlights the first matching word it finds.

If the dialog box covers the highlighted word, position the mouse ⓚ over the blue title bar and then drag the dialog box to a new location.

7 Click one of these options.

Note: Replace All replaces the word and all other matching words on the Web page. Replace replaces the word. Find Next ignores the word.

In this example, FrontPage replaces the word and searches for the next matching word.

8 Replace or ignore matching words until a dialog box appears, telling you the search is complete.

9 Click **OK** to close the dialog box.

10 Click **Cancel** to close the Find and Replace dialog box.

BOLD, ITALICIZE OR UNDERLINE TEXT

You can bold, italicize or underline text to emphasize information and enhance the appearance of a Web page. Be careful when underlining text, since visitors may mistake the text for a link.

BOLD, ITALICIZE OR UNDERLINE TEXT

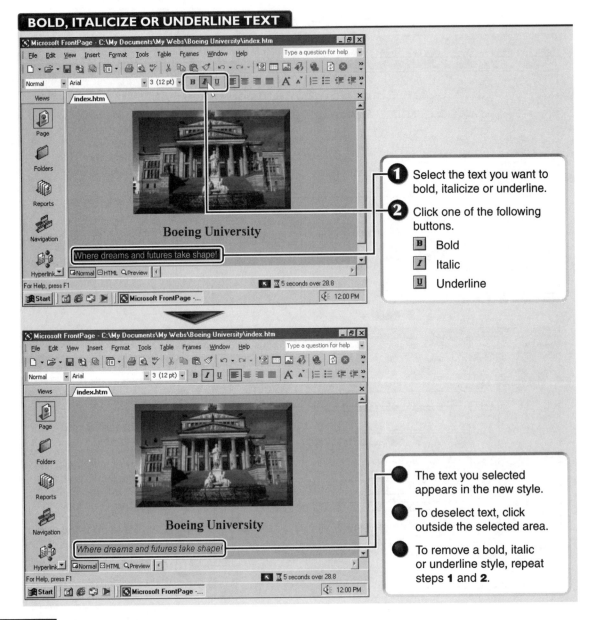

1 Select the text you want to bold, italicize or underline.

2 Click one of the following buttons.

B Bold

I Italic

<u>U</u> Underline

● The text you selected appears in the new style.

● To deselect text, click outside the selected area.

● To remove a bold, italic or underline style, repeat steps **1** and **2**.

You can change the alignment of text on a Web page.
FrontPage automatically left aligns text that you type.
Changing the alignment of text is useful when you
want to center a heading or right align an address.

CHANGE ALIGNMENT OF TEXT

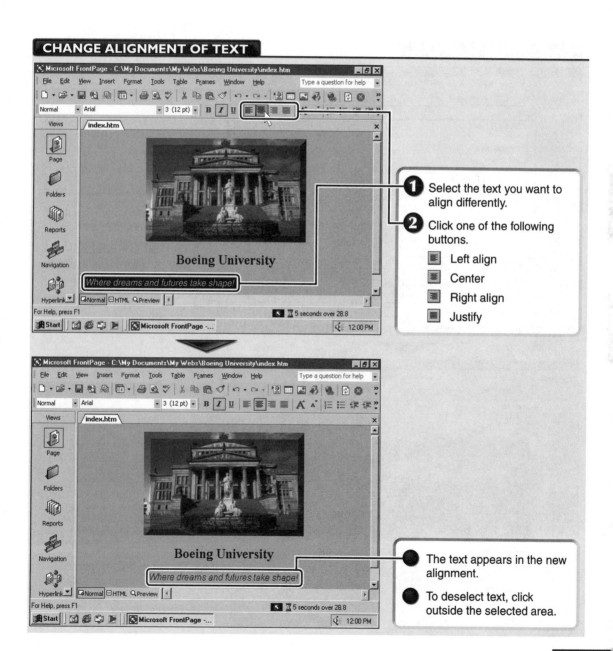

1 Select the text you want to align differently.

2 Click one of the following buttons.

▤ Left align

▤ Center

▤ Right align

▤ Justify

● The text appears in the new alignment.

● To deselect text, click outside the selected area.

CHANGE FONT OF TEXT

You can change the font of text to enhance the appearance of text on a Web page. You should choose common fonts, such as Arial or Times New Roman, to ensure a visitor's Web browser will be able to display your text in the font you select.

CHANGE FONT OF TEXT

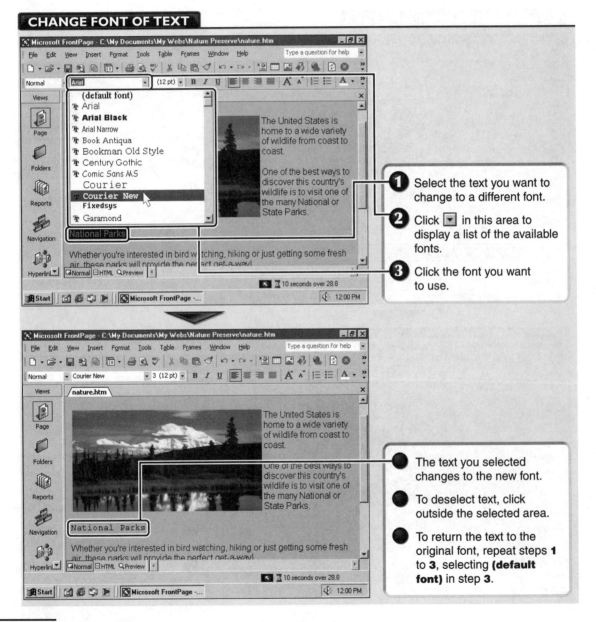

1 Select the text you want to change to a different font.

2 Click ▼ in this area to display a list of the available fonts.

3 Click the font you want to use.

● The text you selected changes to the new font.

● To deselect text, click outside the selected area.

● To return the text to the original font, repeat steps 1 to 3, selecting **(default font)** in step 3.

You can increase or decrease the size of text on a Web page. Larger text is easier to read, but smaller text allows you to fit more information on a screen. FrontPage offers seven font sizes. Size 1 is the smallest and size 7 is the largest.

CHANGE SIZE OF TEXT

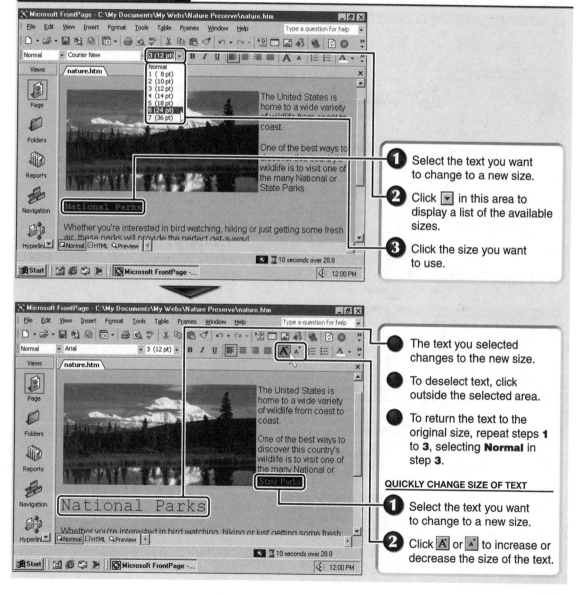

1 Select the text you want to change to a new size.

2 Click ▼ in this area to display a list of the available sizes.

3 Click the size you want to use.

■ The text you selected changes to the new size.

■ To deselect text, click outside the selected area.

■ To return the text to the original size, repeat steps 1 to 3, selecting **Normal** in step 3.

QUICKLY CHANGE SIZE OF TEXT

1 Select the text you want to change to a new size.

2 Click A or A to increase or decrease the size of the text.

CHANGE COLOR OF TEXT

You can change the color of text to draw attention to headings or important information on a Web page. Make sure the text color you choose works well with the background color of the Web page. For example, red text on a blue background can be difficult to read.

CHANGE COLOR OF TEXT

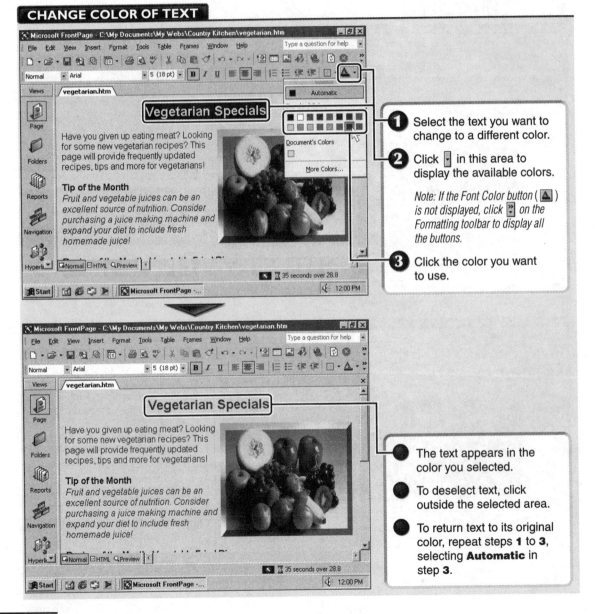

1 Select the text you want to change to a different color.

2 Click ⬝ in this area to display the available colors.

Note: If the Font Color button (🅰) is not displayed, click » on the Formatting toolbar to display all the buttons.

3 Click the color you want to use.

■ The text appears in the color you selected.

■ To deselect text, click outside the selected area.

■ To return text to its original color, repeat steps **1** to **3**, selecting **Automatic** in step **3**.

You can highlight text that you want to stand out from the rest of the text on a Web page. Highlighting text is useful when you want to mark information you want to review or verify later, such as an address.

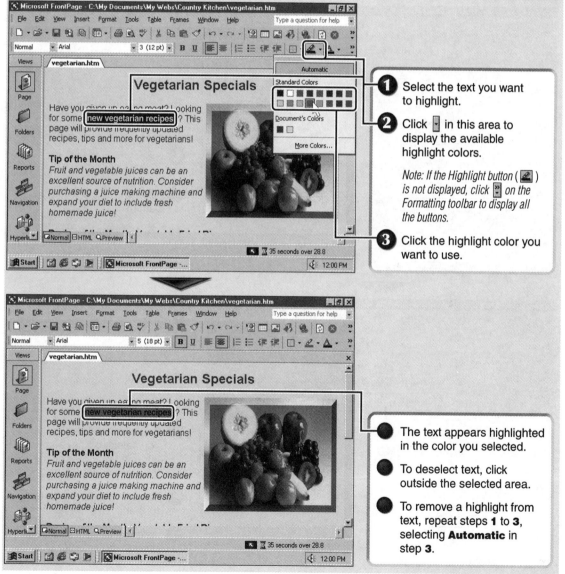

1 Select the text you want to highlight.

2 Click ▾ in this area to display the available highlight colors.

Note: If the Highlight button () is not displayed, click ▾ on the Formatting toolbar to display all the buttons.

3 Click the highlight color you want to use.

● The text appears highlighted in the color you selected.

● To deselect text, click outside the selected area.

● To remove a highlight from text, repeat steps **1** to **3**, selecting **Automatic** in step **3**.

INDENT TEXT

You can indent text to move text away from the left and right edges of a Web page. Indenting text is useful when you want to set paragraphs, such as quotations, apart from the rest of the text on a Web page.

INDENT TEXT

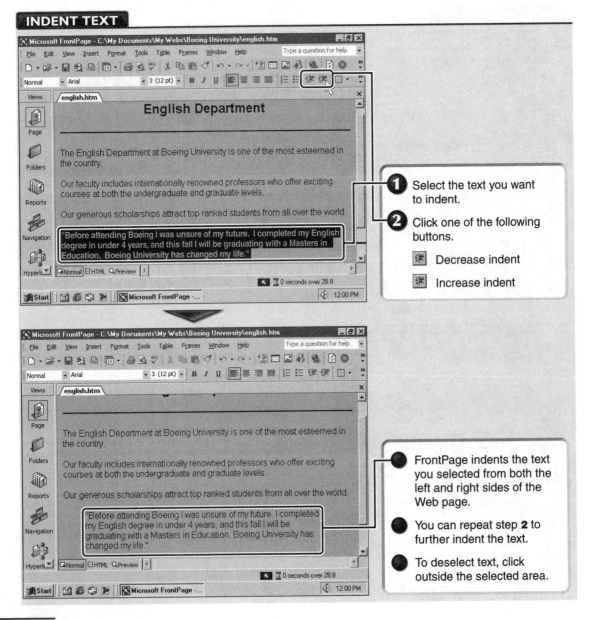

1 Select the text you want to indent.

2 Click one of the following buttons.

⧉ Decrease indent

⧉ Increase indent

● FrontPage indents the text you selected from both the left and right sides of the Web page.

● You can repeat step 2 to further indent the text.

● To deselect text, click outside the selected area.

ADD BORDERS TO TEXT

You can add borders to text to draw attention to information on a Web page. For example, you could add a border to a special announcement on a Web page. FrontPage allows you to add borders to the top, bottom, left, right or all sides of text.

ADD BORDERS TO TEXT

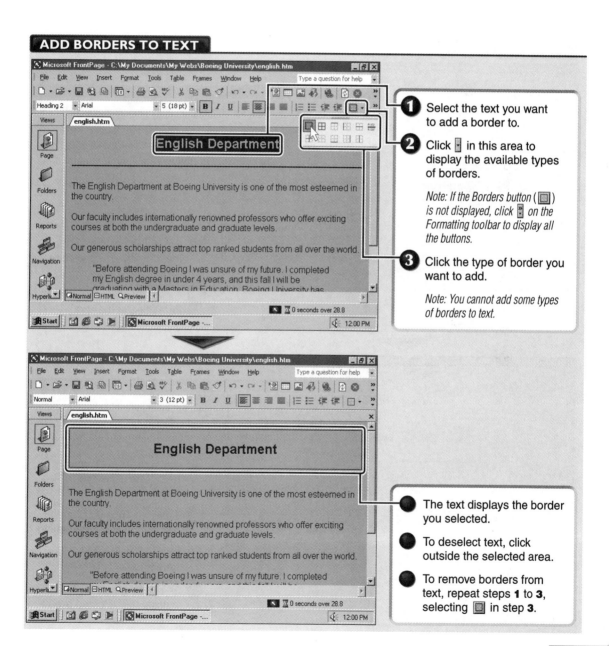

1 Select the text you want to add a border to.

2 Click ⊡ in this area to display the available types of borders.

Note: If the Borders button (▣) is not displayed, click ⁑ on the Formatting toolbar to display all the buttons.

3 Click the type of border you want to add.

Note: You cannot add some types of borders to text.

● The text displays the border you selected.

● To deselect text, click outside the selected area.

● To remove borders from text, repeat steps **1** to **3**, selecting ▣ in step **3**.

COPY FORMATTING

You can copy the formatting of text to make one area of text on a Web page look exactly like another. You may want to copy the formatting of text to make all the headings or important words on a Web page look the same. This can give the text on a Web page a consistent appearance.

COPY FORMATTING

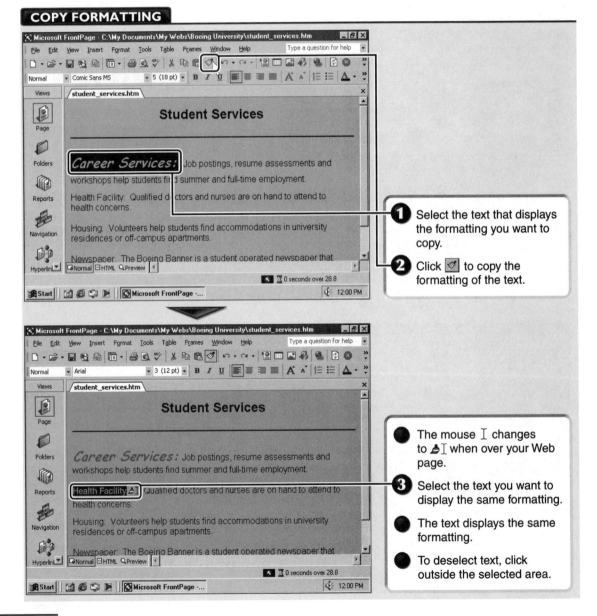

1 Select the text that displays the formatting you want to copy.

2 Click to copy the formatting of the text.

■ The mouse I changes to I when over your Web page.

3 Select the text you want to display the same formatting.

■ The text displays the same formatting.

■ To deselect text, click outside the selected area.

REMOVE FORMATTING

FrontPage allows you to quickly remove all the formatting from text on a Web page. You may want to remove the formatting you applied to a word, sentence, paragraph or your entire Web page. When you remove the formatting from text, FrontPage will display the text in the default font, size and color.

REMOVE FORMATTING

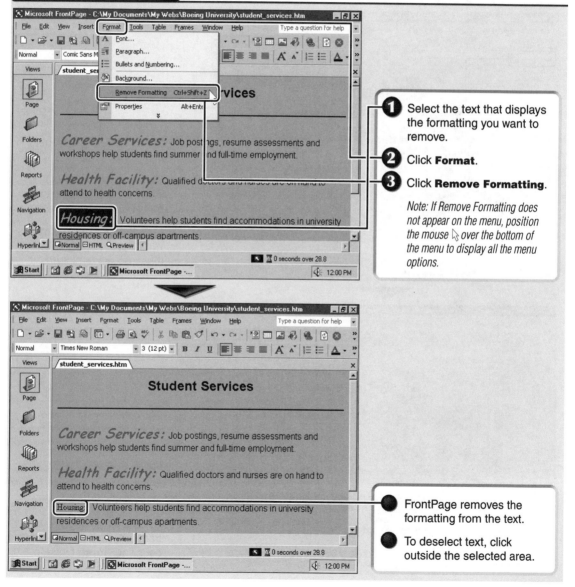

1 Select the text that displays the formatting you want to remove.

2 Click **Format**.

3 Click **Remove Formatting**.

Note: If Remove Formatting does not appear on the menu, position the mouse over the bottom of the menu to display all the menu options.

● FrontPage removes the formatting from the text.

● To deselect text, click outside the selected area.

ADD A HEADING

You can use headings to organize the information on a Web page and help visitors quickly locate topics of interest. Since different Web browsers display headings in slightly different ways, you should use headings to signify the importance of information on a Web page rather than to change the appearance of text.

ADD A HEADING

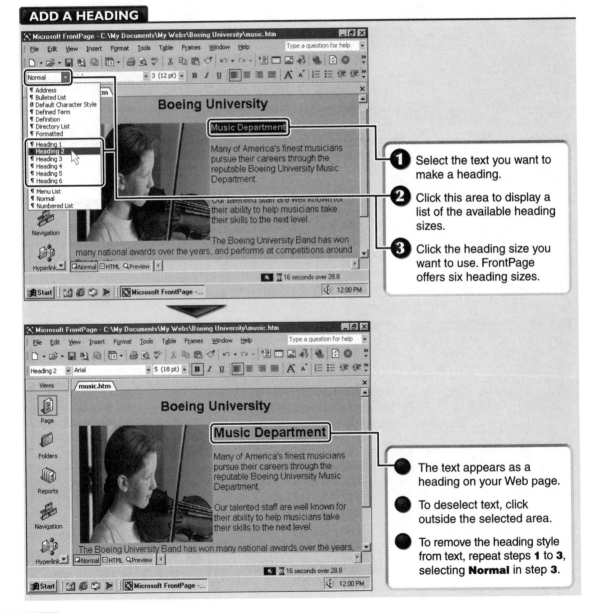

1 Select the text you want to make a heading.

2 Click this area to display a list of the available heading sizes.

3 Click the heading size you want to use. FrontPage offers six heading sizes.

● The text appears as a heading on your Web page.

● To deselect text, click outside the selected area.

● To remove the heading style from text, repeat steps **1** to **3**, selecting **Normal** in step **3**.

You can create a definition list to display terms and their definitions. FrontPage will automatically indent the definitions below each term. A definition list is ideal for displaying a glossary.

CREATE A DEFINITION LIST

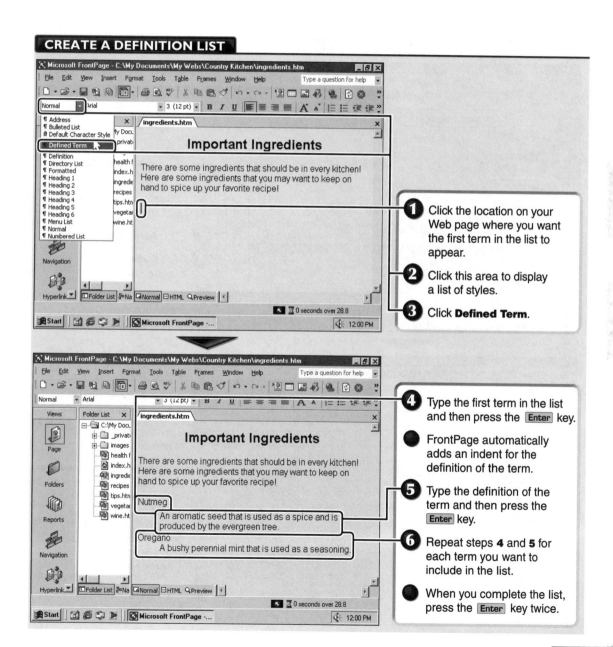

① Click the location on your Web page where you want the first term in the list to appear.

② Click this area to display a list of styles.

③ Click **Defined Term**.

④ Type the first term in the list and then press the Enter key.

● FrontPage automatically adds an indent for the definition of the term.

⑤ Type the definition of the term and then press the Enter key.

⑥ Repeat steps **4** and **5** for each term you want to include in the list.

● When you complete the list, press the Enter key twice.

You can separate items in a list by beginning each item with a bullet or number. Bulleted lists are useful for items in no particular order, such as a list of products. Numbered lists are useful for items in a specific order, such as a set of instructions.

CREATE A BULLETED OR NUMBERED LIST

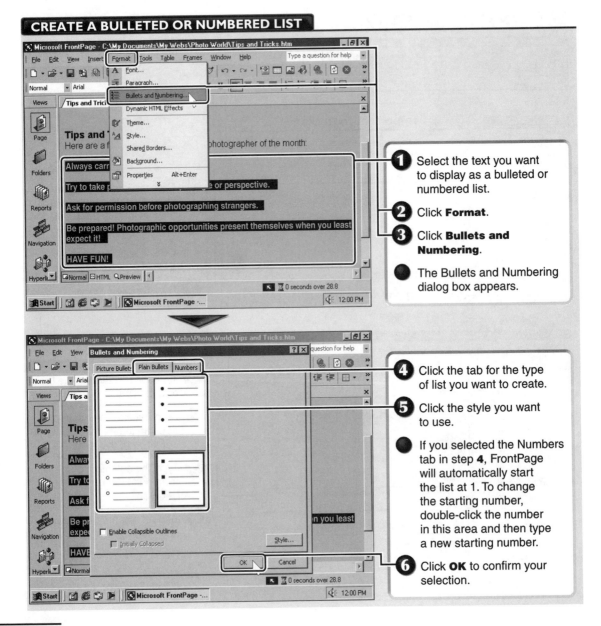

1 Select the text you want to display as a bulleted or numbered list.

2 Click **Format**.

3 Click **Bullets and Numbering**.

● The Bullets and Numbering dialog box appears.

4 Click the tab for the type of list you want to create.

5 Click the style you want to use.

● If you selected the Numbers tab in step **4**, FrontPage will automatically start the list at 1. To change the starting number, double-click the number in this area and then type a new starting number.

6 Click **OK** to confirm your selection.

in an instant

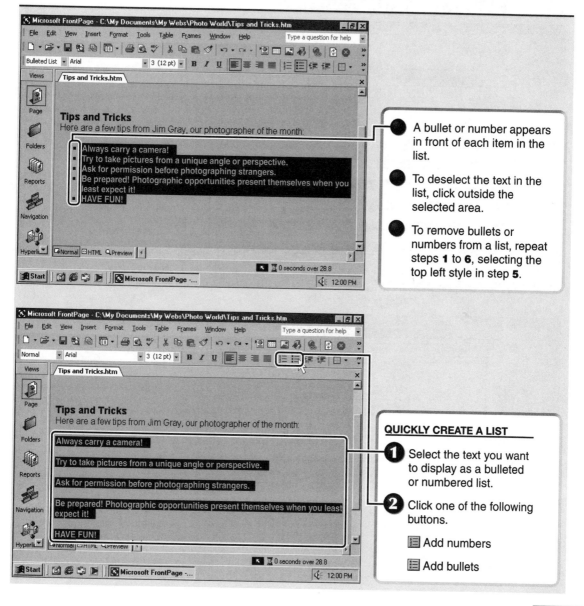

A bullet or number appears in front of each item in the list.

To deselect the text in the list, click outside the selected area.

To remove bullets or numbers from a list, repeat steps **1** to **6**, selecting the top left style in step **5**.

QUICKLY CREATE A LIST

1 Select the text you want to display as a bulleted or numbered list.

2 Click one of the following buttons.

Add numbers

Add bullets

CREATE A LIST WITH PICTURE BULLETS

You can create an eye-catching list on a Web page that uses images as bullets. Many Web sites, such as www.abcgiant.com, offer images that you can use as picture bullets. Make sure the picture bullets you choose are small images that will fit neatly beside each item in a list.

CREATE A LIST WITH PICTURE BULLETS

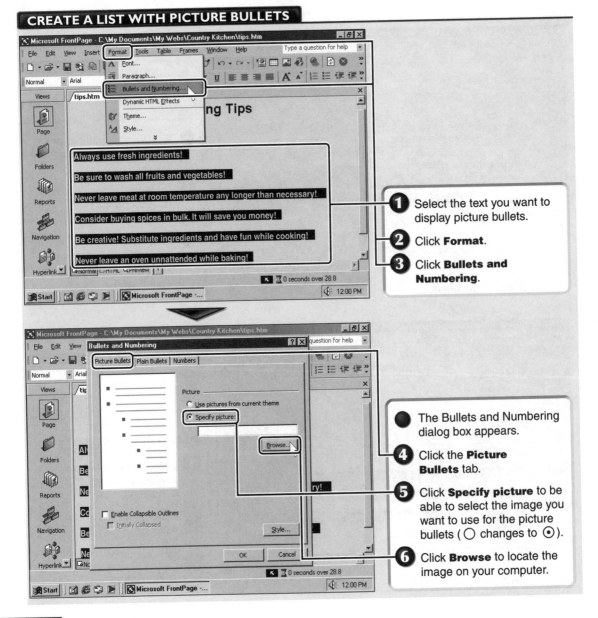

1 Select the text you want to display picture bullets.

2 Click **Format**.

3 Click **Bullets and Numbering**.

● The Bullets and Numbering dialog box appears.

4 Click the **Picture Bullets** tab.

5 Click **Specify picture** to be able to select the image you want to use for the picture bullets (○ changes to ⊙).

6 Click **Browse** to locate the image on your computer.

in an *instant*

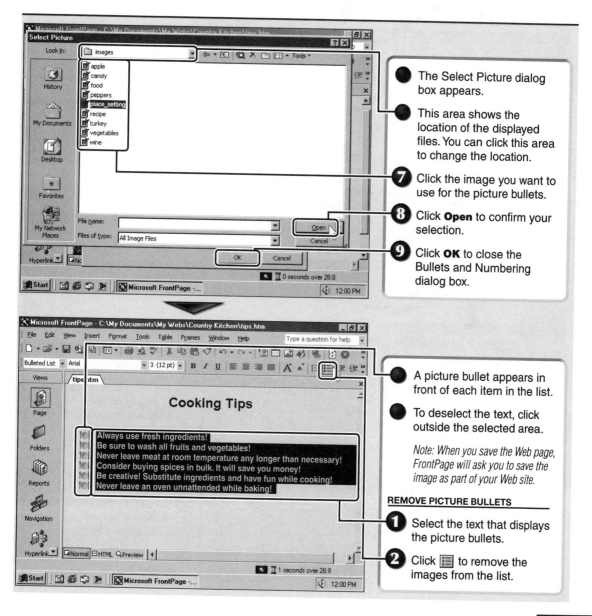

The Select Picture dialog box appears.

This area shows the location of the displayed files. You can click this area to change the location.

7 Click the image you want to use for the picture bullets.

8 Click **Open** to confirm your selection.

9 Click **OK** to close the Bullets and Numbering dialog box.

A picture bullet appears in front of each item in the list.

To deselect the text, click outside the selected area.

Note: When you save the Web page, FrontPage will ask you to save the image as part of your Web site.

REMOVE PICTURE BULLETS

1 Select the text that displays the picture bullets.

2 Click 📋 to remove the images from the list.

CHANGE BACKGROUND COLOR

You can change the background color of a Web page to customize the appearance of the page. Make sure you select a background color that works well with the color of your text. For example, red text on a blue background can be difficult to read.

CHANGE BACKGROUND COLOR

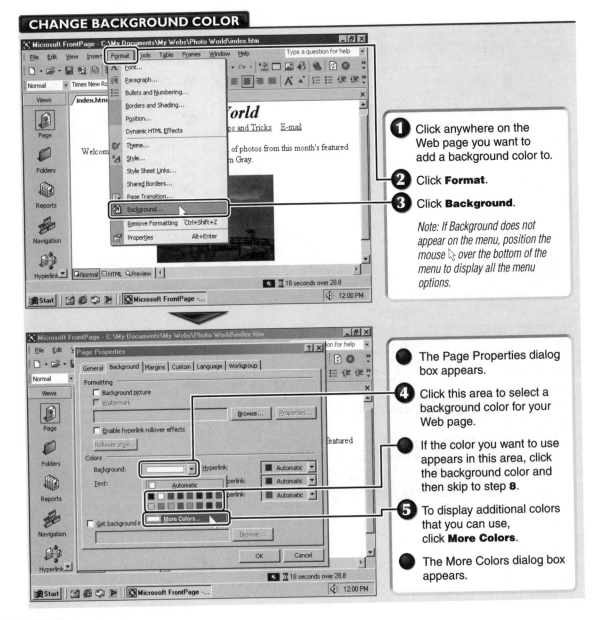

1 Click anywhere on the Web page you want to add a background color to.

2 Click **Format**.

3 Click **Background**.

Note: If Background does not appear on the menu, position the mouse ⩗ over the bottom of the menu to display all the menu options.

■ The Page Properties dialog box appears.

4 Click this area to select a background color for your Web page.

■ If the color you want to use appears in this area, click the background color and then skip to step **8**.

5 To display additional colors that you can use, click **More Colors**.

■ The More Colors dialog box appears.

in an *instant*

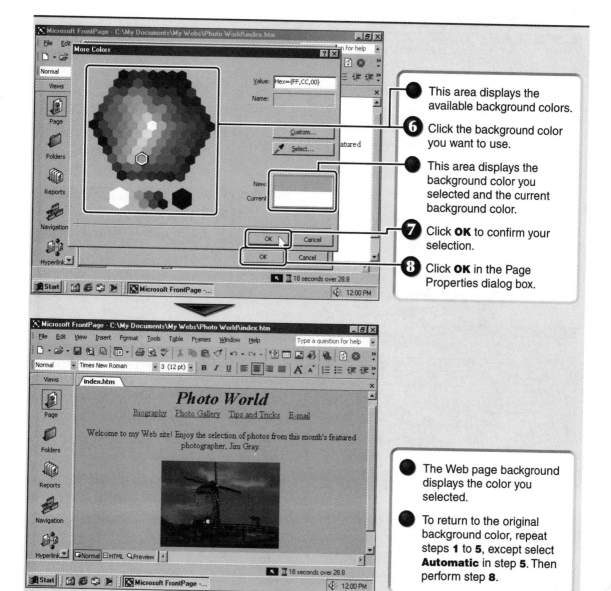

This area displays the available background colors.

6 Click the background color you want to use.

This area displays the background color you selected and the current background color.

7 Click **OK** to confirm your selection.

8 Click **OK** in the Page Properties dialog box.

The Web page background displays the color you selected.

To return to the original background color, repeat steps **1** to **5**, except select **Automatic** in step **5**. Then perform step **8**.

APPLY A THEME

FrontPage offers many themes that you can choose from to give your Web pages a professional appearance. Each theme consists of coordinated design elements, including fonts, colors, bullets and lines. You can apply a theme to all the Web pages in your Web site or to only the displayed page.

APPLY A THEME

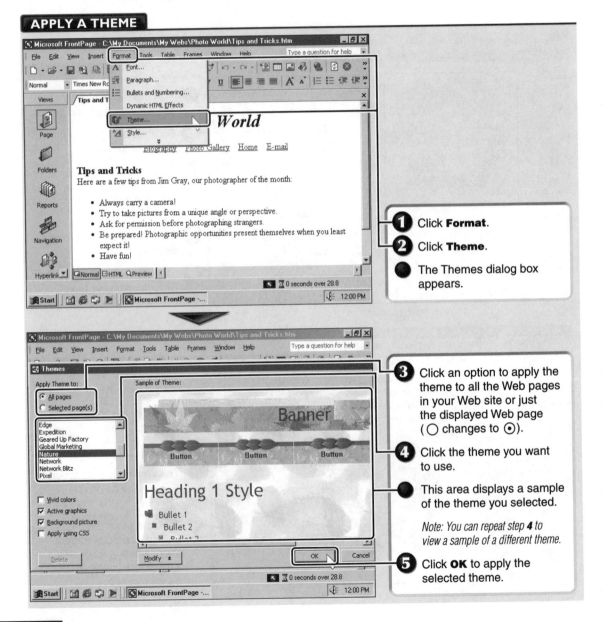

1 Click **Format**.

2 Click **Theme**.

● The Themes dialog box appears.

3 Click an option to apply the theme to all the Web pages in your Web site or just the displayed Web page (○ changes to ⊙).

4 Click the theme you want to use.

● This area displays a sample of the theme you selected.

Note: You can repeat step 4 to view a sample of a different theme.

5 Click **OK** to apply the selected theme.

in an *Instant*

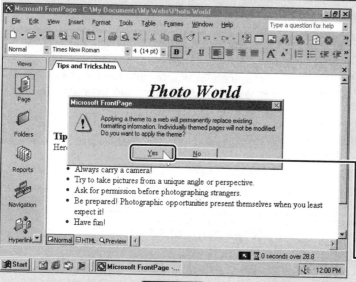

A dialog box may appear, stating that applying a theme will change the appearance of all your Web pages and permanently replace some of the formatting changes you previously made.

6 Click **Yes** to continue.

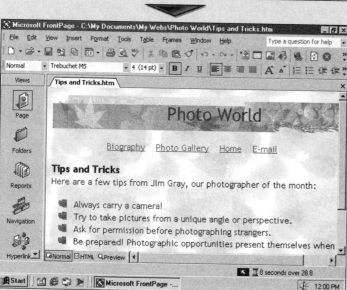

The Web page(s) you specified display the theme.

To remove a theme from Web pages, repeat steps **1** to **6**, selecting **(No Theme)** in step **4**.

INTRODUCTION TO IMAGES

FrontPage allows you to add images, such as photographs, drawings, picture bullets and navigation buttons, to your Web pages. Images can help illustrate ideas, add visual interest and help break up long sections of text on a Web page.

TYPES OF IMAGES

When you save a Web page, FrontPage automatically converts any images you added to the page to the GIF or JPEG format. The GIF and JPEG formats are the most popular image formats on the Web. Most Web browsers can display images in the GIF and JPEG format.

Graphics Interchange Format (GIF) images are limited to 256 colors and are often used for logos, banners and computer-generated art.

GIF images have the .gif extension, such as logo.gif.

Joint Photographic Experts Group (JPEG) images can have millions of colors and are often used for photographs and very large images. JPEG images have the .jpg extension, such as stonehenge.jpg.

OBTAIN IMAGES

INTERNET

Many Web sites offer images, such as computer-generated art and photographs, that you can use for free on your Web pages. Make sure you have permission to use any images you obtain on the Web. You can find images at the following Web sites.

www.allfree-clipart.com

www.free-graphics.com

www.noeticart.com

CREATE IMAGES

You can use an image editing program to create your own images. Creating your own images allows you to design images that best suit your Web pages. Popular image editing programs include Adobe Photoshop (www.adobe.com) and Jasc Paint Shop Pro (www.jasc.com). If you are creating a Web site for your company, you may want to hire a graphic artist to create images for you.

SCAN IMAGES

If you have existing images that you want to add to your Web pages, you can use a scanner to scan the images into your computer. You can scan photographs, logos or drawings and then place the scanned images on your Web pages. If you do not have a scanner, many service bureaus will scan images for a fee.

IMAGE COLLECTIONS

You can purchase collections of ready-made images at computer stores. Image collections can include cartoons, drawings, photographs and computer-generated art. You should try to purchase image collections that contain images in the GIF and JPEG formats, since these formats are the most popular image formats on the Web.

IMAGE CONSIDERATIONS

IMAGE SIZE

Images increase the time Web pages take to transfer and appear on a visitor's screen. If a Web page takes too long to appear, visitors may lose interest and move to another page. Whenever possible, you should use images with small file sizes since these images will transfer faster.

If you want to include a large image on a Web page, consider adding a thumbnail image. A thumbnail image is a small version of an image that visitors can select to display the larger image. Displaying a thumbnail image on a Web page allows visitors to decide if they want to wait to view the larger image.

IMAGE RESOLUTION

The resolution of an image refers to the clarity of the image. Higher resolution images are sharper and more detailed, but take longer to transfer and appear on a visitor's screen. Since most computer monitors display images at a resolution of 72 dots per inch (dpi), images you add to your Web pages do not need to have a resolution higher than 72 dpi.

REUSE IMAGES

If you use the same image on several Web pages in a Web site, the time the pages take to transfer and appear on a visitor's screen will not increase. When the same image appears on several Web pages in a Web site, the image transfers only once to a computer. The computer temporarily stores a copy of the image and displays the copy each time the image appears.

VIEW WEB PAGES WITHOUT IMAGES

Make sure your Web pages will look attractive and make sense if the images do not appear. Some visitors turn off the display of images to browse the Web more quickly, while others use Web browsers that cannot display images. FrontPage allows you to provide alternative text that will appear on a Web page if the images do not appear on a visitor's screen.

COPYRIGHT

You may find images in books, newspapers, magazines and on the Internet that you want to add to your Web pages. If the images you want to use are copyrighted, make sure you have permission to use any of these images on your Web pages.

ADD AN IMAGE

You can add an image to illustrate a concept or enhance the appearance of a Web page. For example, you can add photographs of your family or products, a map to give directions, a diagram or an advertisement.

ADD AN IMAGE

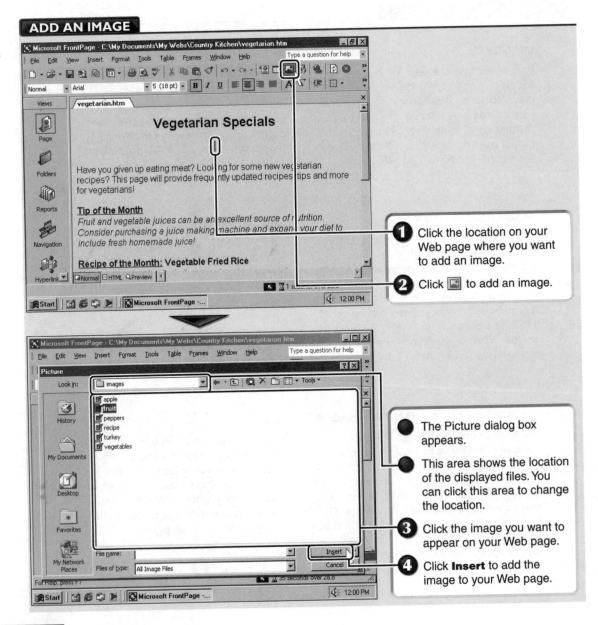

1 Click the location on your Web page where you want to add an image.

2 Click 🖻 to add an image.

● The Picture dialog box appears.

● This area shows the location of the displayed files. You can click this area to change the location.

3 Click the image you want to appear on your Web page.

4 Click **Insert** to add the image to your Web page.

in an *instant*

The image appears on your Web page.

The Pictures toolbar also appears, displaying buttons that allow you to change the appearance of the image.

DELETE AN IMAGE

1. Click the image you want to delete. Handles (■) appear around the image.

2. Press the Delete key to delete the image.

ADD AN AUTOSHAPE

FrontPage provides many ready-made shapes, called AutoShapes, that you can add to a Web page. AutoShapes can enhance a Web page or draw attention to important information. You can add many types of AutoShapes to a Web page, including lines, circles, squares, arrows, stars and banners.

ADD AN AUTOSHAPE

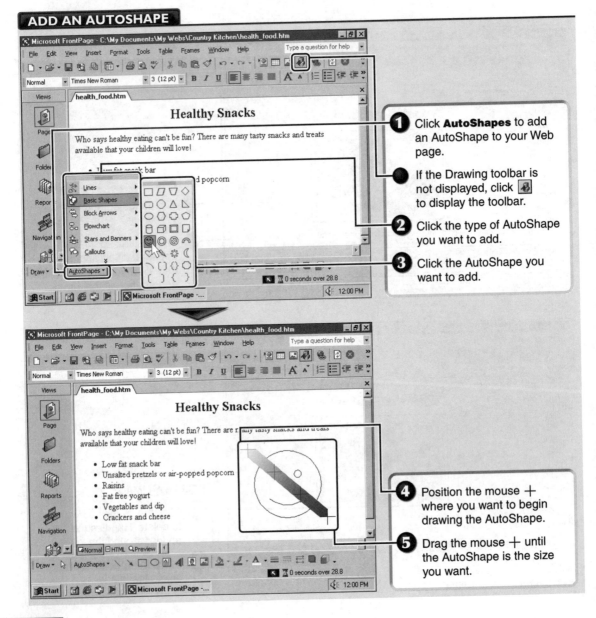

1 Click **AutoShapes** to add an AutoShape to your Web page.

If the Drawing toolbar is not displayed, click to display the toolbar.

2 Click the type of AutoShape you want to add.

3 Click the AutoShape you want to add.

4 Position the mouse + where you want to begin drawing the AutoShape.

5 Drag the mouse + until the AutoShape is the size you want.

in an *instant*

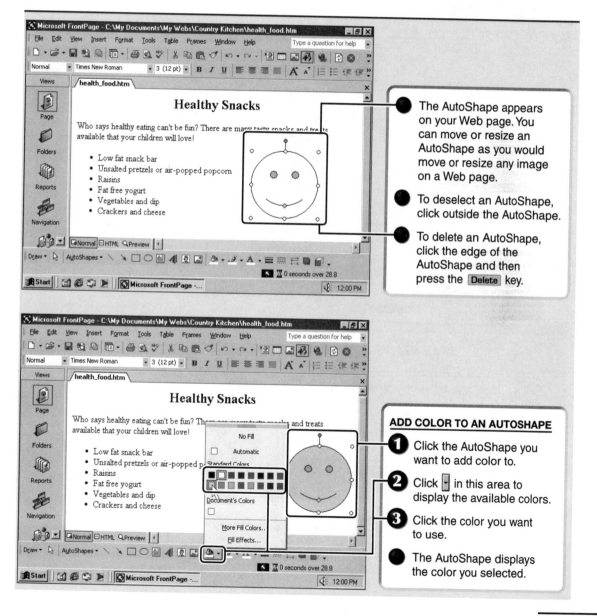

The AutoShape appears on your Web page. You can move or resize an AutoShape as you would move or resize any image on a Web page.

To deselect an AutoShape, click outside the AutoShape.

To delete an AutoShape, click the edge of the AutoShape and then press the **Delete** key.

ADD COLOR TO AN AUTOSHAPE

1 Click the AutoShape you want to add color to.

2 Click ⬝ in this area to display the available colors.

3 Click the color you want to use.

The AutoShape displays the color you selected.

ADD WORDART

You can add WordArt to a Web page to display a decorative title or draw attention to important information. FrontPage offers various WordArt styles that you can choose from, including styles that stretch, rotate, curve or add a shadow to text.

ADD WORDART

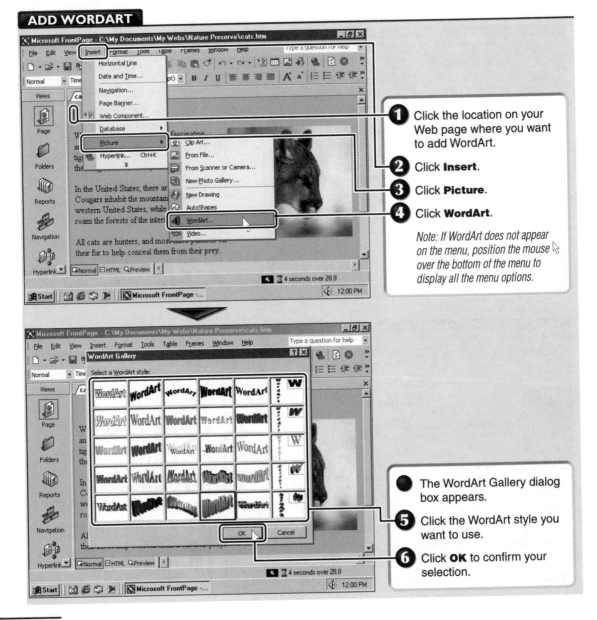

1 Click the location on your Web page where you want to add WordArt.

2 Click **Insert**.

3 Click **Picture**.

4 Click **WordArt**.

Note: If WordArt does not appear on the menu, position the mouse over the bottom of the menu to display all the menu options.

● The WordArt Gallery dialog box appears.

5 Click the WordArt style you want to use.

6 Click **OK** to confirm your selection.

in an *instant*

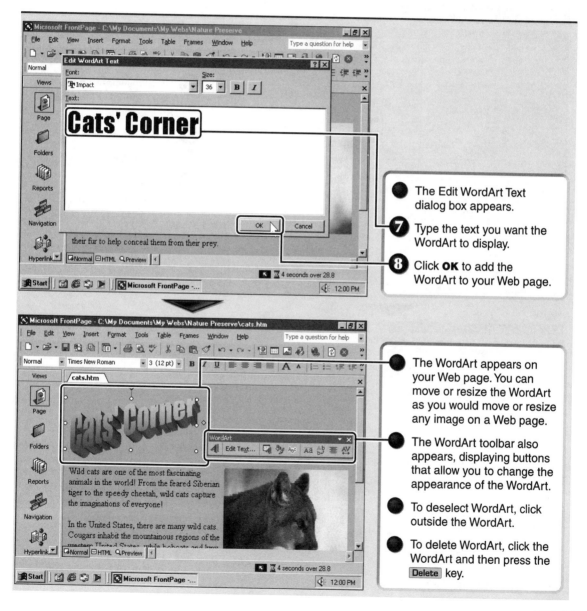

The Edit WordArt Text dialog box appears.

7 Type the text you want the WordArt to display.

8 Click **OK** to add the WordArt to your Web page.

The WordArt appears on your Web page. You can move or resize the WordArt as you would move or resize any image on a Web page.

The WordArt toolbar also appears, displaying buttons that allow you to change the appearance of the WordArt.

To deselect WordArt, click outside the WordArt.

To delete WordArt, click the WordArt and then press the Delete key.

ADD A CLIP ART IMAGE

You can add a professionally designed clip art image to a Web page to make the page more interesting. FrontPage includes the Clip Organizer, which organizes the image, sound and video files on your computer. You can use the Clip Organizer to add a clip art image to a Web page.

ADD A CLIP ART IMAGE

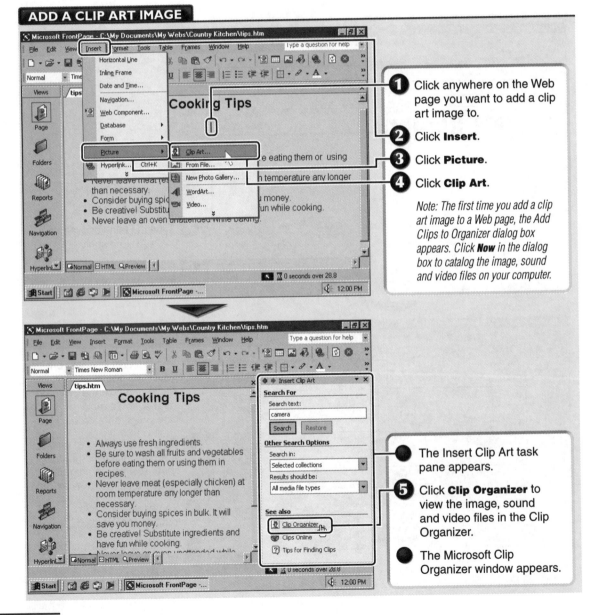

1 Click anywhere on the Web page you want to add a clip art image to.

2 Click **Insert**.

3 Click **Picture**.

4 Click **Clip Art**.

*Note: The first time you add a clip art image to a Web page, the Add Clips to Organizer dialog box appears. Click **Now** in the dialog box to catalog the image, sound and video files on your computer.*

■ The Insert Clip Art task pane appears.

5 Click **Clip Organizer** to view the image, sound and video files in the Clip Organizer.

■ The Microsoft Clip Organizer window appears.

in an instant

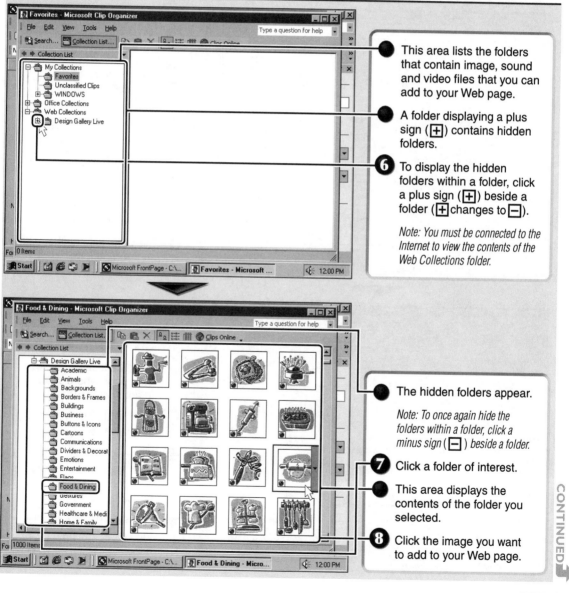

This area lists the folders that contain image, sound and video files that you can add to your Web page.

A folder displaying a plus sign (+) contains hidden folders.

6 To display the hidden folders within a folder, click a plus sign (+) beside a folder (+ changes to −).

Note: You must be connected to the Internet to view the contents of the Web Collections folder.

The hidden folders appear.

Note: To once again hide the folders within a folder, click a minus sign (−) beside a folder.

7 Click a folder of interest.

This area displays the contents of the folder you selected.

8 Click the image you want to add to your Web page.

CONTINUED

After you locate a suitable image in the Clip Organizer, you can copy the image and then place the image on your Web page. If you cannot find a suitable image, you can search for an image by specifying words of interest. FrontPage will search the file names and keywords assigned to clip art images for the words you specify.

ADD A CLIP ART IMAGE (CONTINUED)

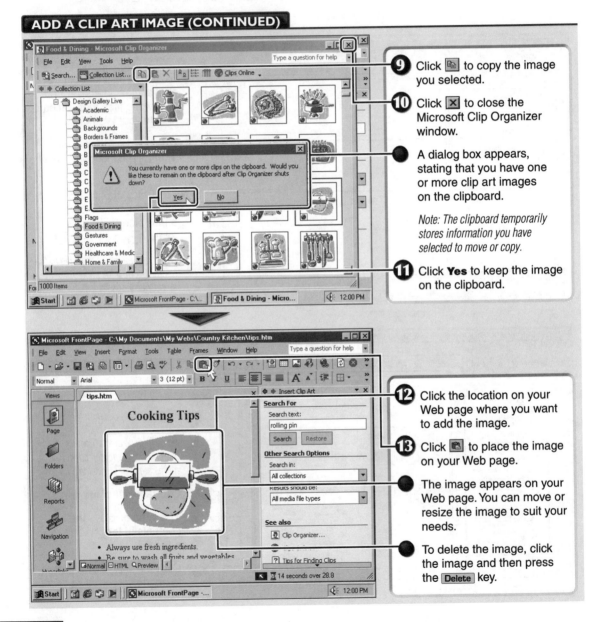

⑨ Click 🔳 to copy the image you selected.

⑩ Click ⊠ to close the Microsoft Clip Organizer window.

● A dialog box appears, stating that you have one or more clip art images on the clipboard.

Note: The clipboard temporarily stores information you have selected to move or copy.

⑪ Click **Yes** to keep the image on the clipboard.

⑫ Click the location on your Web page where you want to add the image.

⑬ Click 🔳 to place the image on your Web page.

● The image appears on your Web page. You can move or resize the image to suit your needs.

● To delete the image, click the image and then press the Delete key.

in an instant

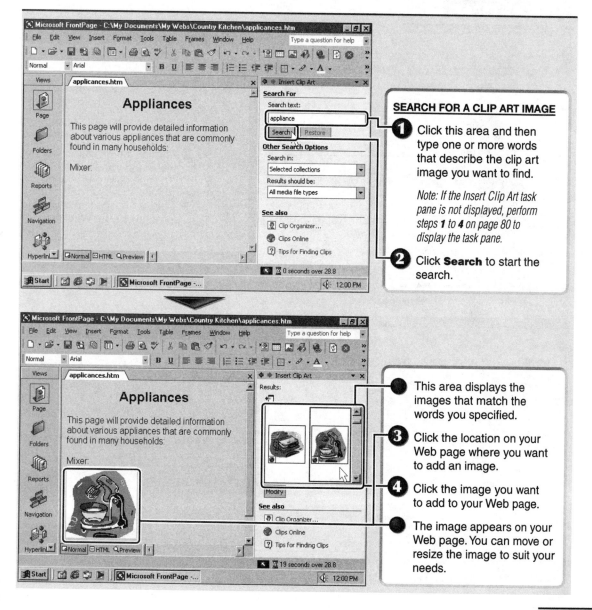

SEARCH FOR A CLIP ART IMAGE

1 Click this area and then type one or more words that describe the clip art image you want to find.

Note: If the Insert Clip Art task pane is not displayed, perform steps 1 to 4 on page 80 to display the task pane.

2 Click **Search** to start the search.

■ This area displays the images that match the words you specified.

3 Click the location on your Web page where you want to add an image.

4 Click the image you want to add to your Web page.

■ The image appears on your Web page. You can move or resize the image to suit your needs.

MOVE OR RESIZE AN IMAGE

You can change the location and size of an image on a Web page. Moving or resizing an image can improve the layout of a Web page. When you resize an image, try not to make the image too large since the image may appear distorted.

MOVE AN IMAGE

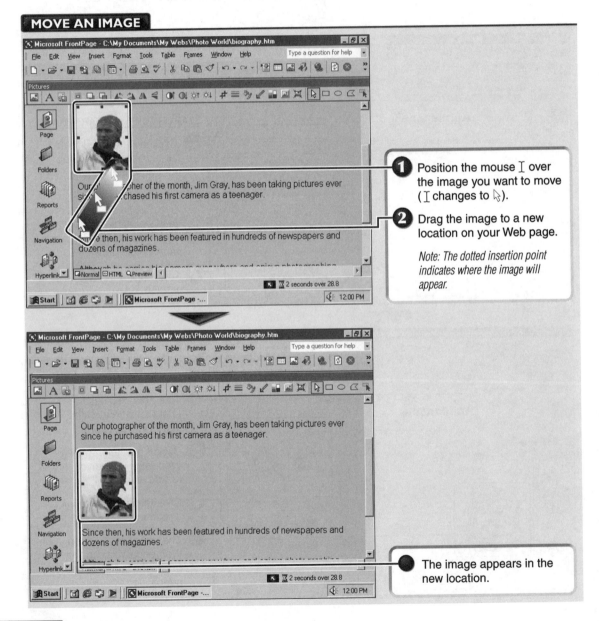

1 Position the mouse I over the image you want to move (I changes to ↳).

2 Drag the image to a new location on your Web page.

Note: The dotted insertion point indicates where the image will appear.

■ The image appears in the new location.

in an instant

RESIZE AN IMAGE

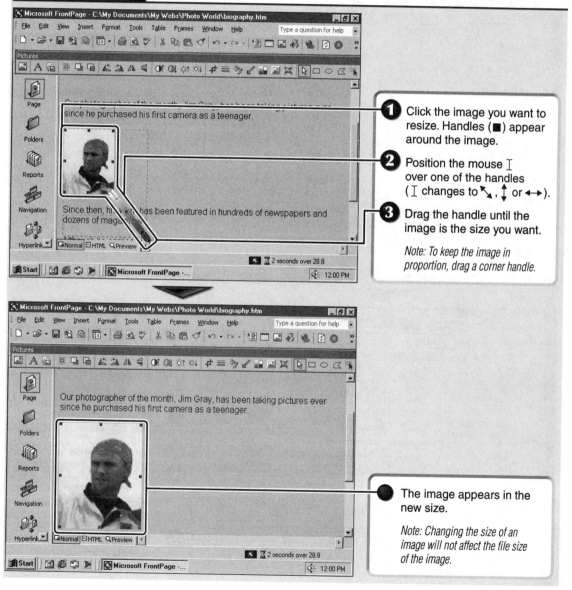

1 Click the image you want to resize. Handles (■) appear around the image.

2 Position the mouse I over one of the handles (I changes to ↖, ↕ or ↔).

3 Drag the handle until the image is the size you want.

Note: To keep the image in proportion, drag a corner handle.

● The image appears in the new size.

Note: Changing the size of an image will not affect the file size of the image.

PROVIDE ALTERNATIVE TEXT

You can provide text that you want to display if an image does not appear on a Web page. This will give visitors information about the missing image. Some visitors use Web browsers that cannot display images, while others turn off the display of images to browse the Web more quickly.

PROVIDE ALTERNATIVE TEXT

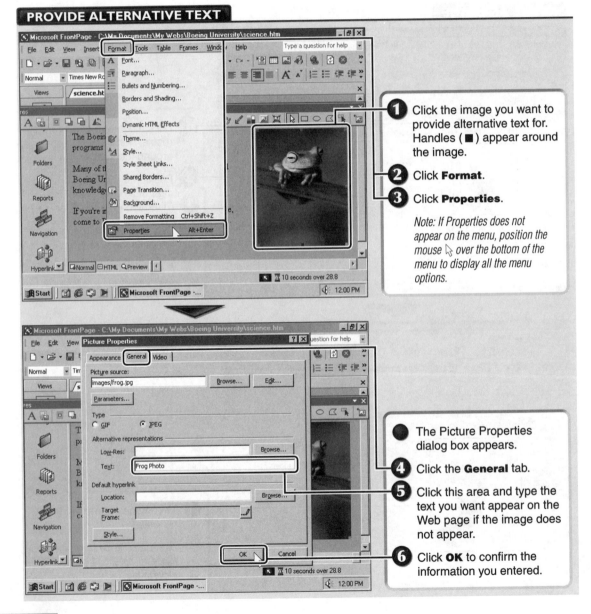

1. Click the image you want to provide alternative text for. Handles (■) appear around the image.
2. Click **Format**.
3. Click **Properties**.

Note: If Properties does not appear on the menu, position the mouse over the bottom of the menu to display all the menu options.

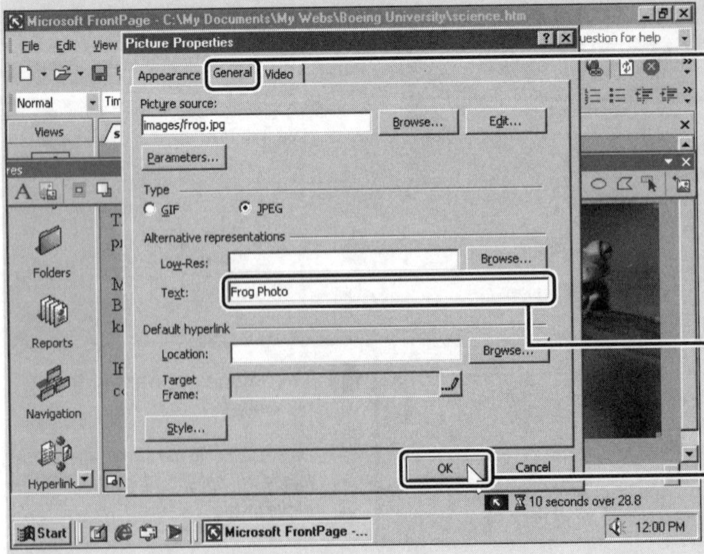

- The Picture Properties dialog box appears.

4. Click the **General** tab.
5. Click this area and type the text you want appear on the Web page if the image does not appear.
6. Click **OK** to confirm the information you entered.

You can add a horizontal line to visually separate sections of a Web page. Make sure you do not overuse horizontal lines on your Web pages since this can distract your visitors and make your Web pages difficult to read. Try not to place more than one horizontal line on each screen.

ADD A HORIZONTAL LINE

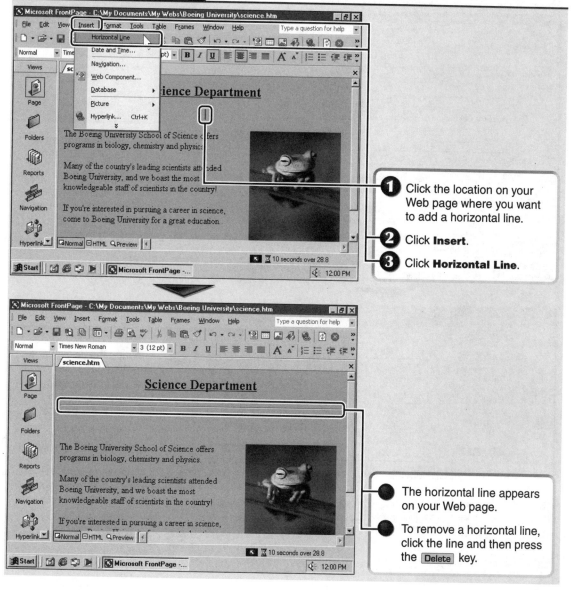

1 Click the location on your Web page where you want to add a horizontal line.

2 Click **Insert**.

3 Click **Horizontal Line**.

● The horizontal line appears on your Web page.

● To remove a horizontal line, click the line and then press the Delete key.

You can customize the appearance of a horizontal line on a Web page. FrontPage allows you to change the width, color, height and alignment of a horizontal line. When you change the color of a horizontal line, consider that the Netscape Navigator Web browser cannot display a horizontal line in color.

CUSTOMIZE A HORIZONTAL LINE

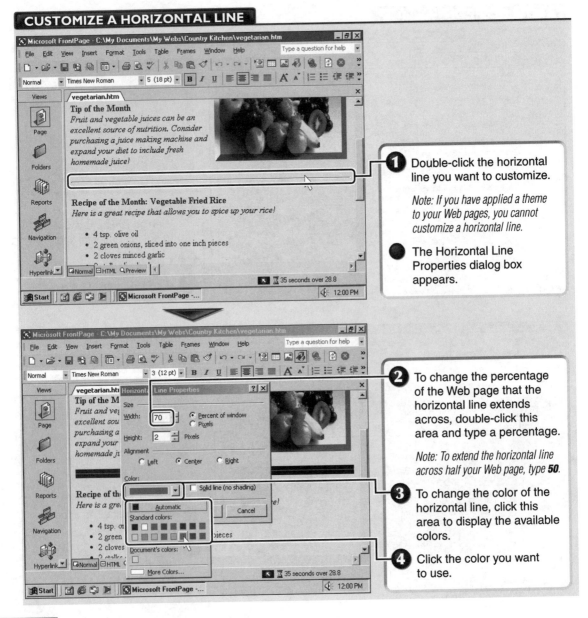

1 Double-click the horizontal line you want to customize.

Note: If you have applied a theme to your Web pages, you cannot customize a horizontal line.

● The Horizontal Line Properties dialog box appears.

2 To change the percentage of the Web page that the horizontal line extends across, double-click this area and type a percentage.

Note: To extend the horizontal line across half your Web page, type 50.

3 To change the color of the horizontal line, click this area to display the available colors.

4 Click the color you want to use.

in an instant

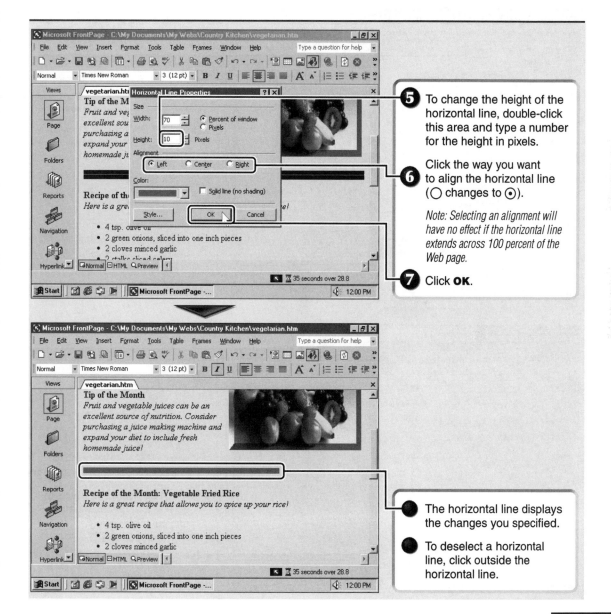

5 To change the height of the horizontal line, double-click this area and type a number for the height in pixels.

6 Click the way you want to align the horizontal line (○ changes to ⊙).

Note: Selecting an alignment will have no effect if the horizontal line extends across 100 percent of the Web page.

7 Click **OK**.

● The horizontal line displays the changes you specified.

● To deselect a horizontal line, click outside the horizontal line.

You can have a small image repeat to fill an entire Web page. This can add an interesting background design to a Web page. Many Web sites, such as imagine.metanet.com, offer background images you can use for free. A good background image has a small file size and will not affect the readability of your Web page.

ADD A BACKGROUND IMAGE

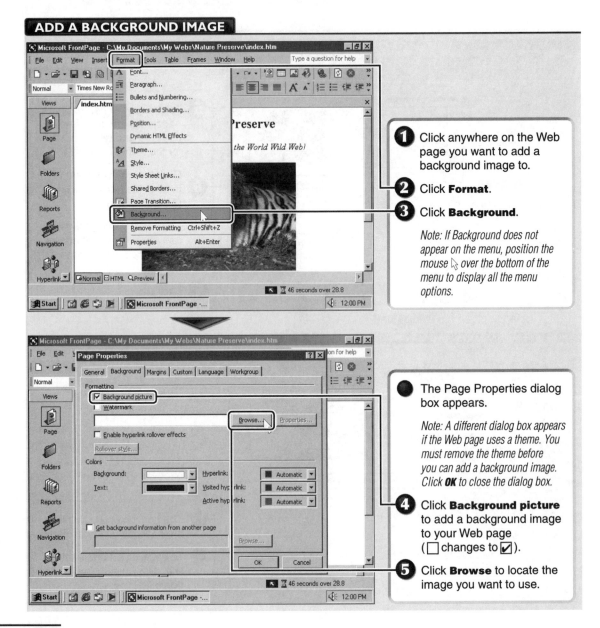

1 Click anywhere on the Web page you want to add a background image to.

2 Click **Format**.

3 Click **Background**.

Note: If Background does not appear on the menu, position the mouse ⓘ over the bottom of the menu to display all the menu options.

● The Page Properties dialog box appears.

Note: A different dialog box appears if the Web page uses a theme. You must remove the theme before you can add a background image. Click OK to close the dialog box.

4 Click **Background picture** to add a background image to your Web page (☐ changes to ☑).

5 Click **Browse** to locate the image you want to use.

in an instant

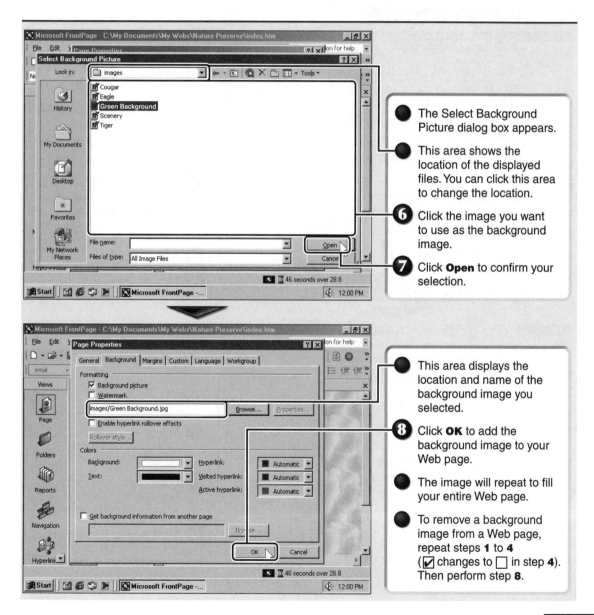

The Select Background Picture dialog box appears.

This area shows the location of the displayed files. You can click this area to change the location.

6 Click the image you want to use as the background image.

7 Click **Open** to confirm your selection.

This area displays the location and name of the background image you selected.

8 Click **OK** to add the background image to your Web page.

The image will repeat to fill your entire Web page.

To remove a background image from a Web page, repeat steps **1** to **4** (☑ changes to ☐ in step **4**). Then perform step **8**.

CREATE A PHOTO GALLERY

You can create a photo gallery to neatly display several images on a Web page. When you create a photo gallery, FrontPage automatically creates thumbnails of your images. A thumbnail image is a small version of an image that visitors can select to display a larger version of the image.

CREATE A PHOTO GALLERY

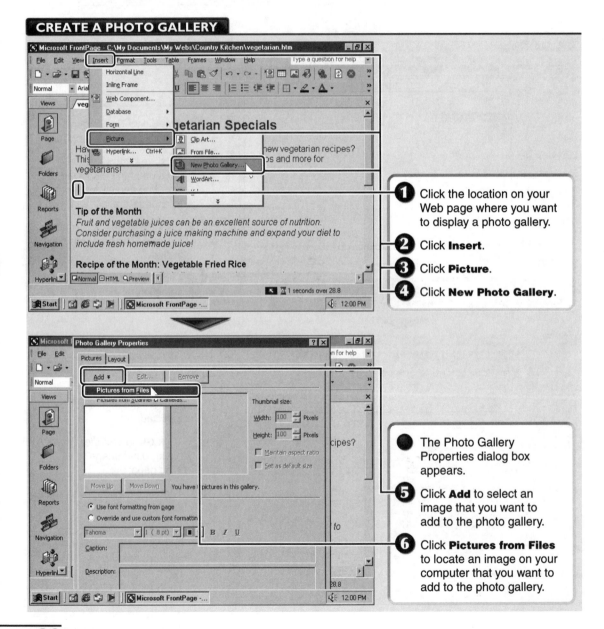

1 Click the location on your Web page where you want to display a photo gallery.

2 Click **Insert**.

3 Click **Picture**.

4 Click **New Photo Gallery**.

■ The Photo Gallery Properties dialog box appears.

5 Click **Add** to select an image that you want to add to the photo gallery.

6 Click **Pictures from Files** to locate an image on your computer that you want to add to the photo gallery.

in an *instant*

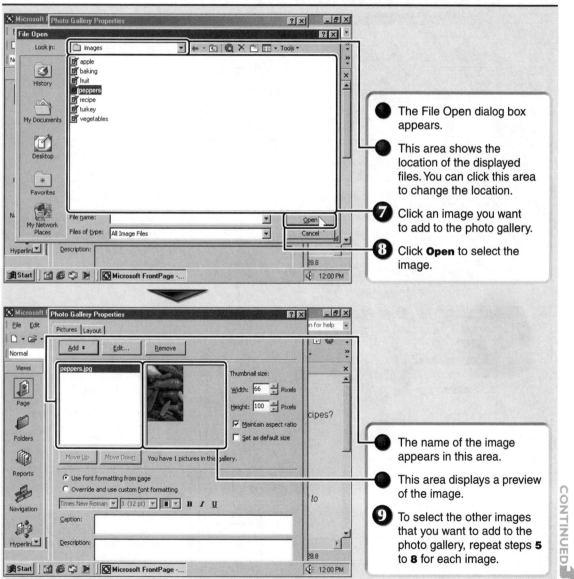

The File Open dialog box appears.

This area shows the location of the displayed files. You can click this area to change the location.

7 Click an image you want to add to the photo gallery.

8 Click **Open** to select the image.

The name of the image appears in this area.

This area displays a preview of the image.

9 To select the other images that you want to add to the photo gallery, repeat steps **5** to **8** for each image.

CONTINUED

When creating a photo gallery, you can provide a title and description that you want to display beside each image. Providing a title and description is useful if your photo gallery displays images you want to describe to your visitors, such as photographs of your products or family vacation.

CREATE A PHOTO GALLERY (CONTINUED)

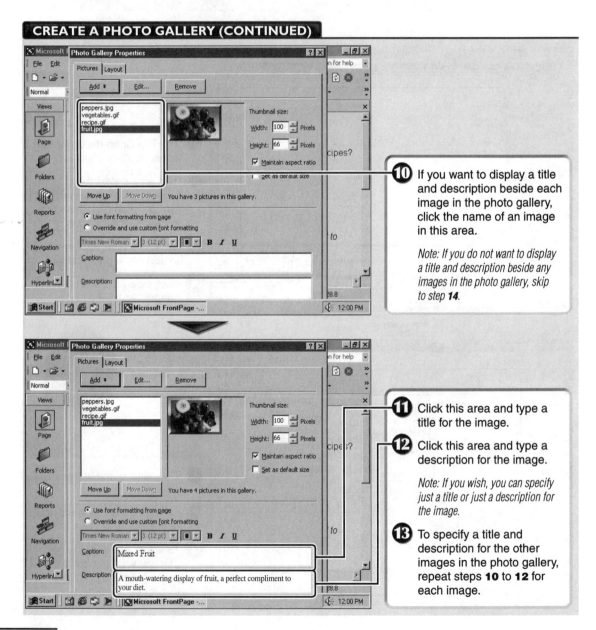

10 If you want to display a title and description beside each image in the photo gallery, click the name of an image in this area.

Note: If you do not want to display a title and description beside any images in the photo gallery, skip to step 14.

11 Click this area and type a title for the image.

12 Click this area and type a description for the image.

Note: If you wish, you can specify just a title or just a description for the image.

13 To specify a title and description for the other images in the photo gallery, repeat steps **10** to **12** for each image.

in an instant

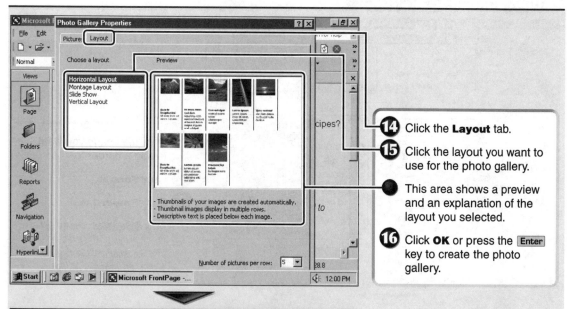

14 Click the **Layout** tab.

15 Click the layout you want to use for the photo gallery.

● This area shows a preview and an explanation of the layout you selected.

16 Click **OK** or press the Enter key to create the photo gallery.

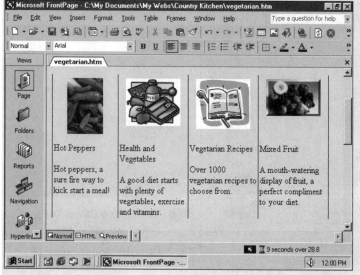

● The photo gallery appears on your Web page.

Note: To test the photo gallery, you can use the Preview view.

● To make changes to the photo gallery, double-click the photo gallery and then repeat steps **5** to **16** starting on page 92.

● To delete a photo gallery, click the photo gallery and then press the Delete key.

ADD A BORDER TO AN IMAGE

You can add a border to an image on a Web page. Adding a border allows you to place a frame around an image. FrontPage will add a black border around an image, unless the image is a link. By default, FrontPage will add a blue border around a linked image to help people quickly recognize that the image is a link.

ADD A BORDER TO AN IMAGE

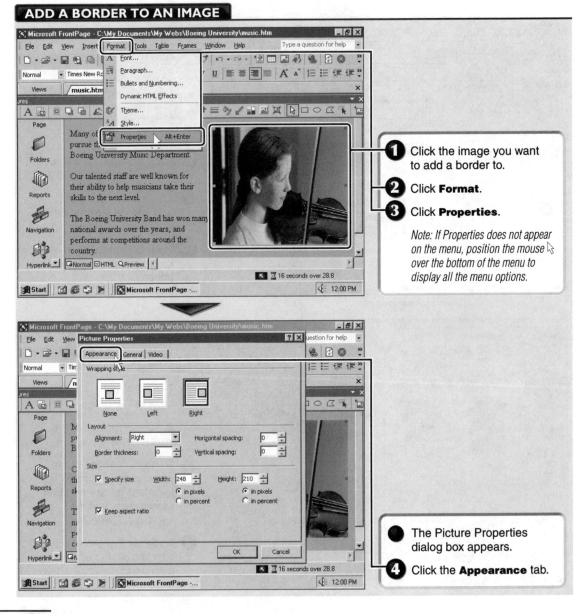

1 Click the image you want to add a border to.

2 Click **Format**.

3 Click **Properties**.

Note: If Properties does not appear on the menu, position the mouse ⌖ over the bottom of the menu to display all the menu options.

● The Picture Properties dialog box appears.

4 Click the **Appearance** tab.

in an instant

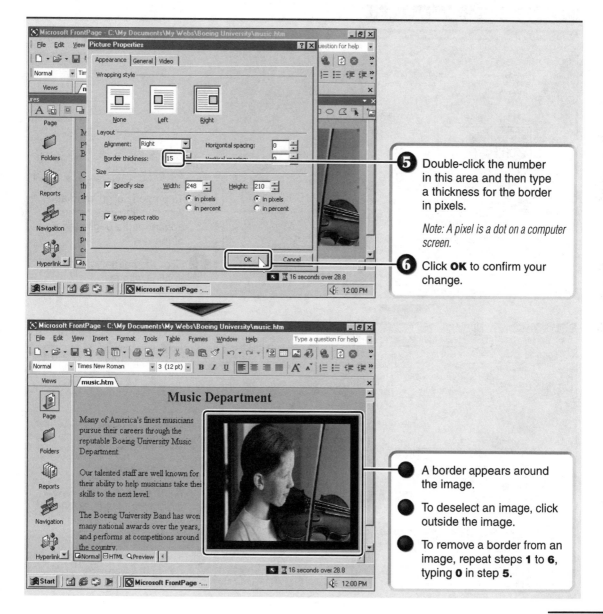

5 Double-click the number in this area and then type a thickness for the border in pixels.

Note: A pixel is a dot on a computer screen.

6 Click **OK** to confirm your change.

● A border appears around the image.

● To deselect an image, click outside the image.

● To remove a border from an image, repeat steps **1** to **6**, typing **0** in step **5**.

ALIGN AN IMAGE WITH TEXT

You can change the way an image appears in relation to surrounding text on a Web page. For example, you can wrap text around the left or right side of an image. You can also align text with the top, middle or bottom part of an image.

ALIGN AN IMAGE WITH TEXT

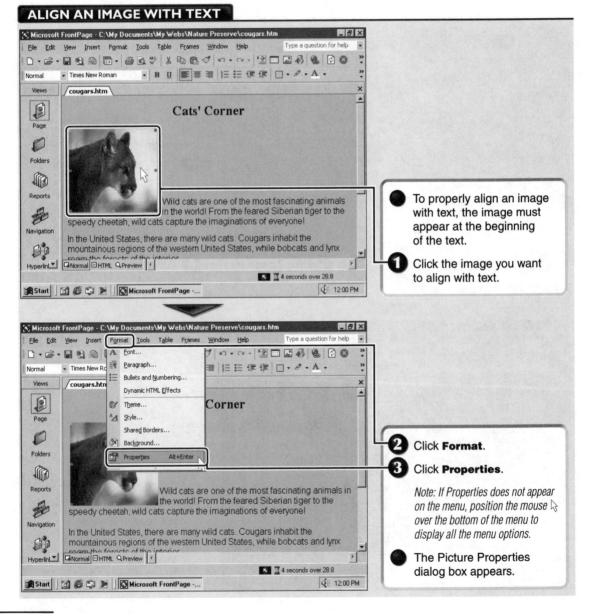

■ To properly align an image with text, the image must appear at the beginning of the text.

1 Click the image you want to align with text.

2 Click **Format**.

3 Click **Properties**.

Note: If Properties does not appear on the menu, position the mouse over the bottom of the menu to display all the menu options.

■ The Picture Properties dialog box appears.

in an *Instant*

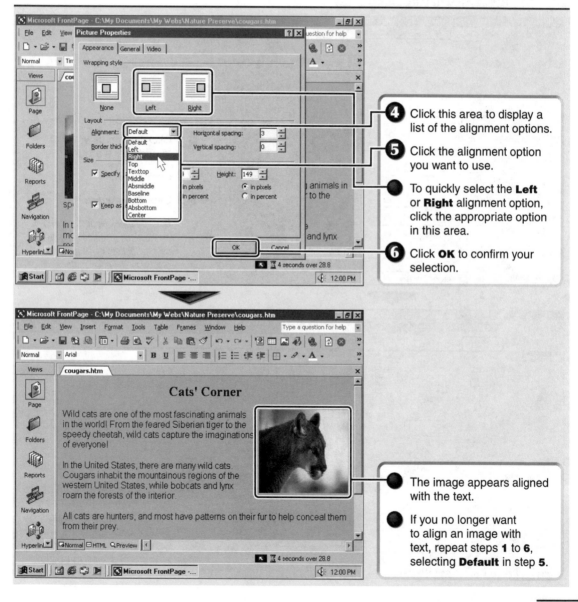

4 Click this area to display a list of the alignment options.

5 Click the alignment option you want to use.

To quickly select the **Left** or **Right** alignment option, click the appropriate option in this area.

6 Click **OK** to confirm your selection.

The image appears aligned with the text.

If you no longer want to align an image with text, repeat steps **1** to **6**, selecting **Default** in step **5**.

ADD SPACE AROUND AN IMAGE

You can increase the amount of space around an image on a Web page. This is useful when you want to add space between an image and text that wraps around the image. FrontPage allows you to add space on both the left and right sides of an image or both above and below an image. You cannot increase the amount of space on just one side of an image.

ADD SPACE AROUND AN IMAGE

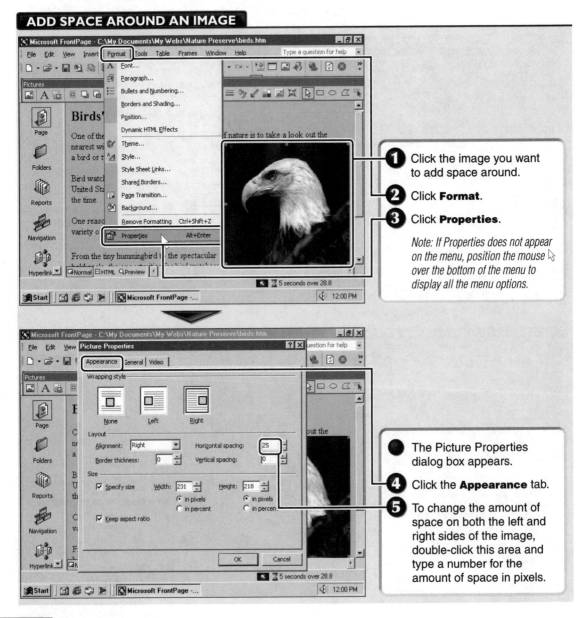

1 Click the image you want to add space around.

2 Click **Format**.

3 Click **Properties**.

Note: If Properties does not appear on the menu, position the mouse over the bottom of the menu to display all the menu options.

■ The Picture Properties dialog box appears.

4 Click the **Appearance** tab.

5 To change the amount of space on both the left and right sides of the image, double-click this area and type a number for the amount of space in pixels.

in an *instant*

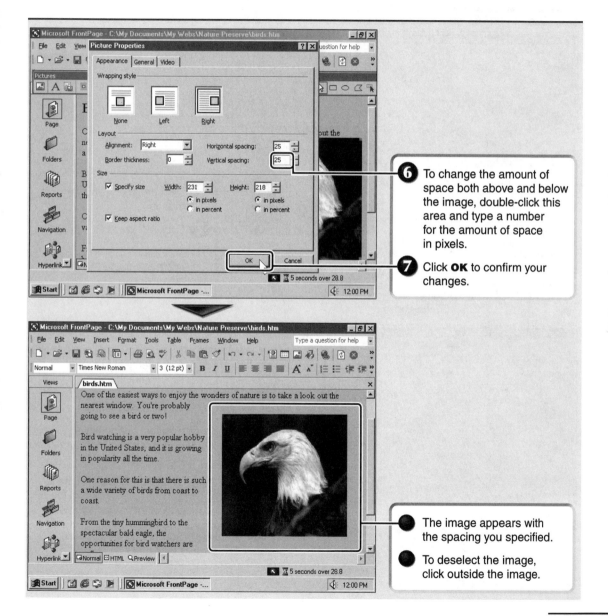

6 To change the amount of space both above and below the image, double-click this area and type a number for the amount of space in pixels.

7 Click **OK** to confirm your changes.

● The image appears with the spacing you specified.

● To deselect the image, click outside the image.

CROP AN IMAGE

You can crop an image to remove parts of an image that you do not want to show on a Web page. Cropping an image is useful when you want to focus a visitor's attention on an important part of an image or make an image fit better on a Web page.

CROP AN IMAGE

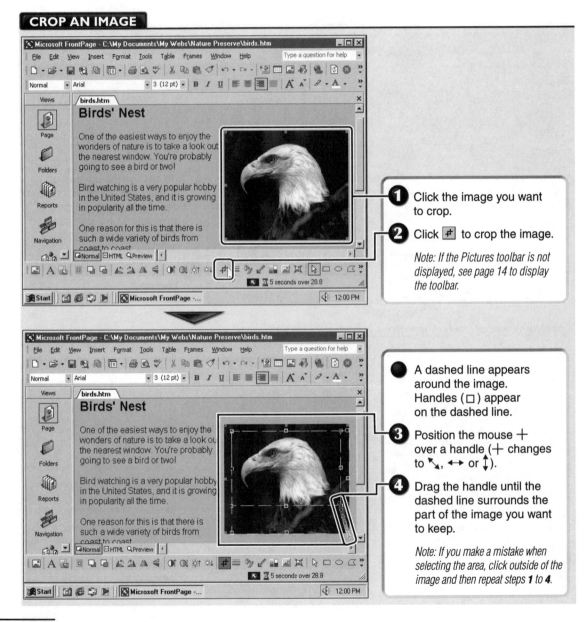

1 Click the image you want to crop.

2 Click [#] to crop the image.

Note: If the Pictures toolbar is not displayed, see page 14 to display the toolbar.

● A dashed line appears around the image. Handles (□) appear on the dashed line.

3 Position the mouse + over a handle (+ changes to ↖, ↔ or ↕).

4 Drag the handle until the dashed line surrounds the part of the image you want to keep.

Note: If you make a mistake when selecting the area, click outside of the image and then repeat steps 1 to 4.

in an *instant*

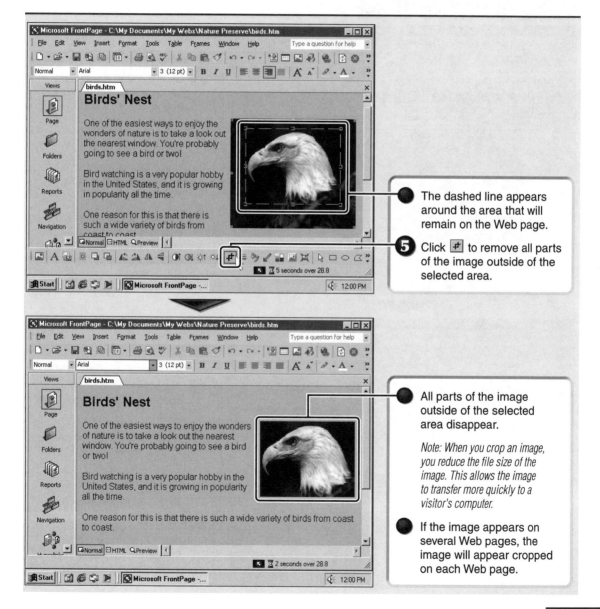

The dashed line appears around the area that will remain on the Web page.

5 Click 🔲 to remove all parts of the image outside of the selected area.

All parts of the image outside of the selected area disappear.

Note: When you crop an image, you reduce the file size of the image. This allows the image to transfer more quickly to a visitor's computer.

If the image appears on several Web pages, the image will appear cropped on each Web page.

CREATE A THUMBNAIL IMAGE

You can create a thumbnail image, which is a small version of an image that visitors can select to display a larger version of the image. A thumbnail image transfers faster and appears on a visitor's screen more quickly than a larger version of the image.

CREATE A THUMBNAIL IMAGE

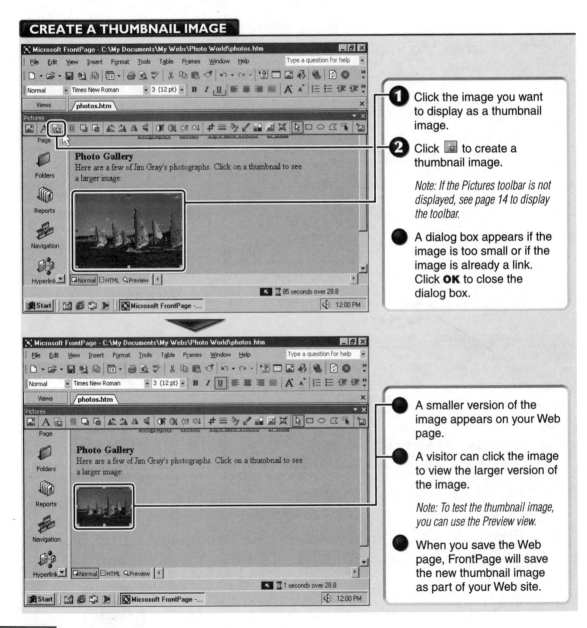

① Click the image you want to display as a thumbnail image.

② Click ⬛ to create a thumbnail image.

Note: If the Pictures toolbar is not displayed, see page 14 to display the toolbar.

● A dialog box appears if the image is too small or if the image is already a link. Click **OK** to close the dialog box.

● A smaller version of the image appears on your Web page.

● A visitor can click the image to view the larger version of the image.

Note: To test the thumbnail image, you can use the Preview view.

● When you save the Web page, FrontPage will save the new thumbnail image as part of your Web site.

104

You can make the background of an image transparent so the background will blend into a Web page. Making an image background transparent works best when the entire background of the image is one color. You can only make the background of a GIF image transparent.

MAKE AN IMAGE BACKGROUND TRANSPARENT

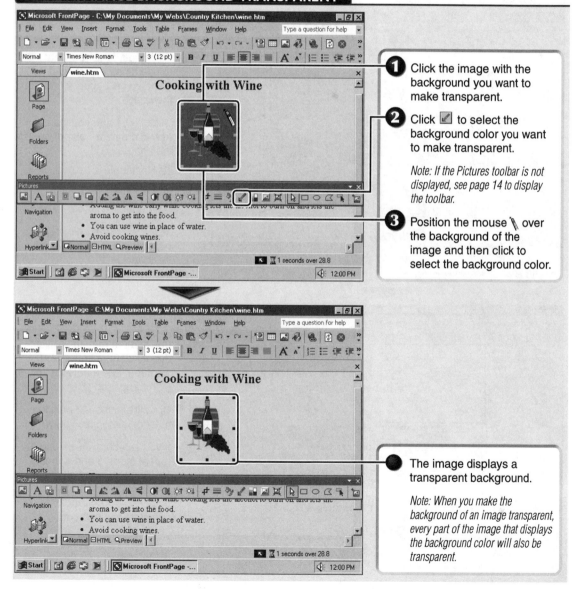

① Click the image with the background you want to make transparent.

② Click 🖉 to select the background color you want to make transparent.

Note: If the Pictures toolbar is not displayed, see page 14 to display the toolbar.

③ Position the mouse ▶ over the background of the image and then click to select the background color.

● The image displays a transparent background.

Note: When you make the background of an image transparent, every part of the image that displays the background color will also be transparent.

105

CREATE AN IMAGE MAP

You can create an image map that divides an image into different areas, called hotspots, that each link to a different Web page. Creating an image map is useful for an image such as a floor plan or map that you want to contain links to different Web pages.

CREATE AN IMAGE MAP

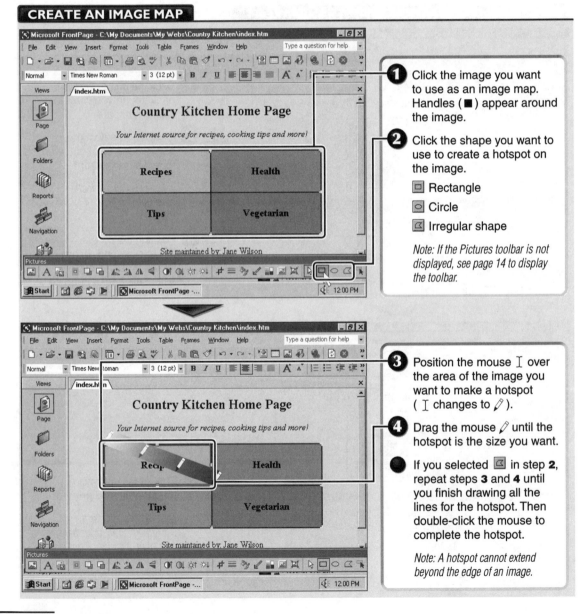

1 Click the image you want to use as an image map. Handles (■) appear around the image.

2 Click the shape you want to use to create a hotspot on the image.

▢ Rectangle

◯ Circle

◪ Irregular shape

Note: If the Pictures toolbar is not displayed, see page 14 to display the toolbar.

3 Position the mouse I over the area of the image you want to make a hotspot (I changes to ✎).

4 Drag the mouse ✎ until the hotspot is the size you want.

● If you selected ◪ in step **2**, repeat steps **3** and **4** until you finish drawing all the lines for the hotspot. Then double-click the mouse to complete the hotspot.

Note: A hotspot cannot extend beyond the edge of an image.

in an *instant*

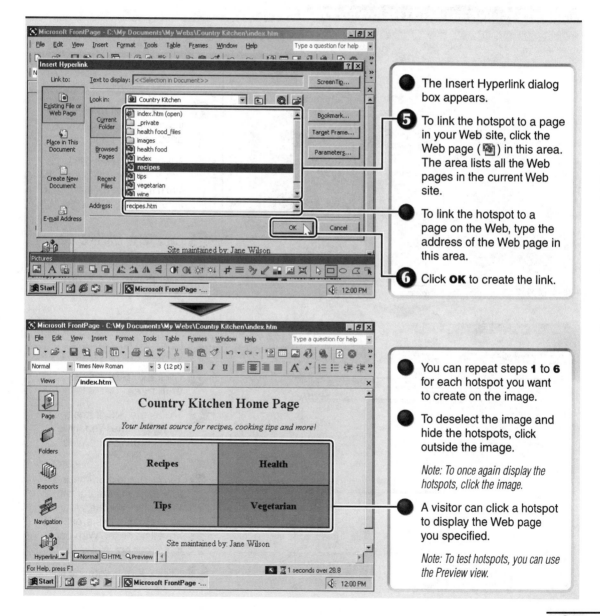

The Insert Hyperlink dialog box appears.

5 To link the hotspot to a page in your Web site, click the Web page (📄) in this area. The area lists all the Web pages in the current Web site.

To link the hotspot to a page on the Web, type the address of the Web page in this area.

6 Click **OK** to create the link.

You can repeat steps **1** to **6** for each hotspot you want to create on the image.

To deselect the image and hide the hotspots, click outside the image.

Note: To once again display the hotspots, click the image.

A visitor can click a hotspot to display the Web page you specified.

Note: To test hotspots, you can use the Preview view.

CREATE A LINK TO ANOTHER WEB PAGE

You can create a link to connect a word, phrase or image on a Web page to another page on the Web. FrontPage allows you to create a link to a Web page in your own Web site or to a Web page created by another person or company.

CREATE A LINK TO ANOTHER WEB PAGE

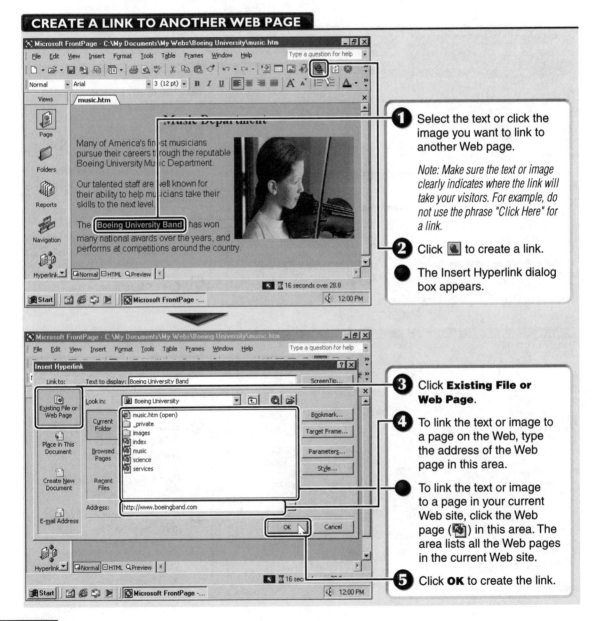

1 Select the text or click the image you want to link to another Web page.

Note: Make sure the text or image clearly indicates where the link will take your visitors. For example, do not use the phrase "Click Here" for a link.

2 Click █ to create a link.

● The Insert Hyperlink dialog box appears.

3 Click **Existing File or Web Page**.

4 To link the text or image to a page on the Web, type the address of the Web page in this area.

● To link the text or image to a page in your current Web site, click the Web page (█) in this area. The area lists all the Web pages in the current Web site.

5 Click **OK** to create the link.

in an instant

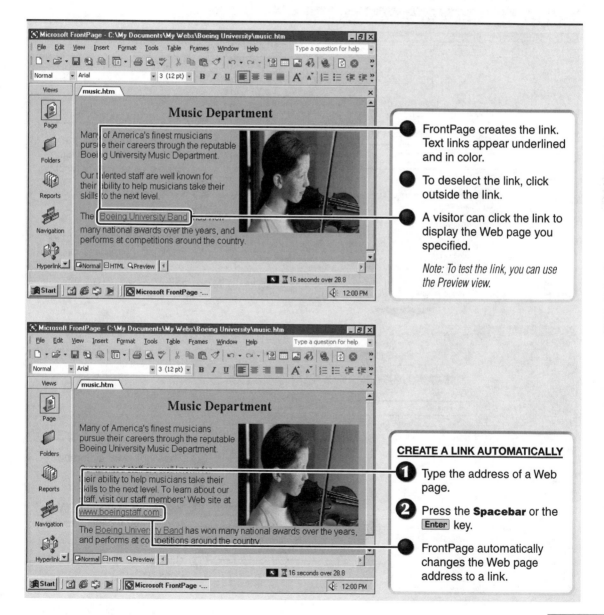

FrontPage creates the link. Text links appear underlined and in color.

To deselect the link, click outside the link.

A visitor can click the link to display the Web page you specified.

Note: To test the link, you can use the Preview view.

CREATE A LINK AUTOMATICALLY

1 Type the address of a Web page.

2 Press the **Spacebar** or the Enter key.

FrontPage automatically changes the Web page address to a link.

CREATE A LINK TO A WEB PAGE AREA

You can create a link that visitors can select to display a specific area on a Web page. This allows visitors to quickly display information of interest. Before you can create a link to a specific Web page area, you must create a bookmark. A bookmark identifies the Web page area that you want visitors to be able to quickly display.

CREATE A LINK TO A WEB PAGE AREA

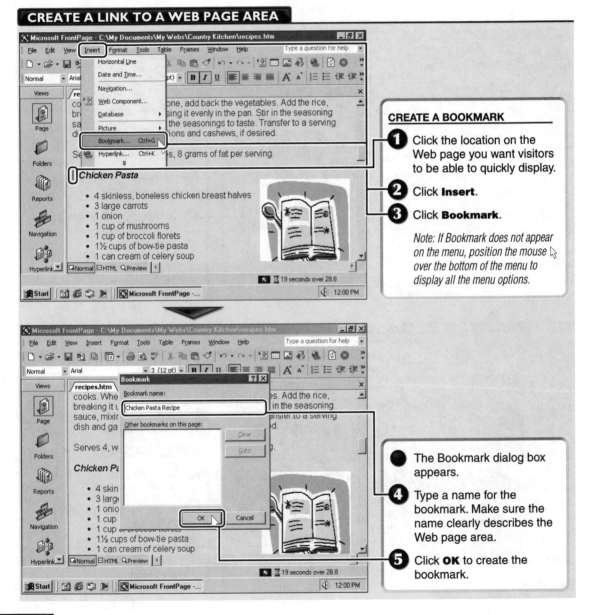

CREATE A BOOKMARK

1 Click the location on the Web page you want visitors to be able to quickly display.

2 Click **Insert**.

3 Click **Bookmark**.

Note: If Bookmark does not appear on the menu, position the mouse over the bottom of the menu to display all the menu options.

■ The Bookmark dialog box appears.

4 Type a name for the bookmark. Make sure the name clearly describes the Web page area.

5 Click **OK** to create the bookmark.

in an *instant*

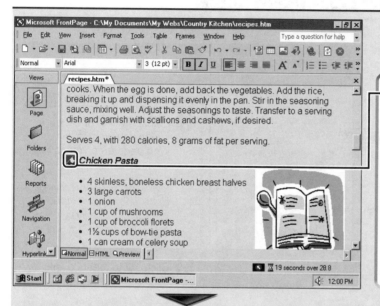

A flag (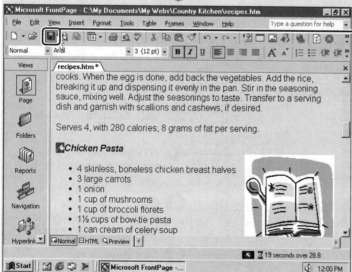) appears on your Web page to indicate the location of the bookmark. The flag will not appear when you publish your Web pages.

Note: If you placed the bookmark in the wrong location, you can delete the bookmark at any time. To delete a bookmark, drag the mouse I over the flag (▣) for the bookmark until you highlight the flag and then press the Delete key.

6 Click ▣ to save the changes you have made to your Web page.

You now need to create a link that visitors can select to display the Web page area you have bookmarked.

CONTINUED➡

CREATE A LINK TO A WEB PAGE AREA

After you bookmark a Web page area, you can create a link that visitors can select to display the area. You can create a link that takes visitors to a bookmarked area within the same Web page. You can also create a link that takes visitors to a bookmarked area on a different Web page in your Web site.

CREATE A LINK TO A WEB PAGE AREA (CONTINUED)

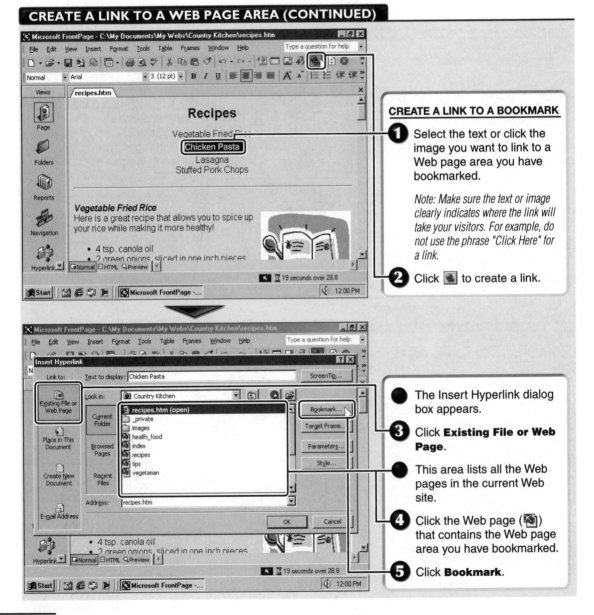

CREATE A LINK TO A BOOKMARK

1 Select the text or click the image you want to link to a Web page area you have bookmarked.

Note: Make sure the text or image clearly indicates where the link will take your visitors. For example, do not use the phrase "Click Here" for a link.

2 Click 🖳 to create a link.

■ The Insert Hyperlink dialog box appears.

3 Click **Existing File or Web Page**.

■ This area lists all the Web pages in the current Web site.

4 Click the Web page (🖳) that contains the Web page area you have bookmarked.

5 Click **Bookmark**.

in an *Instant*

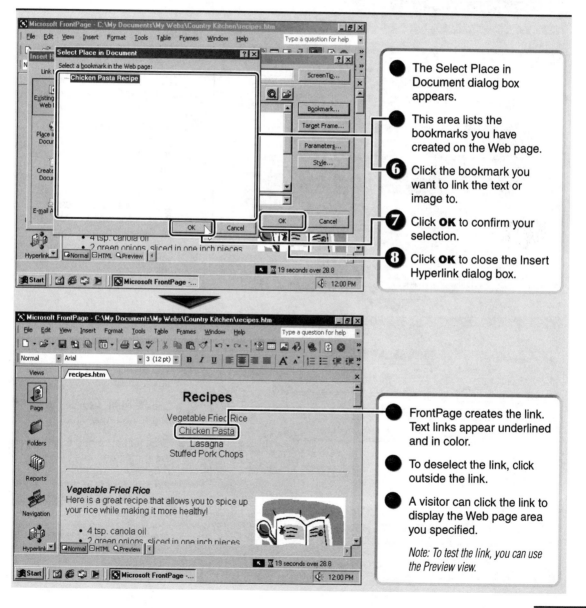

The Select Place in Document dialog box appears.

This area lists the bookmarks you have created on the Web page.

6 Click the bookmark you want to link the text or image to.

7 Click **OK** to confirm your selection.

8 Click **OK** to close the Insert Hyperlink dialog box.

FrontPage creates the link. Text links appear underlined and in color.

To deselect the link, click outside the link.

A visitor can click the link to display the Web page area you specified.

Note: To test the link, you can use the Preview view.

You can create a link on a Web page that visitors can select to send you an e-mail message. This allows visitors to send you questions and comments about your Web pages. When a visitor selects an e-mail link, a blank message addressed to you will appear.

CREATE AN E-MAIL LINK

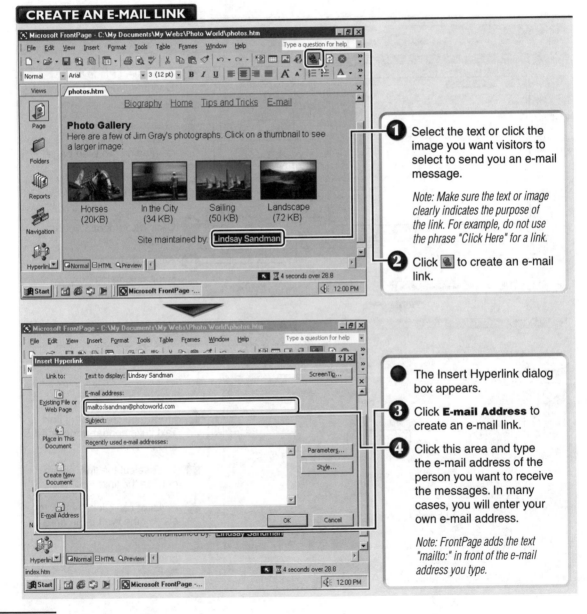

1 Select the text or click the image you want visitors to select to send you an e-mail message.

Note: Make sure the text or image clearly indicates the purpose of the link. For example, do not use the phrase "Click Here" for a link.

2 Click 📧 to create an e-mail link.

● The Insert Hyperlink dialog box appears.

3 Click **E-mail Address** to create an e-mail link.

4 Click this area and type the e-mail address of the person you want to receive the messages. In many cases, you will enter your own e-mail address.

Note: FrontPage adds the text "mailto:" in front of the e-mail address you type.

in an *instant*

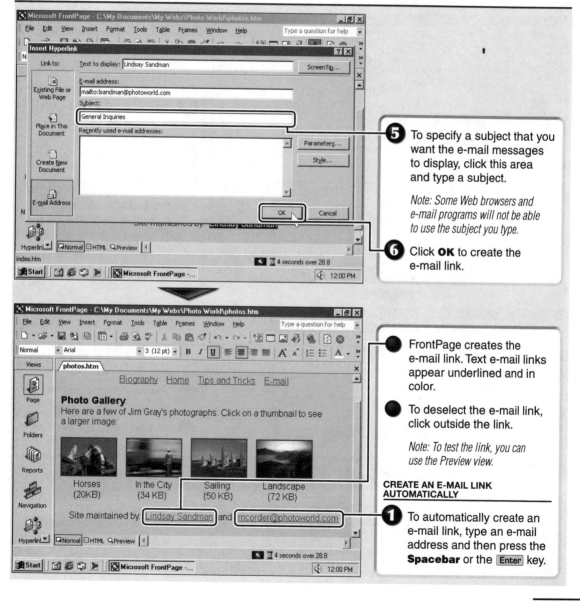

5 To specify a subject that you want the e-mail messages to display, click this area and type a subject.

Note: Some Web browsers and e-mail programs will not be able to use the subject you type.

6 Click **OK** to create the e-mail link.

● FrontPage creates the e-mail link. Text e-mail links appear underlined and in color.

● To deselect the e-mail link, click outside the link.

Note: To test the link, you can use the Preview view.

CREATE AN E-MAIL LINK AUTOMATICALLY

1 To automatically create an e-mail link, type an e-mail address and then press the **Spacebar** or the Enter key.

115

CHANGE LINK COLORS

You can change the color of links on a Web page. A Web page can contain three types of links—unvisited, visited and active links. You should change the link colors only when necessary, since you may confuse some visitors if you do not use the standard link colors. Links are also known as hyperlinks.

CHANGE LINK COLORS

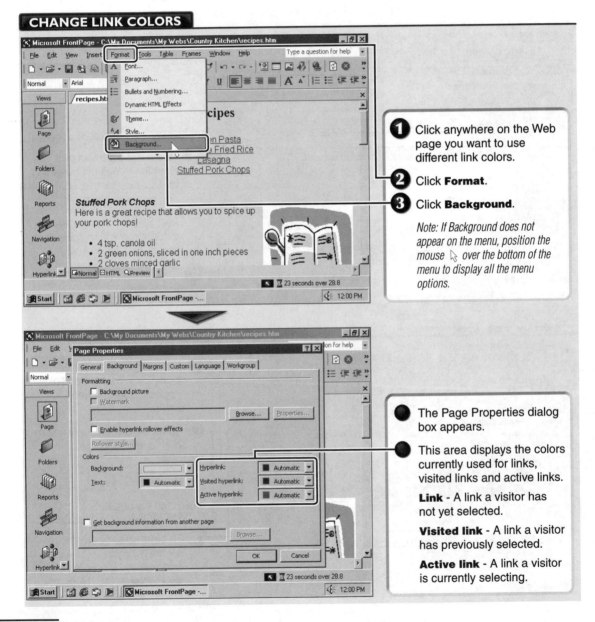

1 Click anywhere on the Web page you want to use different link colors.

2 Click **Format**.

3 Click **Background**.

Note: If Background does not appear on the menu, position the mouse ⤷ over the bottom of the menu to display all the menu options.

● The Page Properties dialog box appears.

● This area displays the colors currently used for links, visited links and active links.

Link - A link a visitor has not yet selected.

Visited link - A link a visitor has previously selected.

Active link - A link a visitor is currently selecting.

in an instant

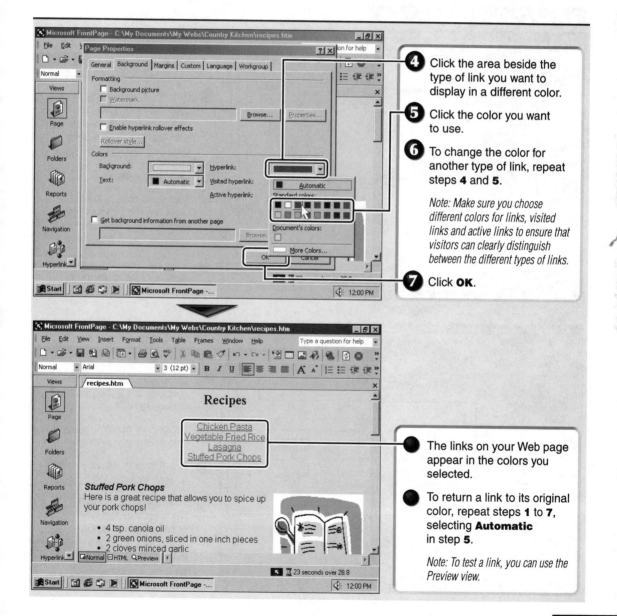

4 Click the area beside the type of link you want to display in a different color.

5 Click the color you want to use.

6 To change the color for another type of link, repeat steps **4** and **5**.

Note: Make sure you choose different colors for links, visited links and active links to ensure that visitors can clearly distinguish between the different types of links.

7 Click **OK**.

■ The links on your Web page appear in the colors you selected.

■ To return a link to its original color, repeat steps **1** to **7**, selecting **Automatic** in step **5**.

Note: To test a link, you can use the Preview view.

USING THE HYPERLINKS VIEW

You can use the Hyperlinks view to display the links that connect the Web pages in your Web site. The Hyperlinks view helps you determine if your Web pages contain the necessary links that will allow visitors to easily navigate through your Web site.

USING THE HYPERLINKS VIEW

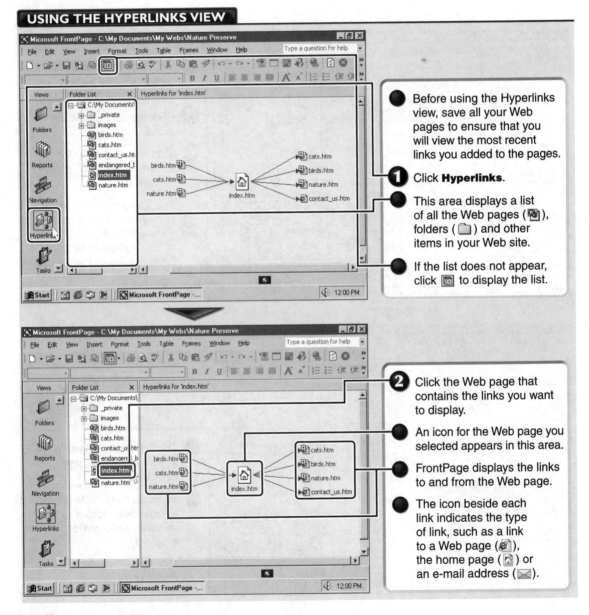

● Before using the Hyperlinks view, save all your Web pages to ensure that you will view the most recent links you added to the pages.

1 Click **Hyperlinks**.

● This area displays a list of all the Web pages (🖳), folders (🗀) and other items in your Web site.

● If the list does not appear, click 🔲 to display the list.

2 Click the Web page that contains the links you want to display.

● An icon for the Web page you selected appears in this area.

● FrontPage displays the links to and from the Web page.

● The icon beside each link indicates the type of link, such as a link to a Web page (🌐), the home page (🏠) or an e-mail address (✉).

in an instant

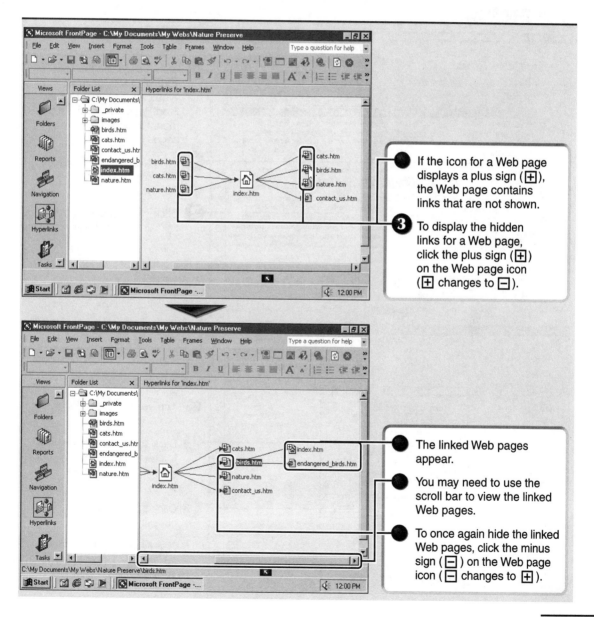

If the icon for a Web page displays a plus sign (⊞), the Web page contains links that are not shown.

3 To display the hidden links for a Web page, click the plus sign (⊞) on the Web page icon (⊞ changes to ⊟).

The linked Web pages appear.

You may need to use the scroll bar to view the linked Web pages.

To once again hide the linked Web pages, click the minus sign (⊟) on the Web page icon (⊟ changes to ⊞).

You can check all the links in your Web site to determine if the links are working properly. An error message will appear if a visitor clicks a broken link in your Web site. A link may be broken if you typed the linked Web page address incorrectly, deleted the linked Web page in your Web site or the linked Web page was moved or deleted on the Web.

CHECK LINKS

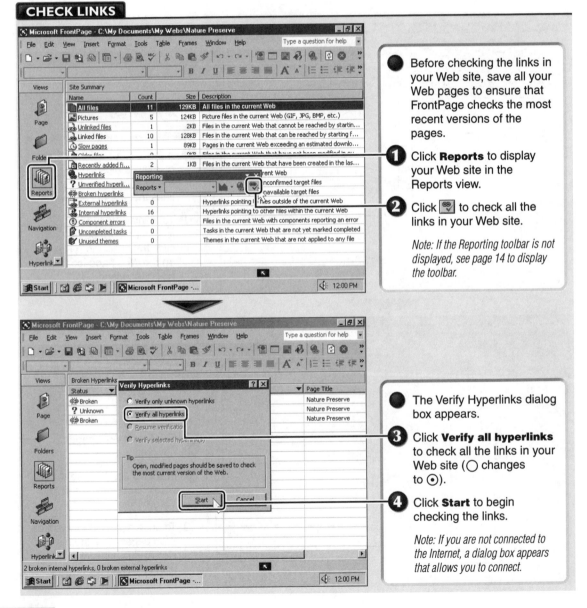

Before checking the links in your Web site, save all your Web pages to ensure that FrontPage checks the most recent versions of the pages.

1 Click **Reports** to display your Web site in the Reports view.

2 Click 🔄 to check all the links in your Web site.

Note: If the Reporting toolbar is not displayed, see page 14 to display the toolbar.

The Verify Hyperlinks dialog box appears.

3 Click **Verify all hyperlinks** to check all the links in your Web site (○ changes to ⊙).

4 Click **Start** to begin checking the links.

Note: If you are not connected to the Internet, a dialog box appears that allows you to connect.

in an instant

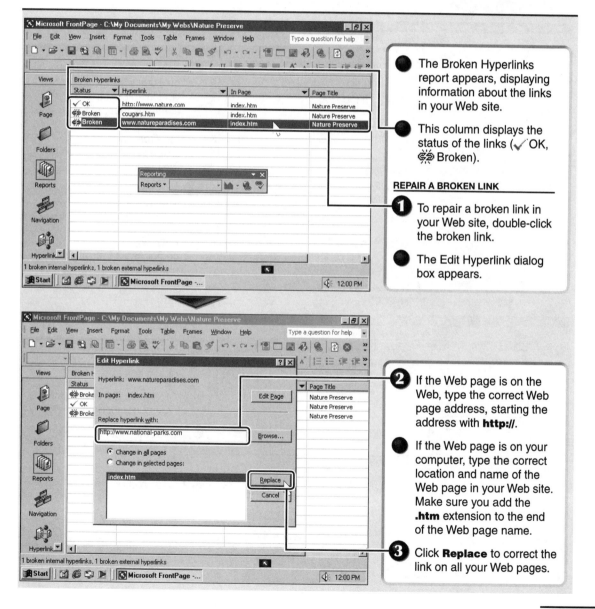

The Broken Hyperlinks report appears, displaying information about the links in your Web site.

This column displays the status of the links (✓ OK, ⚡ Broken).

REPAIR A BROKEN LINK

1 To repair a broken link in your Web site, double-click the broken link.

The Edit Hyperlink dialog box appears.

2 If the Web page is on the Web, type the correct Web page address, starting the address with **http://**.

If the Web page is on your computer, type the correct location and name of the Web page in your Web site. Make sure you add the **.htm** extension to the end of the Web page name.

3 Click **Replace** to correct the link on all your Web pages.

You can add a link bar to a Web page. A link bar displays buttons that visitors can select to display other Web pages. You can create three types of link bars—a link bar that displays a separate link for each Web page you specify, a link bar that displays only a Back and Next link or a link bar based on the navigational structure of your Web site.

ADD A LINK BAR

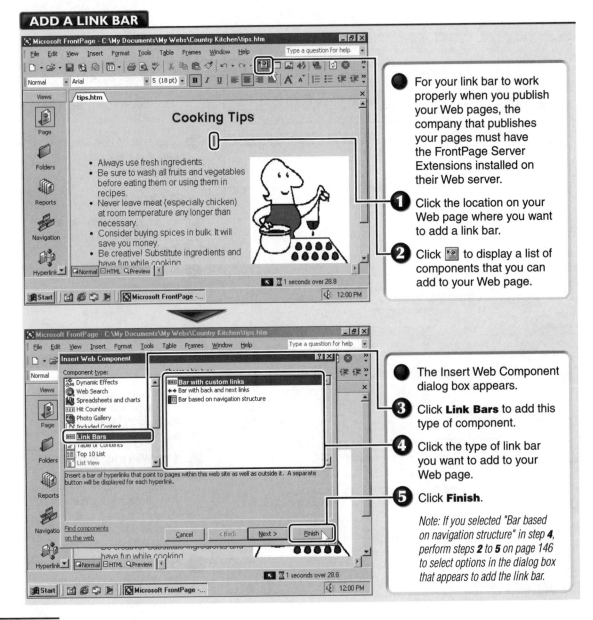

For your link bar to work properly when you publish your Web pages, the company that publishes your pages must have the FrontPage Server Extensions installed on their Web server.

1 Click the location on your Web page where you want to add a link bar.

2 Click ▦ to display a list of components that you can add to your Web page.

The Insert Web Component dialog box appears.

3 Click **Link Bars** to add this type of component.

4 Click the type of link bar you want to add to your Web page.

5 Click **Finish**.

Note: If you selected "Bar based on navigation structure" in step 4, perform steps 2 to 5 on page 146 to select options in the dialog box that appears to add the link bar.

in an *instant*

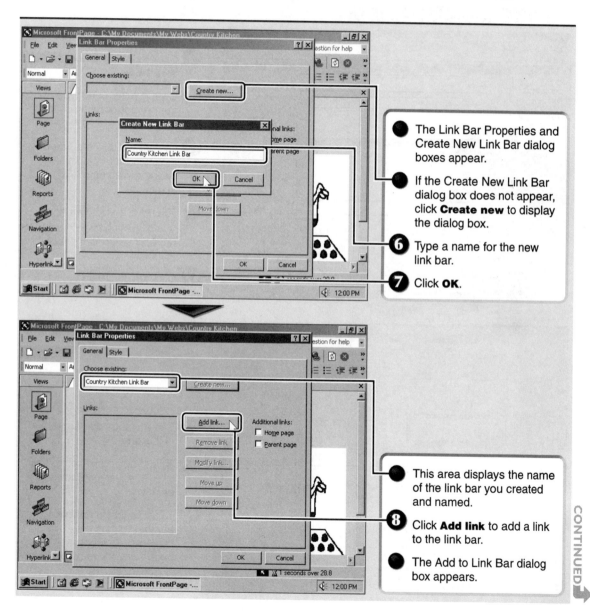

The Link Bar Properties and Create New Link Bar dialog boxes appear.

If the Create New Link Bar dialog box does not appear, click **Create new** to display the dialog box.

6 Type a name for the new link bar.

7 Click **OK**.

This area displays the name of the link bar you created and named.

8 Click **Add link** to add a link to the link bar.

The Add to Link Bar dialog box appears.

CONTINUED

ADD A LINK BAR

You can specify the text you want a link to display on a link bar. You should specify text for a link that will clearly indicate where the link will take your visitors. If you do not specify text for a link, FrontPage will use the file name of the linked Web page to label the link.

ADD A LINK BAR (CONTINUED)

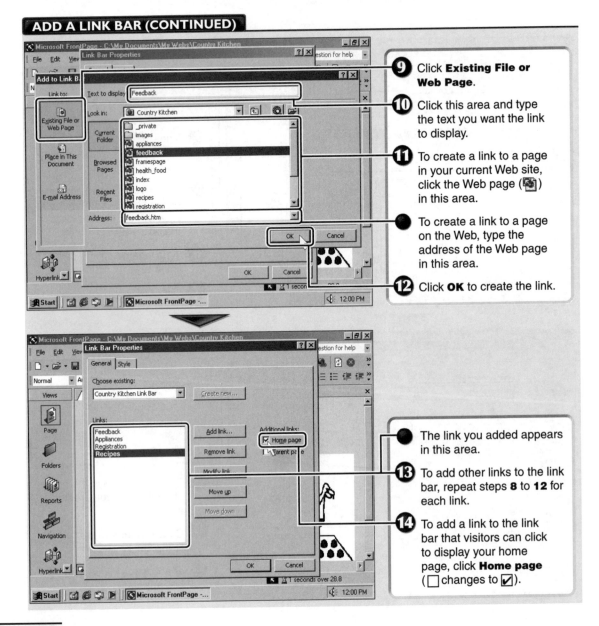

9 Click **Existing File or Web Page**.

10 Click this area and type the text you want the link to display.

11 To create a link to a page in your current Web site, click the Web page (🖳) in this area.

● To create a link to a page on the Web, type the address of the Web page in this area.

12 Click **OK** to create the link.

● The link you added appears in this area.

13 To add other links to the link bar, repeat steps **8** to **12** for each link.

14 To add a link to the link bar that visitors can click to display your home page, click **Home page** (☐ changes to ☑).

124

in an instant

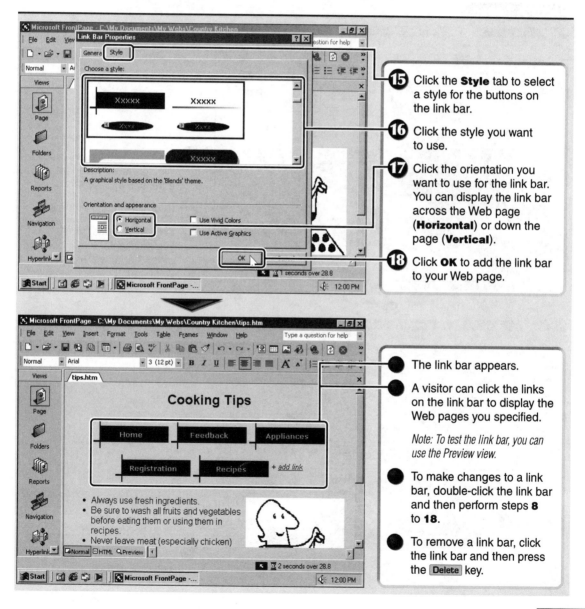

15 Click the **Style** tab to select a style for the buttons on the link bar.

16 Click the style you want to use.

17 Click the orientation you want to use for the link bar. You can display the link bar across the Web page (**Horizontal**) or down the page (**Vertical**).

18 Click **OK** to add the link bar to your Web page.

● The link bar appears.

● A visitor can click the links on the link bar to display the Web pages you specified.

Note: To test the link bar, you can use the Preview view.

● To make changes to a link bar, double-click the link bar and then perform steps **8** to **18**.

● To remove a link bar, click the link bar and then press the Delete key.

ADD A TABLE

You can add a table to neatly display information, such as product information or a timetable, on a Web page. Tables are also useful for controlling the placement of text and images on a Web page. For example, to neatly position two paragraphs and two images, you can create a table with two rows and two columns.

ADD A TABLE

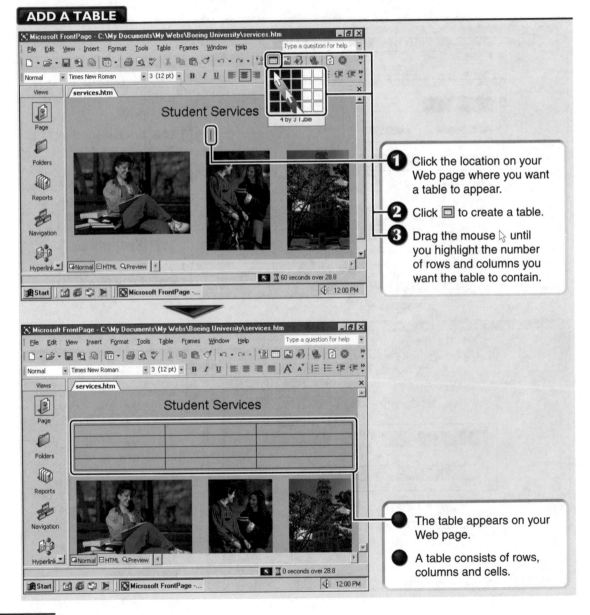

1 Click the location on your Web page where you want a table to appear.

2 Click ▣ to create a table.

3 Drag the mouse ▷ until you highlight the number of rows and columns you want the table to contain.

■ The table appears on your Web page.

■ A table consists of rows, columns and cells.

in an *instant*

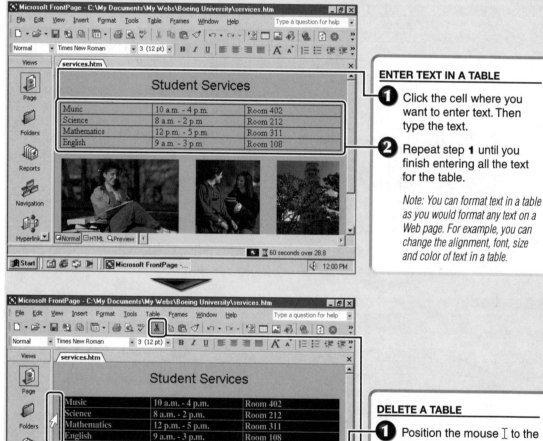

ENTER TEXT IN A TABLE

1 Click the cell where you want to enter text. Then type the text.

2 Repeat step **1** until you finish entering all the text for the table.

Note: You can format text in a table as you would format any text on a Web page. For example, you can change the alignment, font, size and color of text in a table.

DELETE A TABLE

1 Position the mouse I to the left of the table you want to delete (I changes to $\nwarrow$). Then double-click to select the table.

2 Click to delete the table.

● The table disappears from your Web page.

You can add a row or column to a table to insert additional information. When adding a row or column, you can choose to add several rows or columns at once. You can also delete a row or column that you no longer want to display in a table.

ADD OR DELETE A ROW OR COLUMN

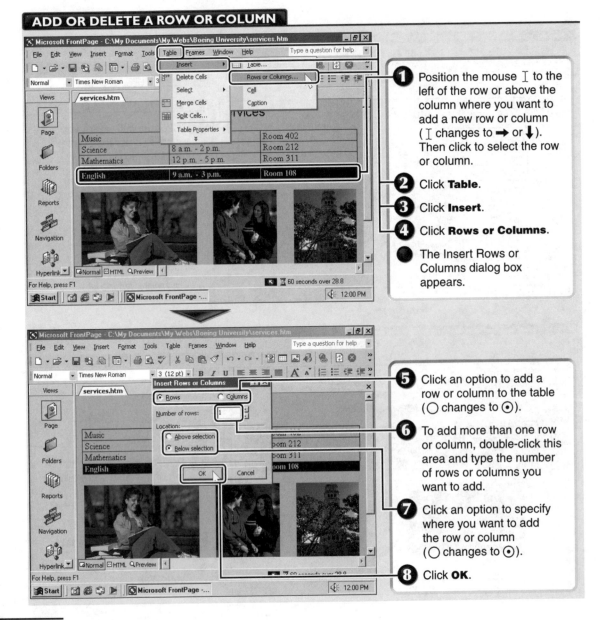

1 Position the mouse I to the left of the row or above the column where you want to add a new row or column (I changes to → or ↓). Then click to select the row or column.

2 Click **Table**.

3 Click **Insert**.

4 Click **Rows or Columns**.

● The Insert Rows or Columns dialog box appears.

5 Click an option to add a row or column to the table (○ changes to ⊙).

6 To add more than one row or column, double-click this area and type the number of rows or columns you want to add.

7 Click an option to specify where you want to add the row or column (○ changes to ⊙).

8 Click **OK**.

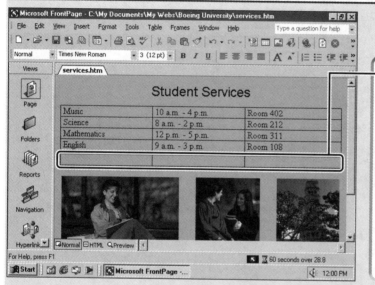

The new row or column appears in your table.

To deselect a row or column, click outside the table.

QUICKLY ADD A ROW

1 To quickly add a row to the bottom of a table, click in the bottom right cell of the table.

2 Press the **Tab** key to create the new row.

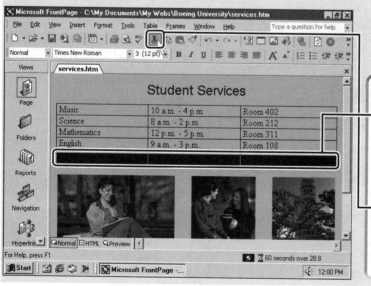

DELETE A ROW OR COLUMN

1 Position the mouse I to the left of the row or above the column you want to delete (I changes to → or ↓). Then click to select the row or column.

2 Click to delete the row or column you selected.

The row or column disappears from your table.

129

CHANGE ROW HEIGHT OR COLUMN WIDTH

You can change the height of rows and the width of columns to improve the layout of a table. You can make a row height or column width any size you want, however, FrontPage will not allow you to make a row or column too small to display the text or image in a cell.

CHANGE ROW HEIGHT OR COLUMN WIDTH

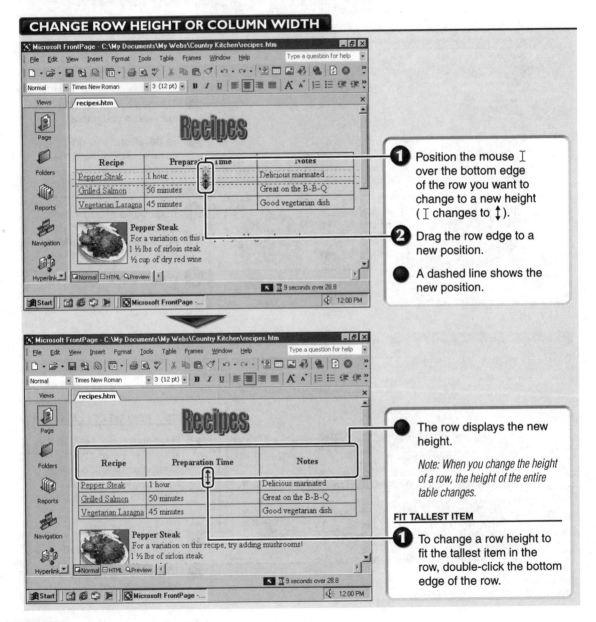

1 Position the mouse I over the bottom edge of the row you want to change to a new height (I changes to ↕).

2 Drag the row edge to a new position.

● A dashed line shows the new position.

● The row displays the new height.

Note: When you change the height of a row, the height of the entire table changes.

FIT TALLEST ITEM

1 To change a row height to fit the tallest item in the row, double-click the bottom edge of the row.

in an instant

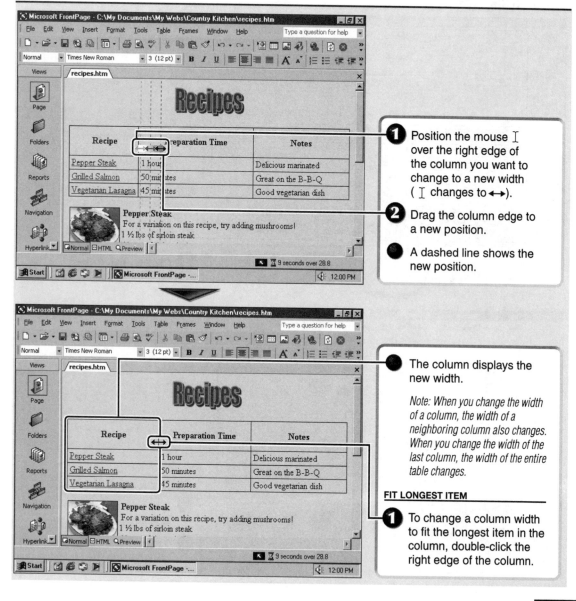

1 Position the mouse I over the right edge of the column you want to change to a new width (I changes to ↔).

2 Drag the column edge to a new position.

● A dashed line shows the new position.

● The column displays the new width.

Note: When you change the width of a column, the width of a neighboring column also changes. When you change the width of the last column, the width of the entire table changes.

FIT LONGEST ITEM

1 To change a column width to fit the longest item in the column, double-click the right edge of the column.

COMBINE CELLS

You can combine, or merge, two or more cells in a table to make one large cell. This is useful if you want to display a title across the top or down the side of a table. When you combine cells, the size of the table does not change.

COMBINE CELLS

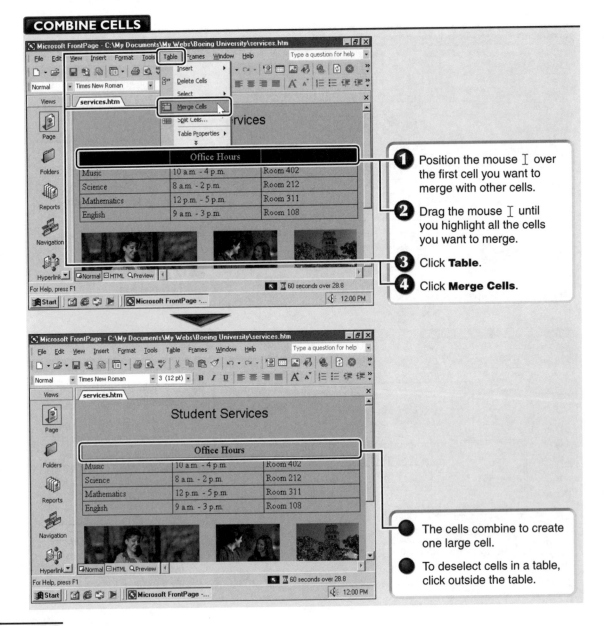

1 Position the mouse I over the first cell you want to merge with other cells.

2 Drag the mouse I until you highlight all the cells you want to merge.

3 Click **Table**.

4 Click **Merge Cells**.

● The cells combine to create one large cell.

● To deselect cells in a table, click outside the table.

132

You can add a caption to a table to provide a title or a description for the table. Captions automatically appear centered at the top of a table. After you add a caption to a table, you can format the caption. For example, you can change the font, size or color of the caption.

ADD A CAPTION TO A TABLE

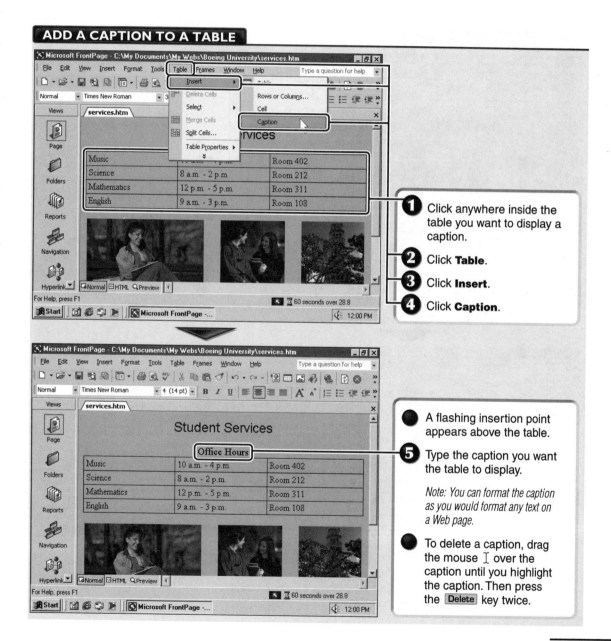

1 Click anywhere inside the table you want to display a caption.

2 Click **Table**.

3 Click **Insert**.

4 Click **Caption**.

● A flashing insertion point appears above the table.

5 Type the caption you want the table to display.

Note: You can format the caption as you would format any text on a Web page.

● To delete a caption, drag the mouse I over the caption until you highlight the caption. Then press the Delete key twice.

CHANGE TABLE BORDER

You can change the size and color of the border that surrounds a table. You can specify a new border size to increase the border thickness or to remove the border. Removing a table border is useful if you are using a table to organize the information on a Web page and you want the border to be invisible.

CHANGE TABLE BORDER

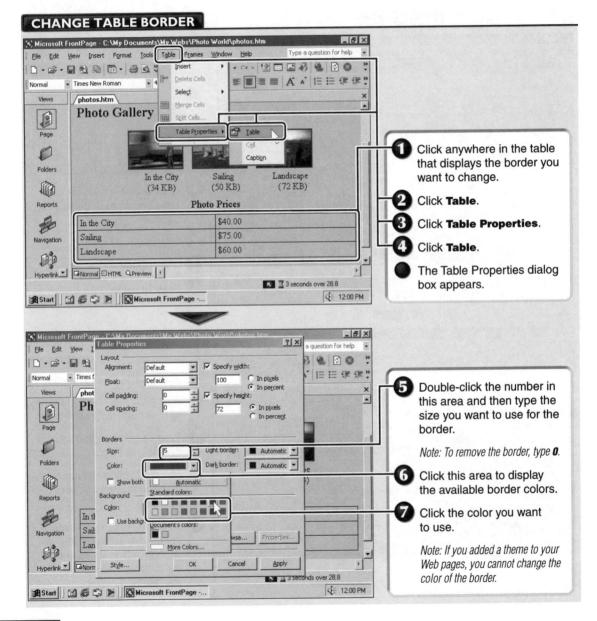

1 Click anywhere in the table that displays the border you want to change.

2 Click **Table**.

3 Click **Table Properties**.

4 Click **Table**.

● The Table Properties dialog box appears.

5 Double-click the number in this area and then type the size you want to use for the border.

*Note: To remove the border, type **0**.*

6 Click this area to display the available border colors.

7 Click the color you want to use.

Note: If you added a theme to your Web pages, you cannot change the color of the border.

in an *instant*

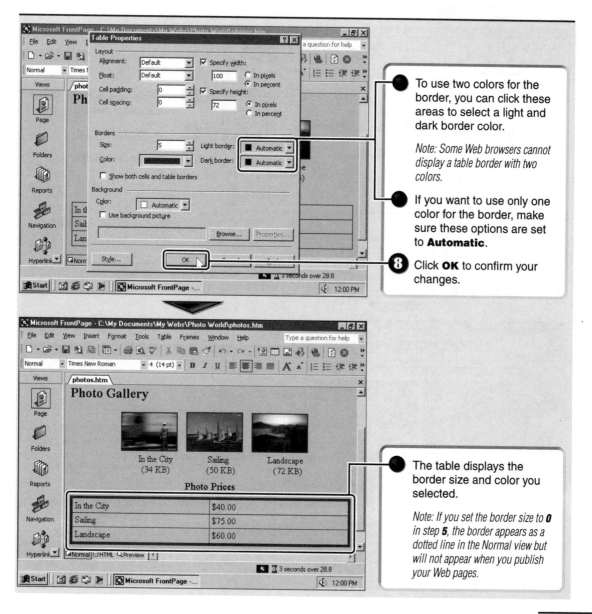

To use two colors for the border, you can click these areas to select a light and dark border color.

Note: Some Web browsers cannot display a table border with two colors.

If you want to use only one color for the border, make sure these options are set to **Automatic**.

8 Click **OK** to confirm your changes.

The table displays the border size and color you selected.

*Note: If you set the border size to **0** in step **5**, the border appears as a dotted line in the Normal view but will not appear when you publish your Web pages.*

FrontPage offers many ready-to-use designs that you can choose from to give a table a new appearance. When selecting a design, you can customize the design. For example, you can apply borders, shading and other formats to a table. You can also apply special formats to specific parts of a table, such as the heading row or first column.

FORMAT A TABLE

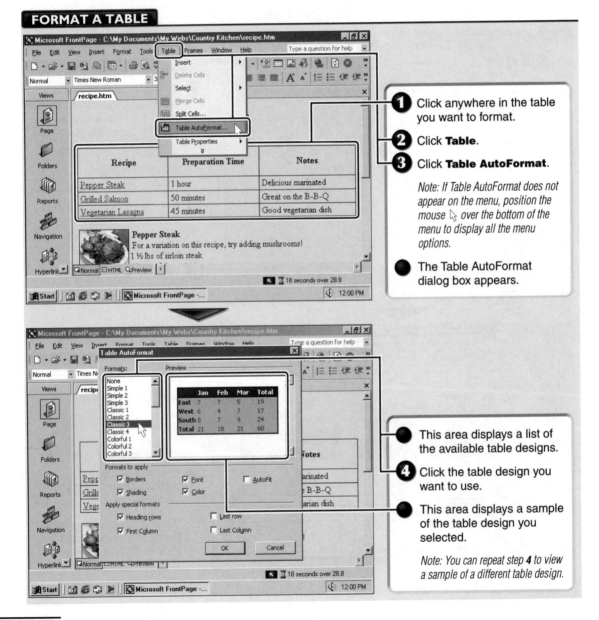

1 Click anywhere in the table you want to format.

2 Click **Table**.

3 Click **Table AutoFormat**.

Note: If Table AutoFormat does not appear on the menu, position the mouse ⬦ over the bottom of the menu to display all the menu options.

● The Table AutoFormat dialog box appears.

● This area displays a list of the available table designs.

4 Click the table design you want to use.

● This area displays a sample of the table design you selected.

Note: You can repeat step 4 to view a sample of a different table design.

in an *instant*

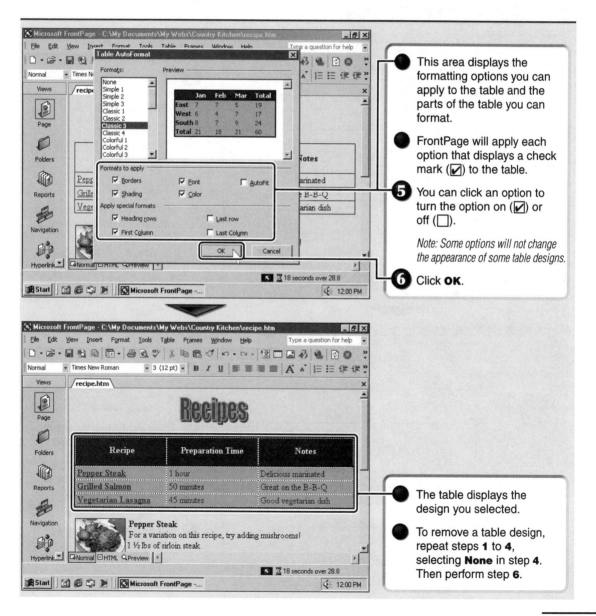

This area displays the formatting options you can apply to the table and the parts of the table you can format.

FrontPage will apply each option that displays a check mark (☑) to the table.

5 You can click an option to turn the option on (☑) or off (☐).

Note: Some options will not change the appearance of some table designs.

6 Click **OK**.

The table displays the design you selected.

To remove a table design, repeat steps **1** to **4**, selecting **None** in step **4**. Then perform step **6**.

The Navigation view shows how the Web pages in your Web site are related. Working in the Navigation view is important if you plan to add navigation buttons that visitors can select to move through your Web pages. FrontPage uses the structure of your Web pages in the Navigation view to determine which navigation buttons should appear on each Web page. To add navigation buttons to your Web pages, see page 144.

USING THE NAVIGATION VIEW

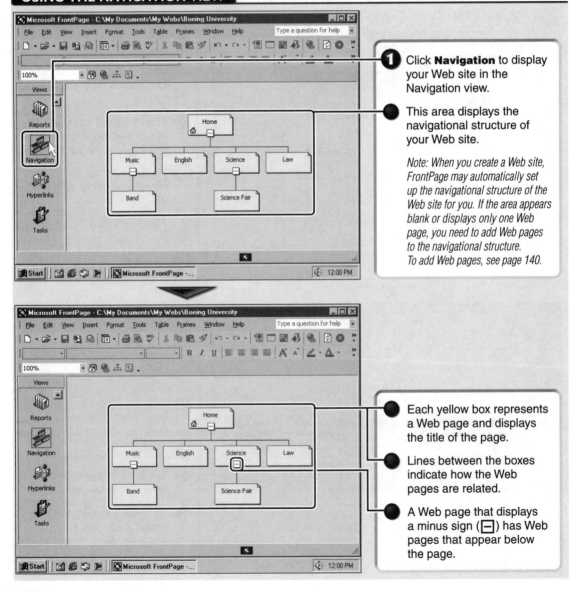

1 Click **Navigation** to display your Web site in the Navigation view.

● This area displays the navigational structure of your Web site.

Note: When you create a Web site, FrontPage may automatically set up the navigational structure of the Web site for you. If the area appears blank or displays only one Web page, you need to add Web pages to the navigational structure. To add Web pages, see page 140.

● Each yellow box represents a Web page and displays the title of the page.

● Lines between the boxes indicate how the Web pages are related.

● A Web page that displays a minus sign (⊟) has Web pages that appear below the page.

138

in an instant

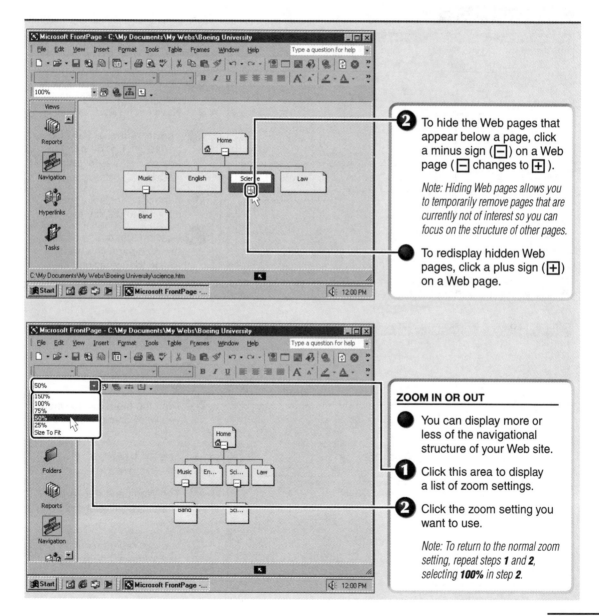

② To hide the Web pages that appear below a page, click a minus sign (□) on a Web page (□ changes to □).

Note: Hiding Web pages allows you to temporarily remove pages that are currently not of interest so you can focus on the structure of other pages.

● To redisplay hidden Web pages, click a plus sign (□) on a Web page.

ZOOM IN OR OUT

● You can display more or less of the navigational structure of your Web site.

① Click this area to display a list of zoom settings.

② Click the zoom setting you want to use.

Note: To return to the normal zoom setting, repeat steps 1 and 2, selecting 100% in step 2.

ADD A WEB PAGE

You can add Web pages to the navigational structure of your Web site. Web pages you add to the navigational structure will appear as navigation buttons on your Web pages. To add navigation buttons to your Web pages, see page 144.

see page 144.

ADD A WEB PAGE

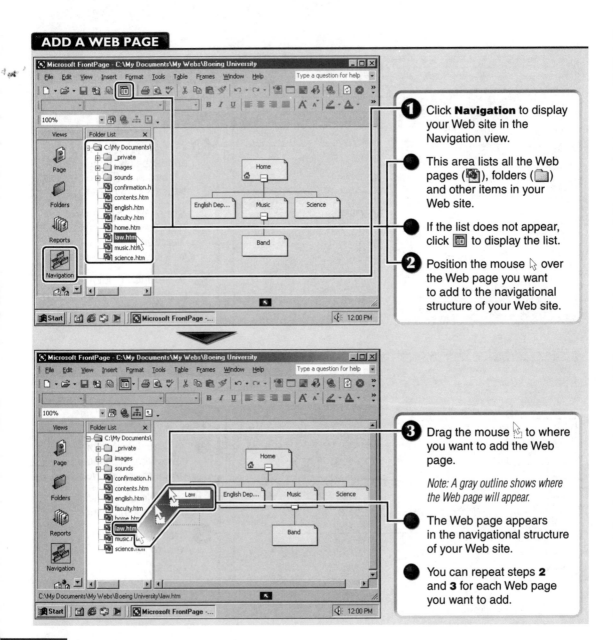

1 Click **Navigation** to display your Web site in the Navigation view.

● This area lists all the Web pages (icon), folders (icon) and other items in your Web site.

● If the list does not appear, click icon to display the list.

2 Position the mouse ᐟ over the Web page you want to add to the navigational structure of your Web site.

3 Drag the mouse ᐟ to where you want to add the Web page.

Note: A gray outline shows where the Web page will appear.

● The Web page appears in the navigational structure of your Web site.

● You can repeat steps **2** and **3** for each Web page you want to add.

You can remove a Web page from the navigational structure of your Web site. Web pages you remove from the navigational structure will no longer appear as navigation buttons on your Web pages. For information on navigation buttons, see page 144.

REMOVE A WEB PAGE

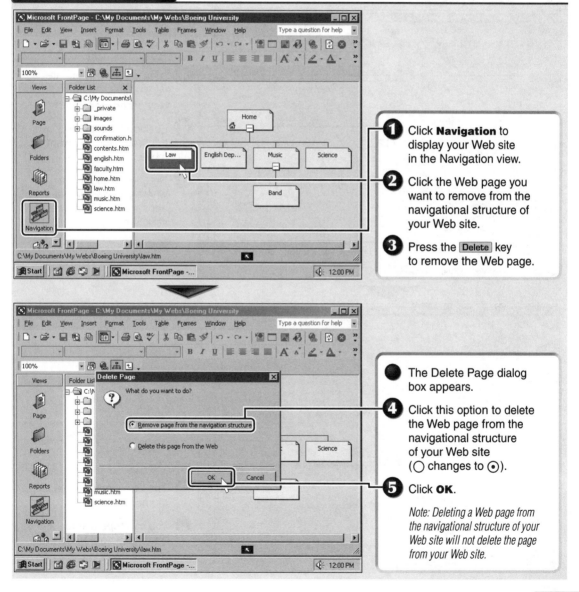

1 Click **Navigation** to display your Web site in the Navigation view.

2 Click the Web page you want to remove from the navigational structure of your Web site.

3 Press the Delete key to remove the Web page.

● The Delete Page dialog box appears.

4 Click this option to delete the Web page from the navigational structure of your Web site (○ changes to ⊙).

5 Click **OK**.

Note: Deleting a Web page from the navigational structure of your Web site will not delete the page from your Web site.

MOVE A WEB PAGE

You can re-arrange Web pages to re-organize the navigational structure of your Web site. Re-arranging Web pages in the navigational structure will change which navigation buttons appear on each Web page and the order of the navigation buttons. To add navigation buttons to your Web pages, see page 144.

MOVE A WEB PAGE

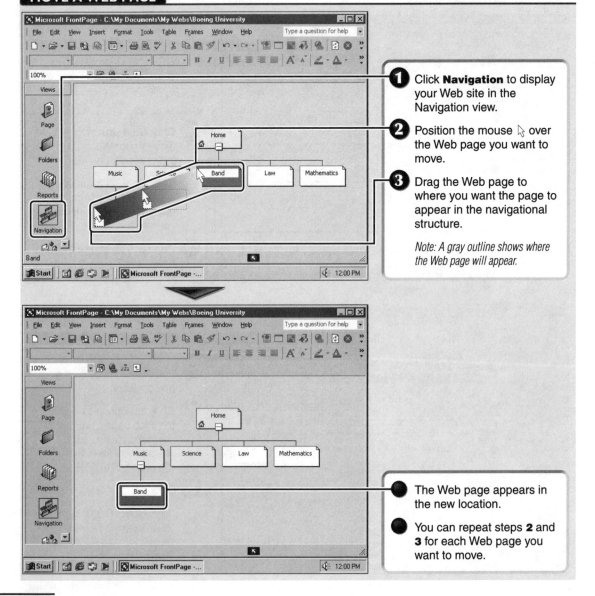

1 Click **Navigation** to display your Web site in the Navigation view.

2 Position the mouse ☐ over the Web page you want to move.

3 Drag the Web page to where you want the page to appear in the navigational structure.

Note: A gray outline shows where the Web page will appear.

■ The Web page appears in the new location.

■ You can repeat steps **2** and **3** for each Web page you want to move.

CHANGE A WEB PAGE TITLE

You can change the title of a Web page in the Navigation view to better describe the contents of the page. FrontPage will use the Web page titles you specify as the labels for the navigation buttons on your Web pages. To add navigation buttons to your Web pages, see page 144.

CHANGE A WEB PAGE TITLE

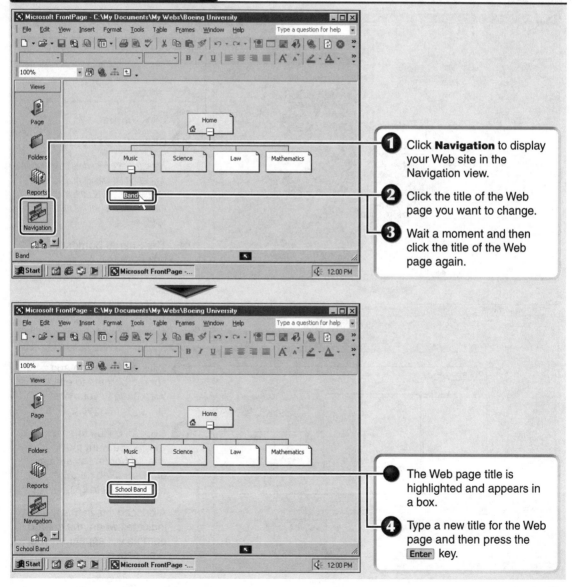

1 Click **Navigation** to display your Web site in the Navigation view.

2 Click the title of the Web page you want to change.

3 Wait a moment and then click the title of the Web page again.

■ The Web page title is highlighted and appears in a box.

4 Type a new title for the Web page and then press the Enter key.

ADD SHARED BORDERS

You can add shared borders to every page in your Web site. Shared borders allow you to display the same information, such as a company logo, on every Web page. When you add shared borders, you can choose to display navigation buttons in the shared borders. Navigation buttons are links visitors can select to move through the pages in your Web site.

ADD SHARED BORDERS

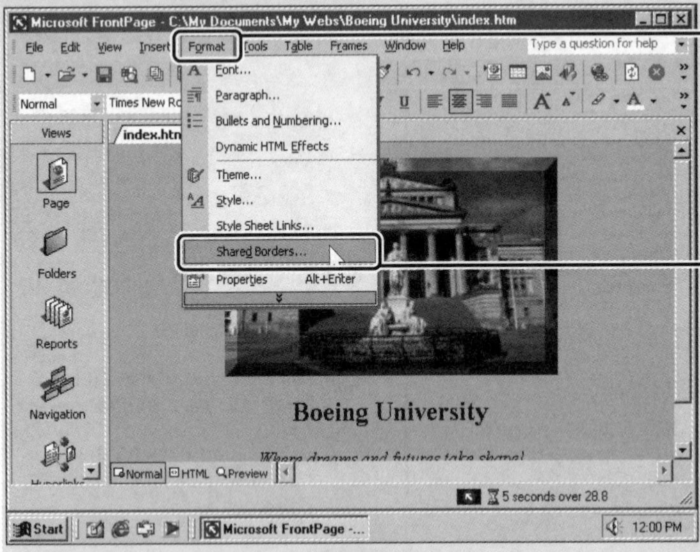

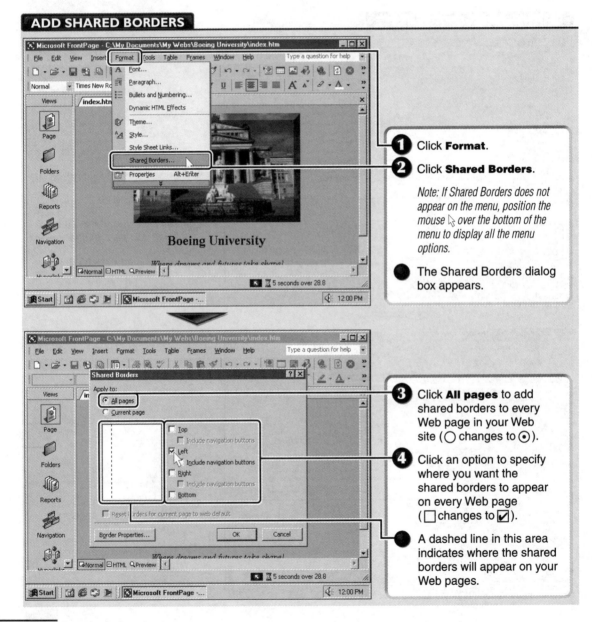

1 Click **Format**.

2 Click **Shared Borders**.

Note: If Shared Borders does not appear on the menu, position the mouse over the bottom of the menu to display all the menu options.

- The Shared Borders dialog box appears.

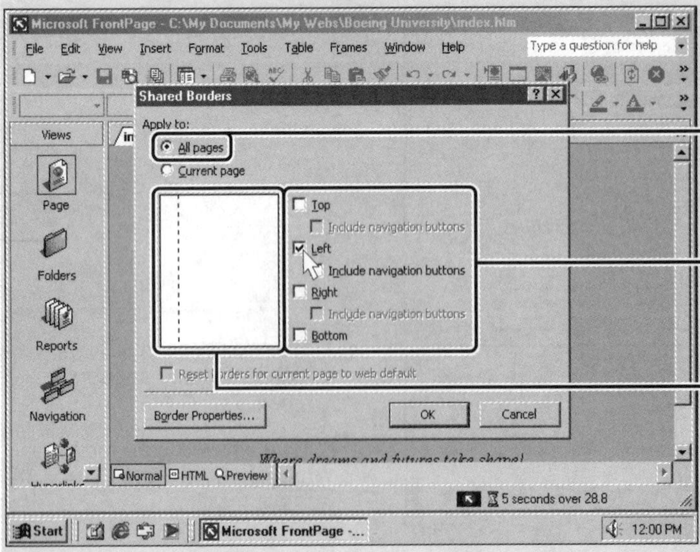

3 Click **All pages** to add shared borders to every Web page in your Web site (○ changes to ⊙).

4 Click an option to specify where you want the shared borders to appear on every Web page (☐ changes to ☑).

- A dashed line in this area indicates where the shared borders will appear on your Web pages.

in an *instant*

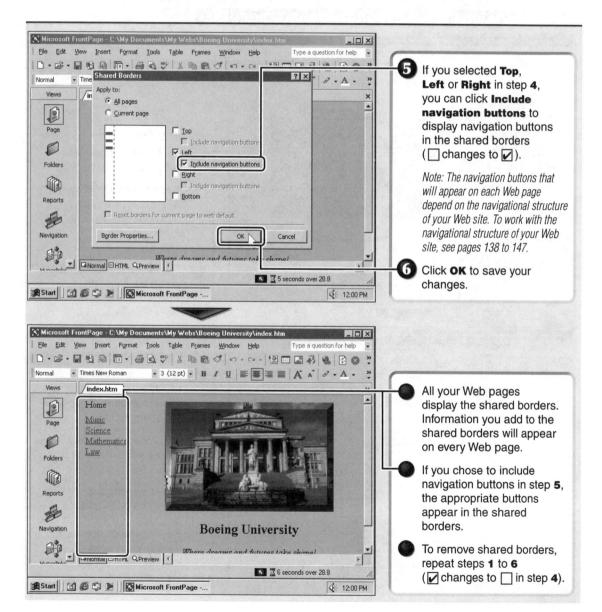

5 If you selected **Top**, **Left** or **Right** in step **4**, you can click **Include navigation buttons** to display navigation buttons in the shared borders (☐ changes to ☑).

Note: The navigation buttons that will appear on each Web page depend on the navigational structure of your Web site. To work with the navigational structure of your Web site, see pages 138 to 147.

6 Click **OK** to save your changes.

● All your Web pages display the shared borders. Information you add to the shared borders will appear on every Web page.

● If you chose to include navigation buttons in step **5**, the appropriate buttons appear in the shared borders.

● To remove shared borders, repeat steps **1** to **6** (☑ changes to ☐ in step **4**).

CHANGE NAVIGATION BUTTONS IN SHARED BORDERS

You can make changes to navigation buttons that you added to shared borders. FrontPage allows you to specify which navigation buttons you want to display on your Web pages. For example, you can choose to display navigation buttons that link to Web pages directly above each page. You can also change the appearance of navigation buttons. To add navigation buttons to your Web pages, see page 144.

CHANGE NAVIGATION BUTTONS IN SHARED BORDERS

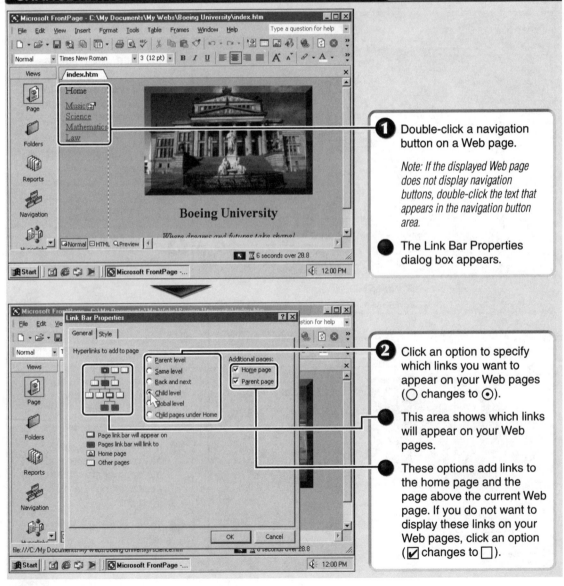

1 Double-click a navigation button on a Web page.

Note: If the displayed Web page does not display navigation buttons, double-click the text that appears in the navigation button area.

● The Link Bar Properties dialog box appears.

2 Click an option to specify which links you want to appear on your Web pages (○ changes to ⊙).

● This area shows which links will appear on your Web pages.

● These options add links to the home page and the page above the current Web page. If you do not want to display these links on your Web pages, click an option (☑ changes to ☐).

in an *instant*

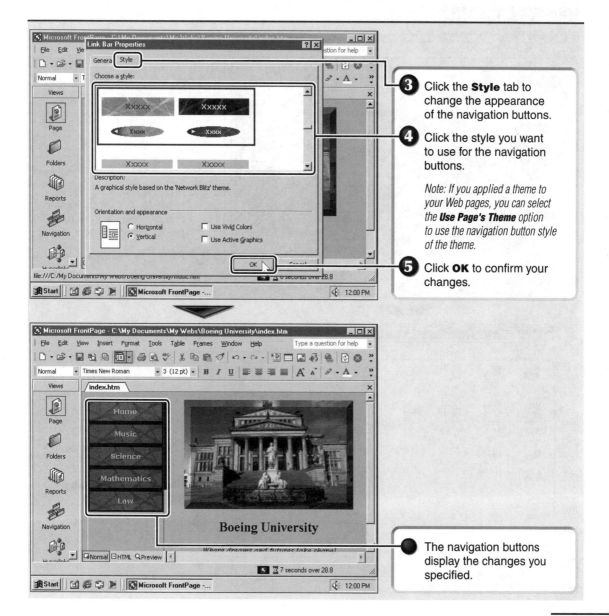

3 Click the **Style** tab to change the appearance of the navigation buttons.

4 Click the style you want to use for the navigation buttons.

*Note: If you applied a theme to your Web pages, you can select the **Use Page's Theme** option to use the navigation button style of the theme.*

5 Click **OK** to confirm your changes.

● The navigation buttons display the changes you specified.

CREATE FRAMES

You can create frames to divide a Web browser window into sections. Each section will display a different Web page. Frames allow you to keep information on the screen while visitors browse through your Web pages. For example, you can use frames to keep an advertisement, company logo or navigational tools on the screen at all times.

CREATE FRAMES

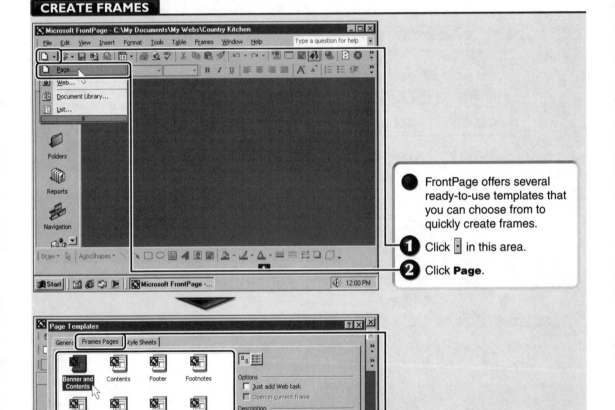

FrontPage offers several ready-to-use templates that you can choose from to quickly create frames.

1 Click ⋅ in this area.

2 Click **Page**.

The Page Templates dialog box appears.

3 Click the **Frames Pages** tab.

This area displays the available frames templates.

4 Click the frames template you want to use.

in an Instant

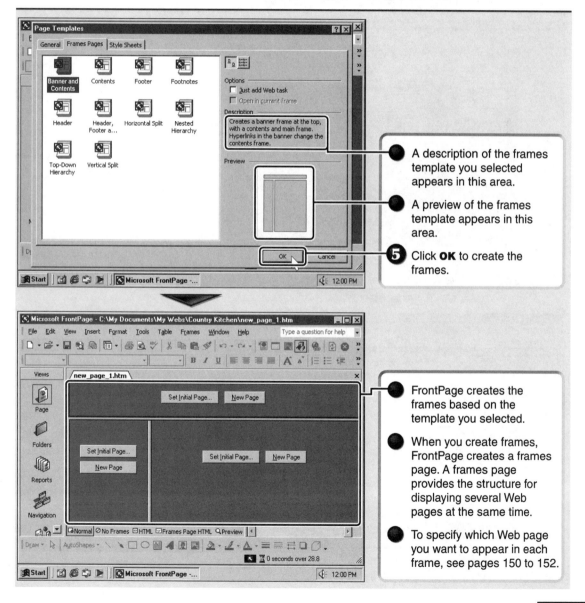

A description of the frames template you selected appears in this area.

A preview of the frames template appears in this area.

5 Click **OK** to create the frames.

FrontPage creates the frames based on the template you selected.

When you create frames, FrontPage creates a frames page. A frames page provides the structure for displaying several Web pages at the same time.

To specify which Web page you want to appear in each frame, see pages 150 to 152.

You can add a Web page you previously created to a frame. When you add an existing Web page to a frame, the amount of information that the frame can display at once depends on the size of the frame. You can edit the contents of a Web page you add to a frame as you would edit any page.

ADD AN EXISTING WEB PAGE TO A FRAME

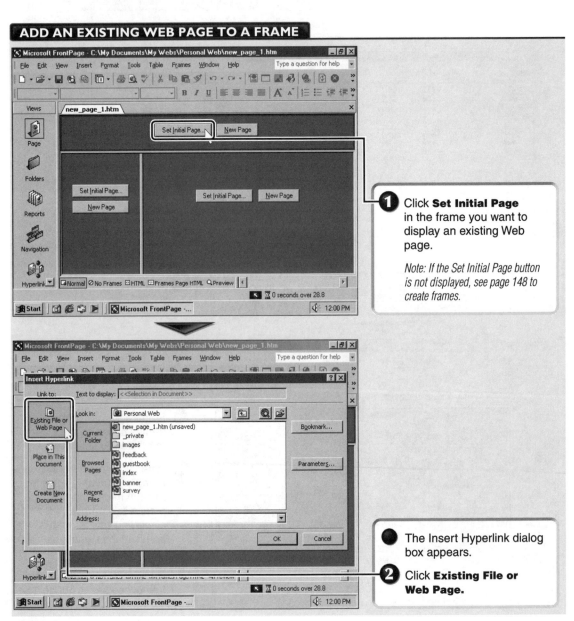

1 Click **Set Initial Page** in the frame you want to display an existing Web page.

Note: If the Set Initial Page button is not displayed, see page 148 to create frames.

● The Insert Hyperlink dialog box appears.

2 Click **Existing File or Web Page.**

in an instant

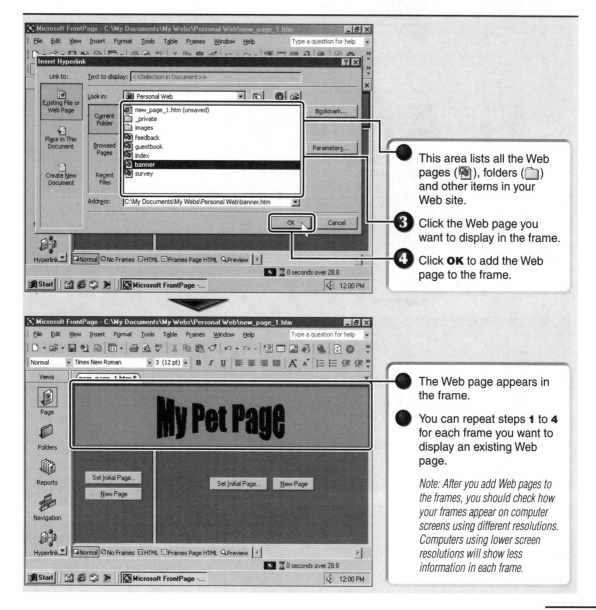

This area lists all the Web pages (📄), folders (📁) and other items in your Web site.

3 Click the Web page you want to display in the frame.

4 Click **OK** to add the Web page to the frame.

The Web page appears in the frame.

You can repeat steps **1** to **4** for each frame you want to display an existing Web page.

Note: After you add Web pages to the frames, you should check how your frames appear on computer screens using different resolutions. Computers using lower screen resolutions will show less information in each frame.

ADD A NEW WEB PAGE TO A FRAME

After you create frames, you can add a new Web page to a frame. This is useful if you want a frame to display a Web page you have not yet created. You can immediately add information to the new Web page.

ADD A NEW WEB PAGE TO A FRAME

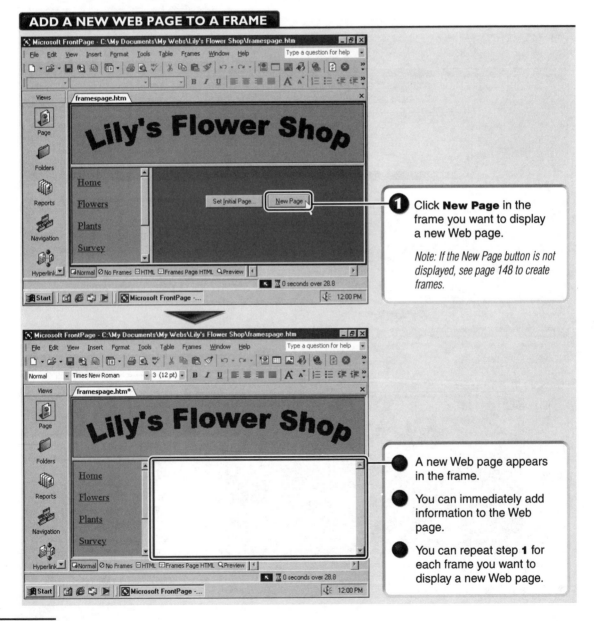

1 Click **New Page** in the frame you want to display a new Web page.

Note: If the New Page button is not displayed, see page 148 to create frames.

● A new Web page appears in the frame.

● You can immediately add information to the Web page.

● You can repeat step **1** for each frame you want to display a new Web page.

RESIZE A FRAME

You can change the size of a frame to show more or less
information in the frame. Resizing a frame will not change
the information displayed in the frame. Resizing a frame
only changes the amount of information the frame displays.

RESIZE A FRAME

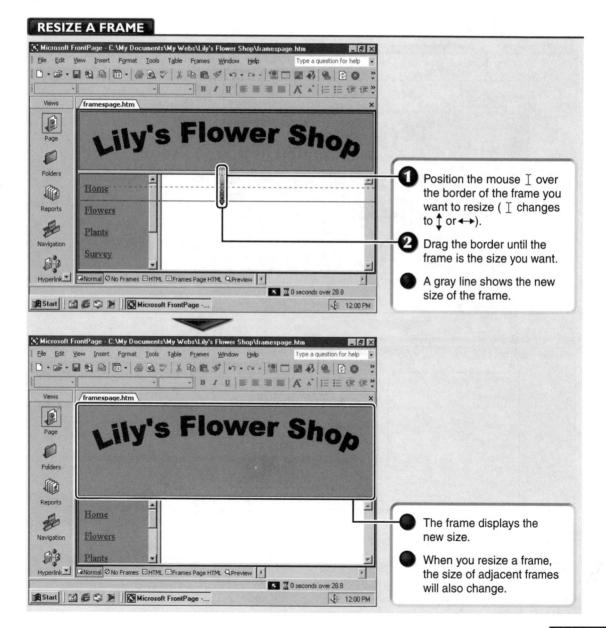

1 Position the mouse I over
the border of the frame you
want to resize (I changes
to ↕ or ↔).

2 Drag the border until the
frame is the size you want.

● A gray line shows the new
size of the frame.

● The frame displays the
new size.

● When you resize a frame,
the size of adjacent frames
will also change.

153

SAVE FRAMES

You should save your frames to store the frames for future use. This allows you to later review and edit the Web pages in the frames. When you save frames, FrontPage will ask you to save each new Web page you added to the frames and the frames page. The frames page provides the structure for displaying several Web pages at the same time.

SAVE FRAMES

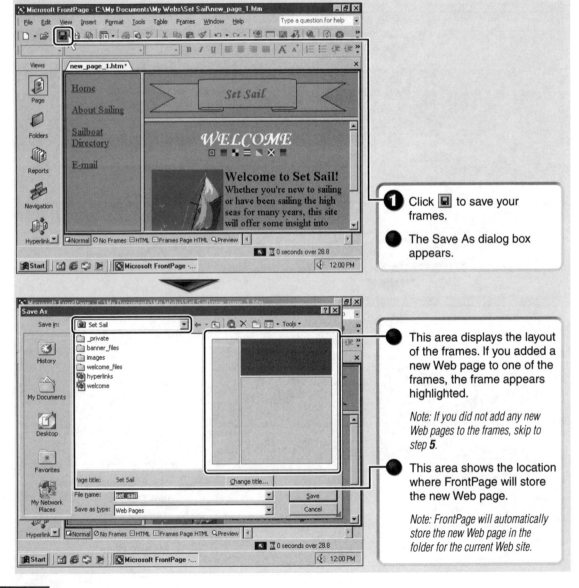

1 Click  to save your frames.

● The Save As dialog box appears.

● This area displays the layout of the frames. If you added a new Web page to one of the frames, the frame appears highlighted.

Note: If you did not add any new Web pages to the frames, skip to step 5.

● This area shows the location where FrontPage will store the new Web page.

Note: FrontPage will automatically store the new Web page in the folder for the current Web site.

in an *Instant*

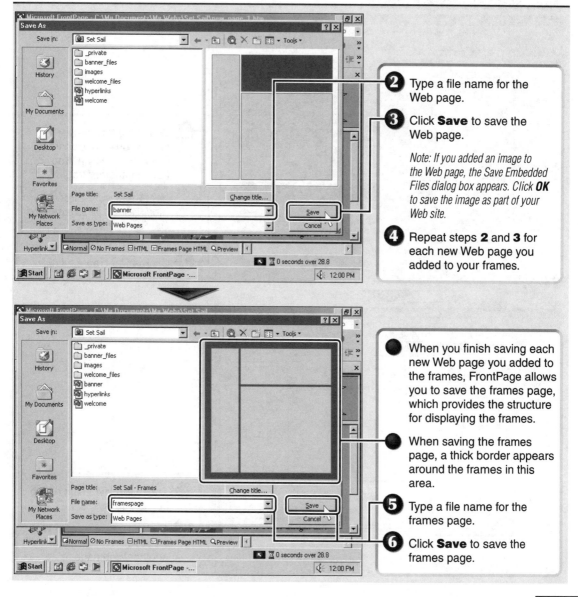

2 Type a file name for the Web page.

3 Click **Save** to save the Web page.

*Note: If you added an image to the Web page, the Save Embedded Files dialog box appears. Click **OK** to save the image as part of your Web site.*

4 Repeat steps **2** and **3** for each new Web page you added to your frames.

● When you finish saving each new Web page you added to the frames, FrontPage allows you to save the frames page, which provides the structure for displaying the frames.

● When saving the frames page, a thick border appears around the frames in this area.

5 Type a file name for the frames page.

6 Click **Save** to save the frames page.

CREATE A LINK TO A FRAME

You can create a link that visitors can select to display a Web page in another frame. Creating a link to a frame is useful when you place a table of contents or navigational tools in one frame and you want the linked Web pages to appear in another frame.

CREATE A LINK TO A FRAME

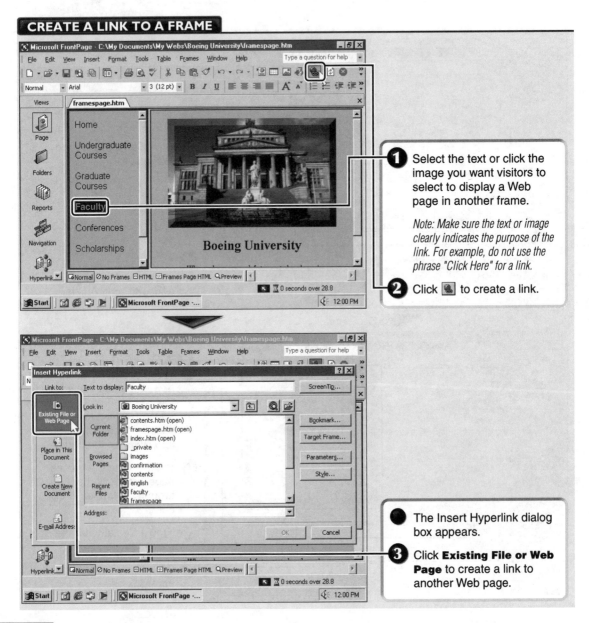

1 Select the text or click the image you want visitors to select to display a Web page in another frame.

Note: Make sure the text or image clearly indicates the purpose of the link. For example, do not use the phrase "Click Here" for a link.

2 Click 🔗 to create a link.

● The Insert Hyperlink dialog box appears.

3 Click **Existing File or Web Page** to create a link to another Web page.

in an *instant*

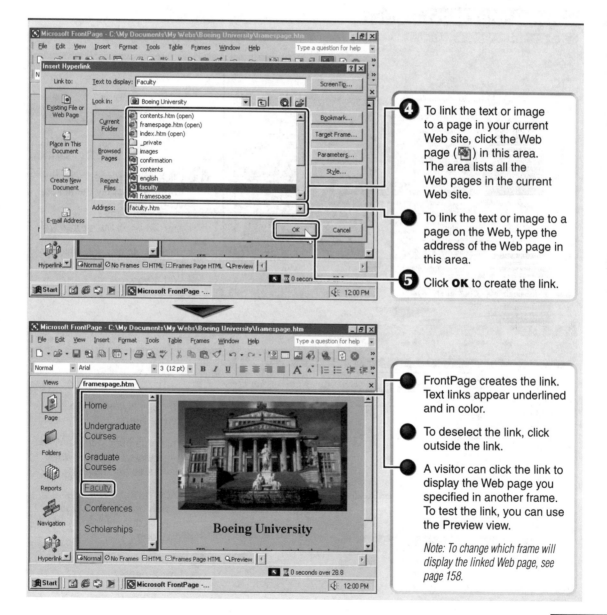

4 To link the text or image to a page in your current Web site, click the Web page (📄) in this area. The area lists all the Web pages in the current Web site.

● To link the text or image to a page on the Web, type the address of the Web page in this area.

5 Click **OK** to create the link.

● FrontPage creates the link. Text links appear underlined and in color.

● To deselect the link, click outside the link.

● A visitor can click the link to display the Web page you specified in another frame. To test the link, you can use the Preview view.

Note: To change which frame will display the linked Web page, see page 158.

CHANGE THE TARGET FRAME

You can change the frame that will display a Web page when visitors select a link. For example, you can choose to display a linked Web page in a specific frame or select a destination that FrontPage suggests, such as a new Web browser window. The frame you select to display a linked Web page is called the target frame.

CHANGE THE TARGET FRAME

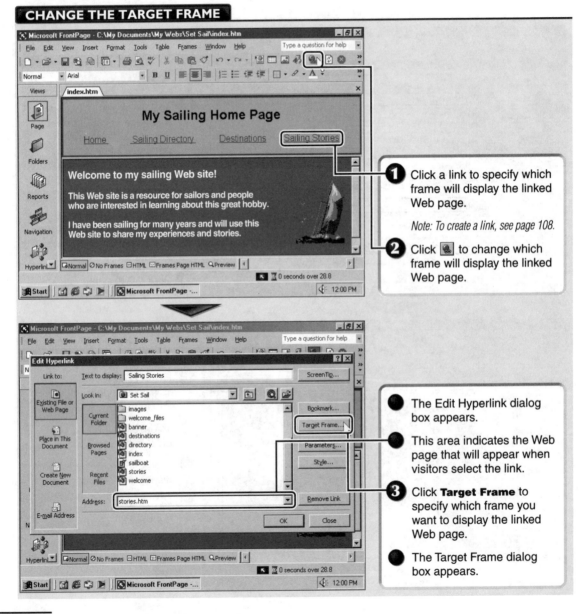

1 Click a link to specify which frame will display the linked Web page.

Note: To create a link, see page 108.

2 Click 🔲 to change which frame will display the linked Web page.

● The Edit Hyperlink dialog box appears.

● This area indicates the Web page that will appear when visitors select the link.

3 Click **Target Frame** to specify which frame you want to display the linked Web page.

● The Target Frame dialog box appears.

158

in an *instant*

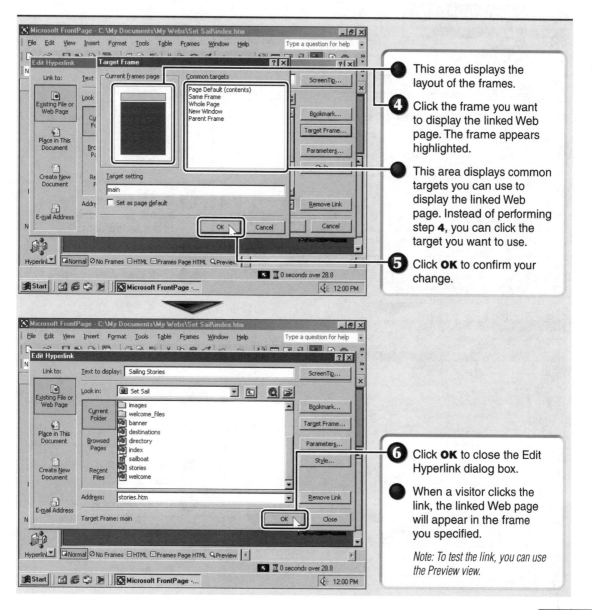

This area displays the layout of the frames.

4 Click the frame you want to display the linked Web page. The frame appears highlighted.

This area displays common targets you can use to display the linked Web page. Instead of performing step **4**, you can click the target you want to use.

5 Click **OK** to confirm your change.

6 Click **OK** to close the Edit Hyperlink dialog box.

When a visitor clicks the link, the linked Web page will appear in the frame you specified.

Note: To test the link, you can use the Preview view.

HIDE FRAME BORDERS

You can hide the borders between your frames to make the frames invisible. When you hide the frame borders, the contents of the frames will appear as one Web page. This is useful when you want information in one frame, such as a company logo or table of contents, to appear as part of another frame.

HIDE FRAME BORDERS

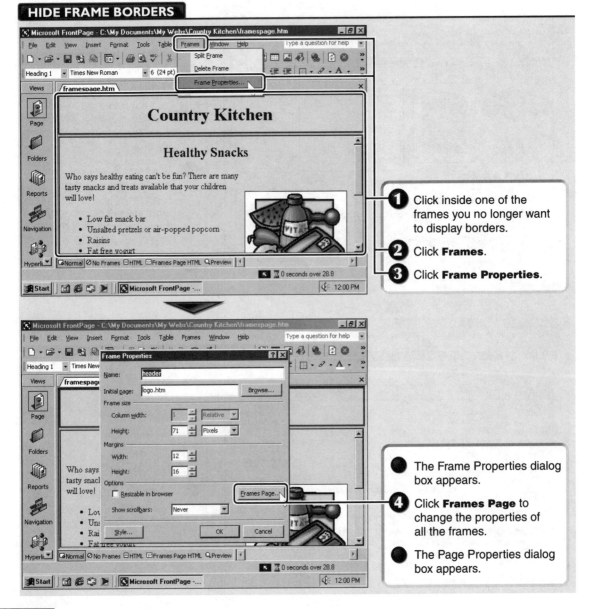

1 Click inside one of the frames you no longer want to display borders.

2 Click **Frames**.

3 Click **Frame Properties**.

■ The Frame Properties dialog box appears.

4 Click **Frames Page** to change the properties of all the frames.

■ The Page Properties dialog box appears.

in an INSTANT

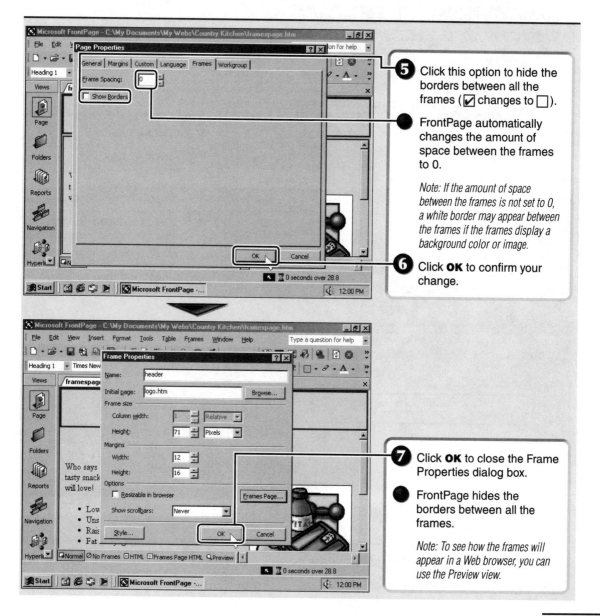

5 Click this option to hide the borders between all the frames (☑ changes to ☐).

● FrontPage automatically changes the amount of space between the frames to 0.

Note: If the amount of space between the frames is not set to 0, a white border may appear between the frames if the frames display a background color or image.

6 Click **OK** to confirm your change.

7 Click **OK** to close the Frame Properties dialog box.

● FrontPage hides the borders between all the frames.

Note: To see how the frames will appear in a Web browser, you can use the Preview view.

FrontPage provides text that will appear on a Web page if a visitor's Web browser cannot display your frames. You can change the text that FrontPage provides to give visitors personalized information about the missing frames.

PROVIDE ALTERNATIVE TEXT FOR FRAMES

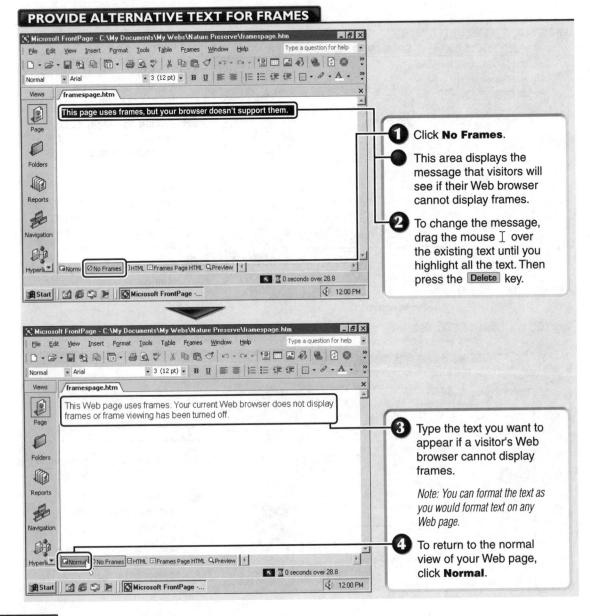

1 Click **No Frames**.

● This area displays the message that visitors will see if their Web browser cannot display frames.

2 To change the message, drag the mouse I over the existing text until you highlight all the text. Then press the Delete key.

3 Type the text you want to appear if a visitor's Web browser cannot display frames.

Note: You can format the text as you would format text on any Web page.

4 To return to the normal view of your Web page, click **Normal**.

If you do not want the layout of your frames to change, you can prevent visitors from resizing a frame. Visitors may want to change the size of a frame to display more information in the frame. FrontPage automatically prevents visitors from resizing some frames, such as a frame that displays a banner.

PREVENT VISITORS FROM RESIZING A FRAME

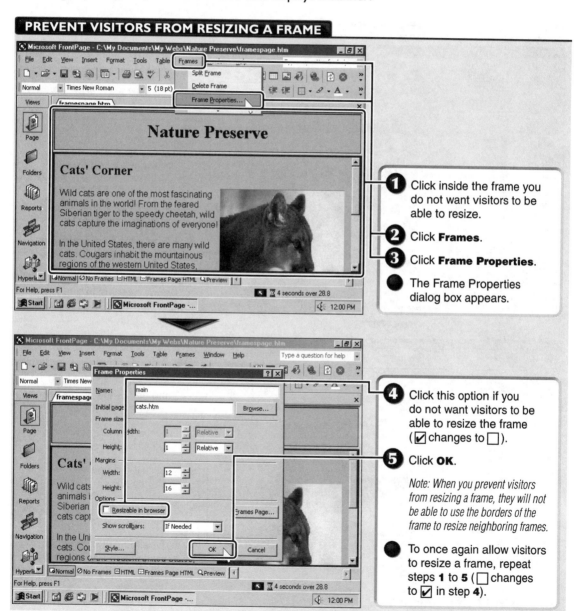

1 Click inside the frame you do not want visitors to be able to resize.

2 Click **Frames**.

3 Click **Frame Properties**.

● The Frame Properties dialog box appears.

4 Click this option if you do not want visitors to be able to resize the frame (☑ changes to ☐).

5 Click **OK**.

Note: When you prevent visitors from resizing a frame, they will not be able to use the borders of the frame to resize neighboring frames.

● To once again allow visitors to resize a frame, repeat steps **1** to **5** (☐ changes to ☑ in step **4**).

SET A FRAMES PAGE AS YOUR HOME PAGE

If you want your frames page to appear when people first visit your Web site, you need to set the frames page as your home page. The home page is usually the first page people will see when they visit a Web site. When you create a Web site, FrontPage automatically names your home page index.htm.

SET A FRAMES PAGE AS YOUR HOME PAGE

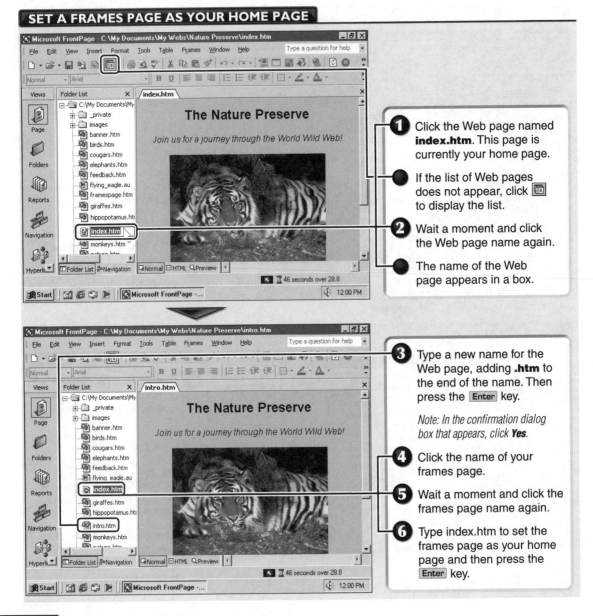

1 Click the Web page named **index.htm**. This page is currently your home page.

● If the list of Web pages does not appear, click 🔲 to display the list.

2 Wait a moment and click the Web page name again.

● The name of the Web page appears in a box.

3 Type a new name for the Web page, adding **.htm** to the end of the name. Then press the Enter key.

Note: In the confirmation dialog box that appears, click **Yes**.

4 Click the name of your frames page.

5 Wait a moment and click the frames page name again.

6 Type index.htm to set the frames page as your home page and then press the Enter key.

CREATE AN INLINE FRAME

You can create an inline frame on a Web page. Creating an inline frame allows you to display a Web page within another Web page. You may want to create an inline frame to display information such as a questionnaire or product descriptions.

CREATE AN INLINE FRAME

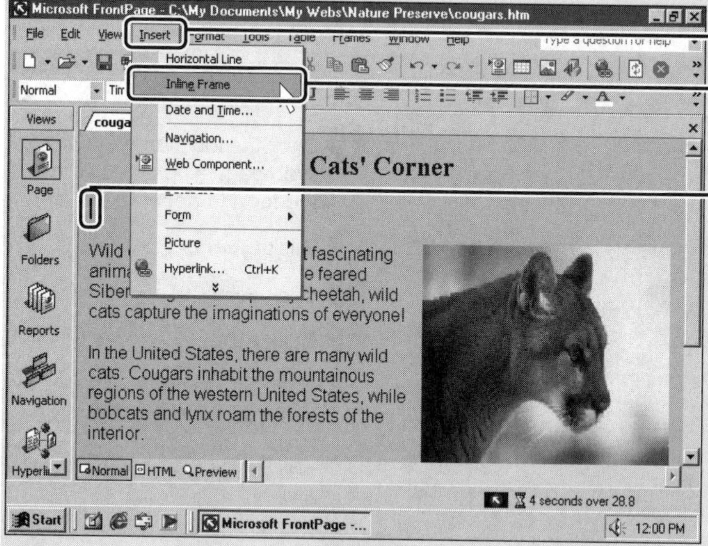

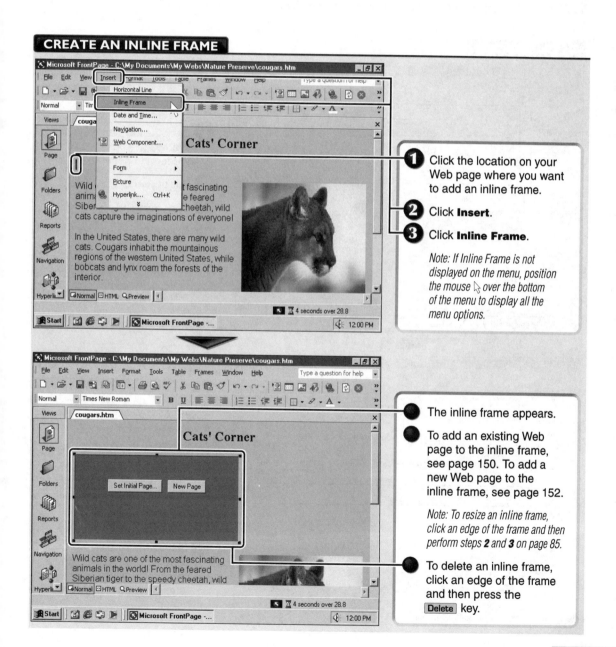

1. Click the location on your Web page where you want to add an inline frame.
2. Click **Insert**.
3. Click **Inline Frame**.

Note: If Inline Frame is not displayed on the menu, position the mouse over the bottom of the menu to display all the menu options.

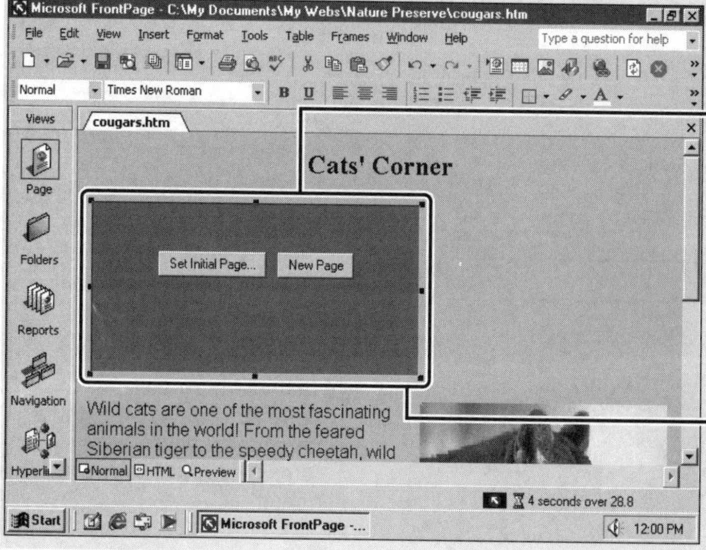

- The inline frame appears.
- To add an existing Web page to the inline frame, see page 150. To add a new Web page to the inline frame, see page 152.

*Note: To resize an inline frame, click an edge of the frame and then perform steps **2** and **3** on page 85.*

- To delete an inline frame, click an edge of the frame and then press the Delete key.

SET UP A FORM

Forms allow you to gather information from visitors who view your Web pages. Setting up a form allows you to create the basic structure of a form. Forms are useful when you want to allow visitors to send you questions and comments about your Web pages or purchase your products and services on the Web.

SET UP A FORM

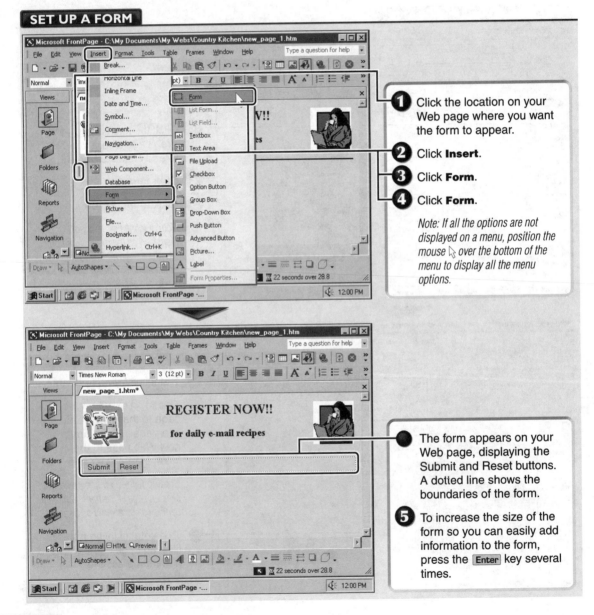

1 Click the location on your Web page where you want the form to appear.

2 Click **Insert**.

3 Click **Form**.

4 Click **Form**.

Note: If all the options are not displayed on a menu, position the mouse ⌖ over the bottom of the menu to display all the menu options.

● The form appears on your Web page, displaying the Submit and Reset buttons. A dotted line shows the boundaries of the form.

5 To increase the size of the form so you can easily add information to the form, press the Enter key several times.

in an instant

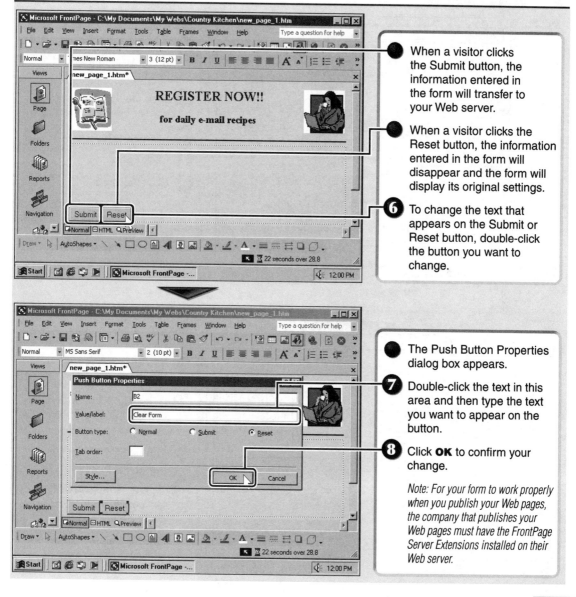

When a visitor clicks the Submit button, the information entered in the form will transfer to your Web server.

When a visitor clicks the Reset button, the information entered in the form will disappear and the form will display its original settings.

6 To change the text that appears on the Submit or Reset button, double-click the button you want to change.

The Push Button Properties dialog box appears.

7 Double-click the text in this area and then type the text you want to appear on the button.

8 Click **OK** to confirm your change.

Note: For your form to work properly when you publish your Web pages, the company that publishes your Web pages must have the FrontPage Server Extensions installed on their Web server.

ADD A TEXT BOX

You can add a text box to a form that allows visitors to enter a small amount of text, such as a name or mailing address. You will need to specify a name for a text box. When you view the form results, the name will identify the information that a visitor entered in the text box.

ADD A TEXT BOX

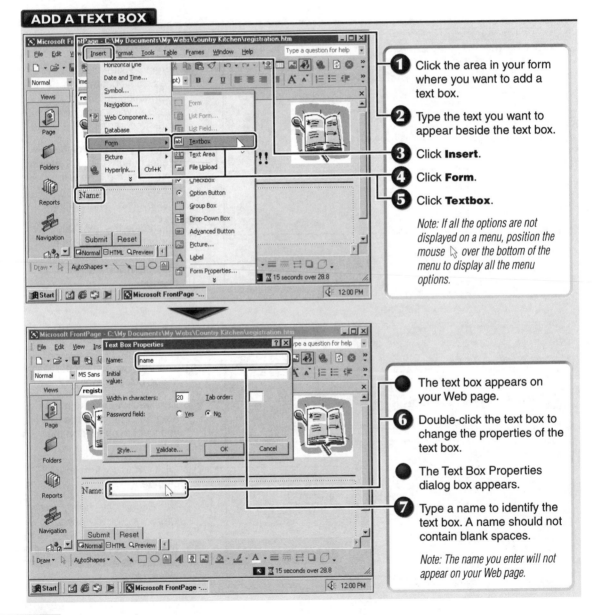

1 Click the area in your form where you want to add a text box.

2 Type the text you want to appear beside the text box.

3 Click **Insert**.

4 Click **Form**.

5 Click **Textbox**.

Note: If all the options are not displayed on a menu, position the mouse ⟍ over the bottom of the menu to display all the menu options.

■ The text box appears on your Web page.

6 Double-click the text box to change the properties of the text box.

■ The Text Box Properties dialog box appears.

7 Type a name to identify the text box. A name should not contain blank spaces.

Note: The name you enter will not appear on your Web page.

in an *instant*

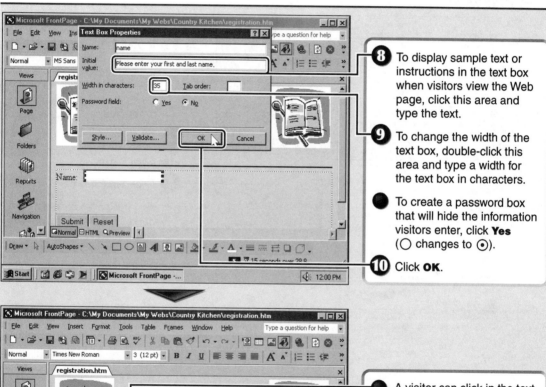

8 To display sample text or instructions in the text box when visitors view the Web page, click this area and type the text.

9 To change the width of the text box, double-click this area and type a width for the text box in characters.

● To create a password box that will hide the information visitors enter, click **Yes** (○ changes to ⊙).

10 Click **OK**.

● A visitor can click in the text box and type the requested information. If you entered sample text or instructions in step **8**, the information appears in the text box.

Note: To try entering information into the text box, you can use the Preview view.

● To delete a text box, click the text box and then press the Delete key.

ADD A TEXT AREA

You can add a text area to a form that allows visitors to enter several lines or paragraphs of text. A text area is ideal for gathering comments or questions from your visitors. You will need to specify a name for a text area. When you view the form results, the name will identify the information that a visitor entered in the text area.

ADD A TEXT AREA

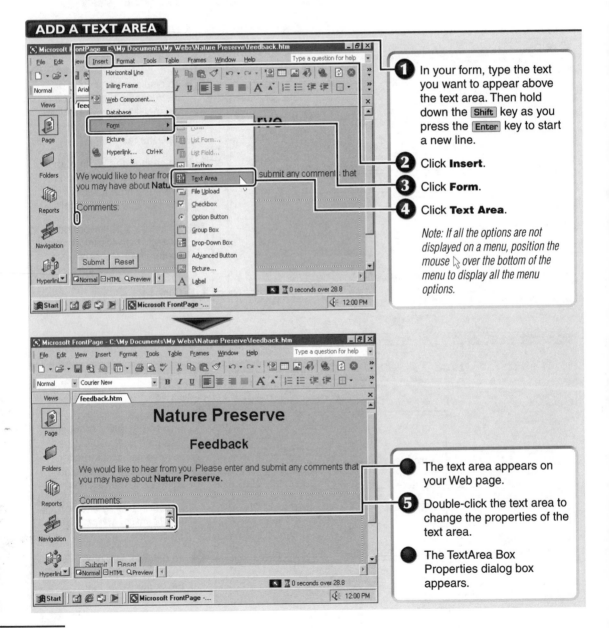

1 In your form, type the text you want to appear above the text area. Then hold down the **Shift** key as you press the **Enter** key to start a new line.

2 Click **Insert**.

3 Click **Form**.

4 Click **Text Area**.

Note: If all the options are not displayed on a menu, position the mouse ↳ over the bottom of the menu to display all the menu options.

■ The text area appears on your Web page.

5 Double-click the text area to change the properties of the text area.

■ The TextArea Box Properties dialog box appears.

in an *instant*

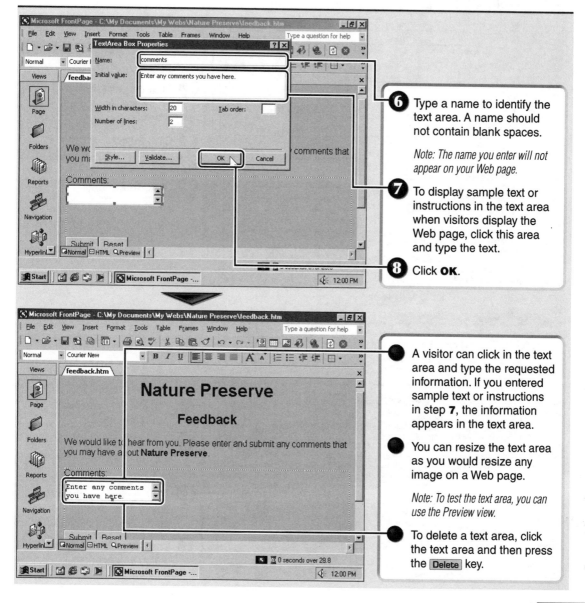

6 Type a name to identify the text area. A name should not contain blank spaces.

Note: The name you enter will not appear on your Web page.

7 To display sample text or instructions in the text area when visitors display the Web page, click this area and type the text.

8 Click **OK**.

■ A visitor can click in the text area and type the requested information. If you entered sample text or instructions in step **7**, the information appears in the text area.

■ You can resize the text area as you would resize any image on a Web page.

Note: To test the text area, you can use the Preview view.

■ To delete a text area, click the text area and then press the Delete key.

You can include check boxes on a form if you want visitors to be able to select one or more options. You will need to specify a name and value for each check box. When you view the form results, the value appears with the name to indicate that a visitor selected the check box.

ADD CHECK BOXES

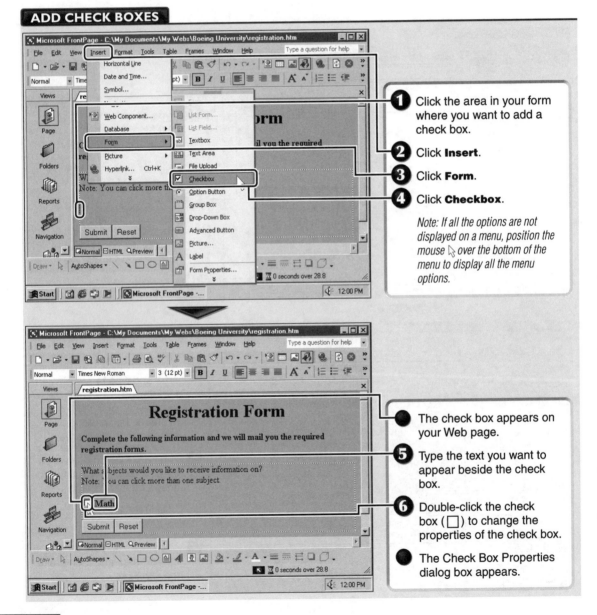

1 Click the area in your form where you want to add a check box.

2 Click **Insert**.

3 Click **Form**.

4 Click **Checkbox**.

Note: If all the options are not displayed on a menu, position the mouse over the bottom of the menu to display all the menu options.

● The check box appears on your Web page.

5 Type the text you want to appear beside the check box.

6 Double-click the check box (☐) to change the properties of the check box.

● The Check Box Properties dialog box appears.

in an *instant*

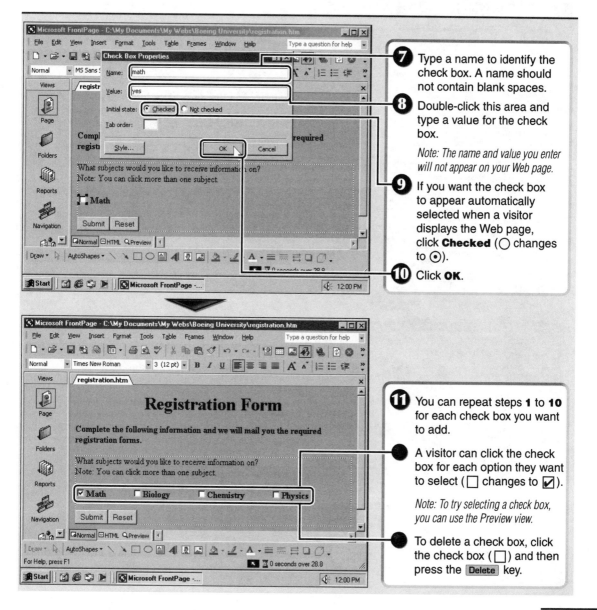

ADD OPTION BUTTONS

You can include option buttons on a form to allow visitors to select only one of several options. You will need to specify a name to identify the group of option buttons and a value for each option button. When you view the form results, a value appears with the group name to indicate which option button a visitor selected.

ADD OPTION BUTTONS

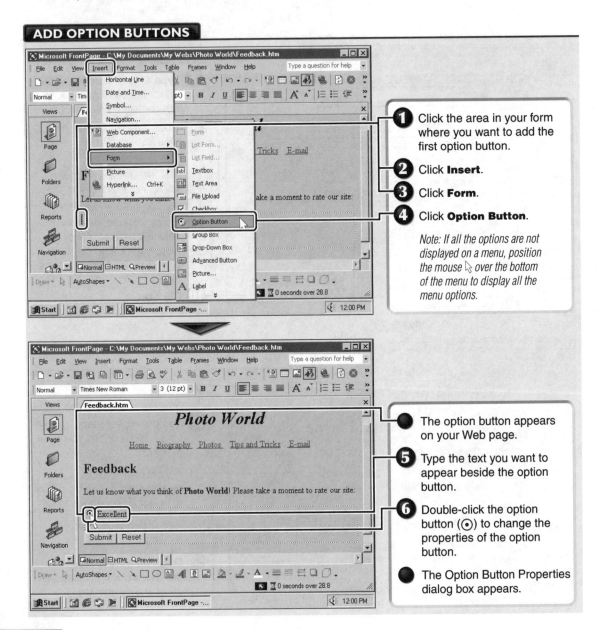

1 Click the area in your form where you want to add the first option button.

2 Click **Insert**.

3 Click **Form**.

4 Click **Option Button**.

Note: If all the options are not displayed on a menu, position the mouse over the bottom of the menu to display all the menu options.

■ The option button appears on your Web page.

5 Type the text you want to appear beside the option button.

6 Double-click the option button (⊙) to change the properties of the option button.

■ The Option Button Properties dialog box appears.

in an *Instant*

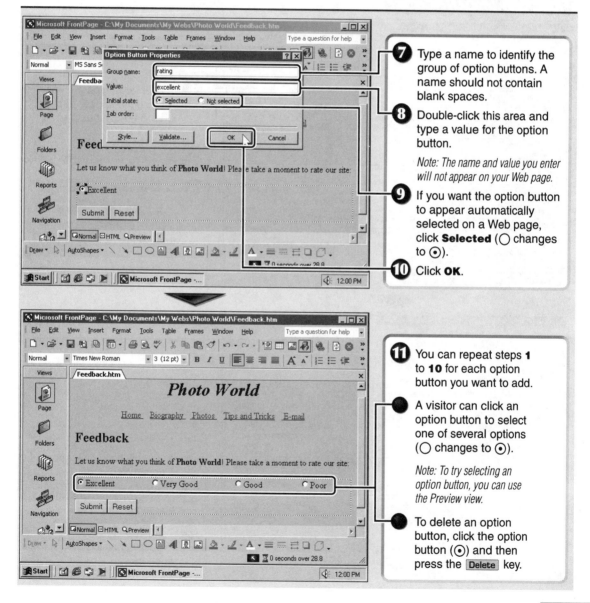

7 Type a name to identify the group of option buttons. A name should not contain blank spaces.

8 Double-click this area and type a value for the option button.

Note: The name and value you enter will not appear on your Web page.

9 If you want the option button to appear automatically selected on a Web page, click **Selected** (○ changes to ⊙).

10 Click **OK**.

11 You can repeat steps **1** to **10** for each option button you want to add.

● A visitor can click an option button to select one of several options (○ changes to ⊙).

Note: To try selecting an option button, you can use the Preview view.

● To delete an option button, click the option button (⊙) and then press the Delete key.

ADD A DROP-DOWN BOX

You can add a drop-down box to a form to provide a list of items that visitors can choose from. You need to specify a name for a drop-down box, the text for each item in a drop-down box and a value for each item. When you view the form results, a value appears with the name to indicate which item a visitor selected.

ADD A DROP-DOWN BOX

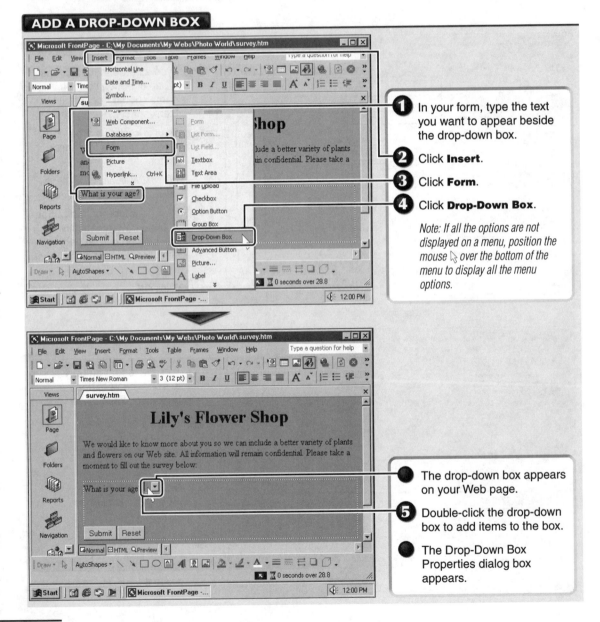

1 In your form, type the text you want to appear beside the drop-down box.

2 Click **Insert**.

3 Click **Form**.

4 Click **Drop-Down Box**.

Note: If all the options are not displayed on a menu, position the mouse ⍗ over the bottom of the menu to display all the menu options.

■ The drop-down box appears on your Web page.

5 Double-click the drop-down box to add items to the box.

■ The Drop-Down Box Properties dialog box appears.

in an *instant*

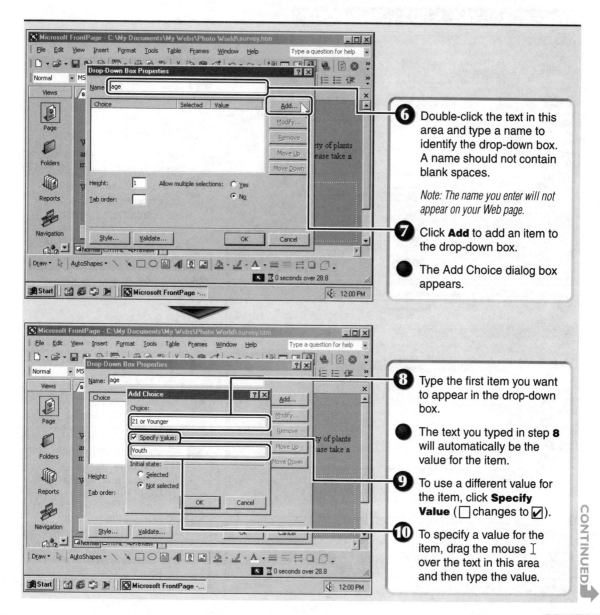

6 Double-click the text in this area and type a name to identify the drop-down box. A name should not contain blank spaces.

Note: The name you enter will not appear on your Web page.

7 Click **Add** to add an item to the drop-down box.

● The Add Choice dialog box appears.

8 Type the first item you want to appear in the drop-down box.

● The text you typed in step **8** will automatically be the value for the item.

9 To use a different value for the item, click **Specify Value** (☐ changes to ☑).

10 To specify a value for the item, drag the mouse I over the text in this area and then type the value.

CONTINUED

177

ADD A DROP-DOWN BOX

You can have an item in a drop-down box appear automatically selected on your form. This is useful if most people will select the item. You can also change the number of items that visitors initially see in a drop-down box. This is useful when you want to display all the items in a short list at once.

ADD A DROP-DOWN BOX (CONTINUED)

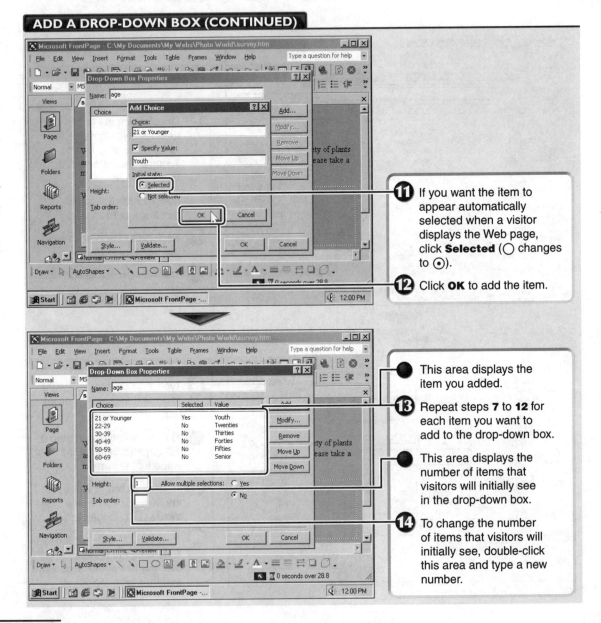

11 If you want the item to appear automatically selected when a visitor displays the Web page, click **Selected** (○ changes to ⊙).

12 Click **OK** to add the item.

● This area displays the item you added.

13 Repeat steps **7** to **12** for each item you want to add to the drop-down box.

● This area displays the number of items that visitors will initially see in the drop-down box.

14 To change the number of items that visitors will initially see, double-click this area and type a new number.

178

in an instant

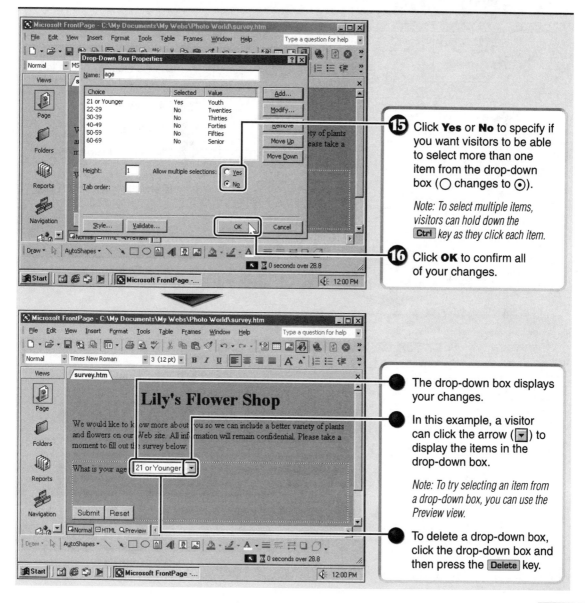

15 Click **Yes** or **No** to specify if you want visitors to be able to select more than one item from the drop-down box (○ changes to ⊙).

Note: To select multiple items, visitors can hold down the **Ctrl** *key as they click each item.*

16 Click **OK** to confirm all of your changes.

● The drop-down box displays your changes.

● In this example, a visitor can click the arrow (▼) to display the items in the drop-down box.

Note: To try selecting an item from a drop-down box, you can use the Preview view.

● To delete a drop-down box, click the drop-down box and then press the **Delete** key.

After you create a form, you need to specify how you want to access the results of the form. You can store the form results in a file on your Web server and/or send the form results in e-mail messages. When visitors submit the form, the information they entered will be added to the file and/or sent to the e-mail address you specify.

ACCESS FORM RESULTS

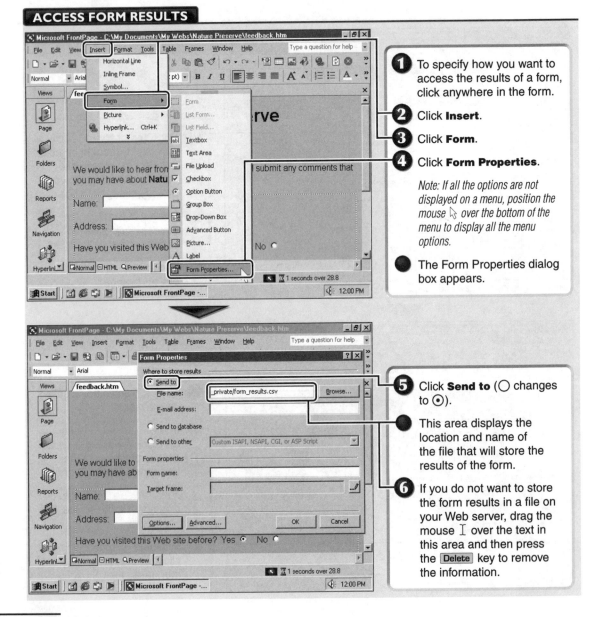

1 To specify how you want to access the results of a form, click anywhere in the form.

2 Click **Insert**.

3 Click **Form**.

4 Click **Form Properties**.

Note: If all the options are not displayed on a menu, position the mouse ⫶ over the bottom of the menu to display all the menu options.

● The Form Properties dialog box appears.

5 Click **Send to** (○ changes to ⊙).

● This area displays the location and name of the file that will store the results of the form.

6 If you do not want to store the form results in a file on your Web server, drag the mouse I over the text in this area and then press the Delete key to remove the information.

in an *instant*

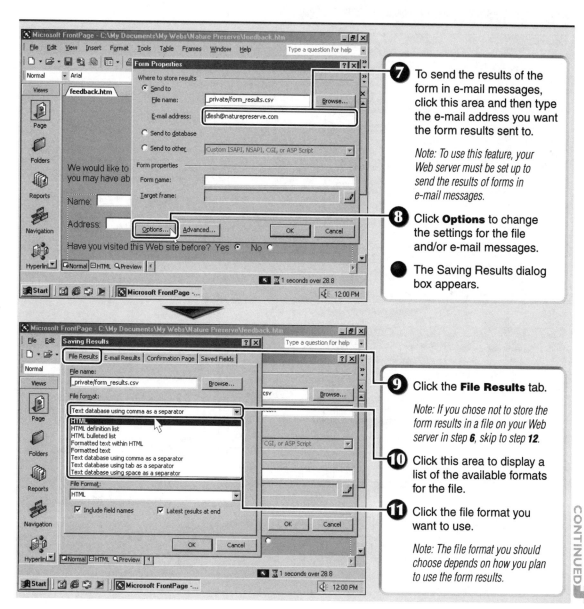

7 To send the results of the form in e-mail messages, click this area and then type the e-mail address you want the form results sent to.

Note: To use this feature, your Web server must be set up to send the results of forms in e-mail messages.

8 Click **Options** to change the settings for the file and/or e-mail messages.

● The Saving Results dialog box appears.

9 Click the **File Results** tab.

Note: If you chose not to store the form results in a file on your Web server in step 6, skip to step 12.

10 Click this area to display a list of the available formats for the file.

11 Click the file format you want to use.

Note: The file format you should choose depends on how you plan to use the form results.

CONTINUED➜

If you set up your form to send the results in e-mail messages, you can choose the subject you want each e-mail message to display. The subject for an e-mail message identifies the contents of the message. You can also choose the file format that you want to use for the e-mail messages, such as HTML or formatted text.

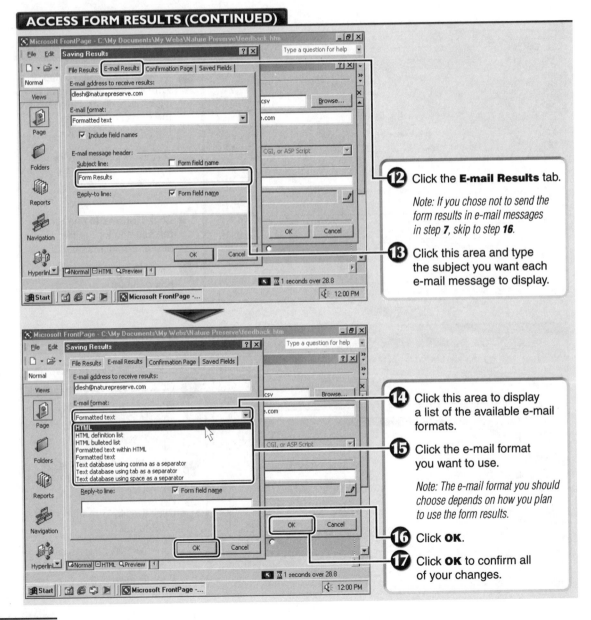

12 Click the **E-mail Results** tab.

Note: If you chose not to send the form results in e-mail messages in step 7, skip to step 16.

13 Click this area and type the subject you want each e-mail message to display.

14 Click this area to display a list of the available e-mail formats.

15 Click the e-mail format you want to use.

Note: The e-mail format you should choose depends on how you plan to use the form results.

16 Click **OK**.

17 Click **OK** to confirm all of your changes.

in an instant

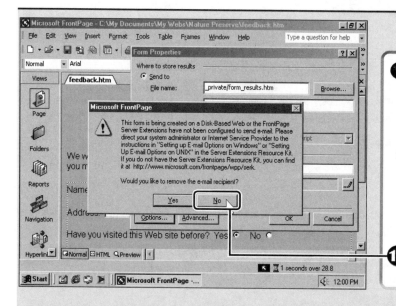

- If you entered an e-mail address in step **7**, a dialog box appears, stating that your computer is not set up to send the results of your form in e-mail messages.

  Note: This dialog box only applies to people who will use their own computer to publish their Web pages. If you are using a company to publish your Web pages, you can ignore this message.

- **18** Click **No** to keep the e-mail address you specified.

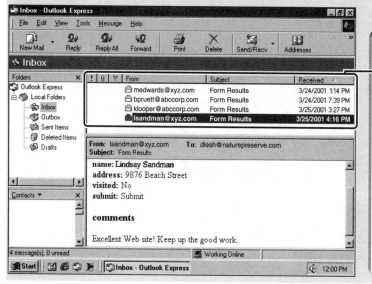

VIEW FORM RESULTS

- If you chose to send the form results in e-mail messages, you will receive a message from each person that submits the form.

- If you chose to store the form results in a file on your Web server, you can use an FTP program, such as WS_FTP Pro, to transfer the file to your computer.

  Note: You can obtain WS_FTP Pro at the www.ipswitch.com Web site.

CREATE A CONFIRMATION PAGE

You can create a confirmation page that will appear after visitors submit a form. A confirmation page allows visitors to review the information they entered in a form. If you do not create a confirmation page, FrontPage will automatically display a basic confirmation page that lists all the information visitors entered in a form.

CREATE A CONFIRMATION PAGE

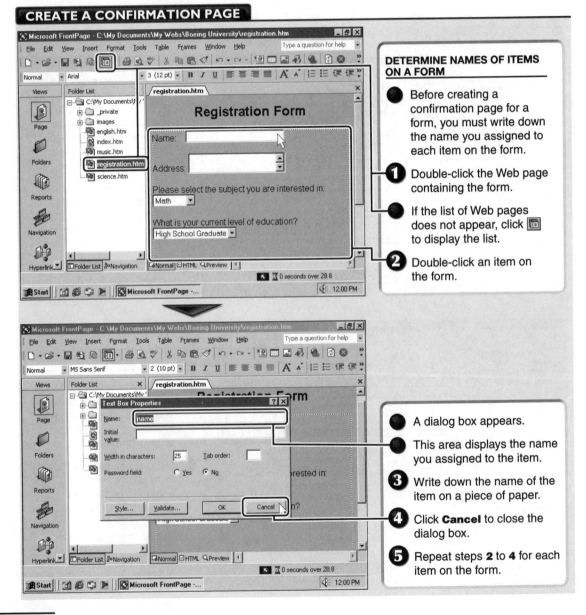

DETERMINE NAMES OF ITEMS ON A FORM

● Before creating a confirmation page for a form, you must write down the name you assigned to each item on the form.

1 Double-click the Web page containing the form.

● If the list of Web pages does not appear, click 🗐 to display the list.

2 Double-click an item on the form.

● A dialog box appears.

● This area displays the name you assigned to the item.

3 Write down the name of the item on a piece of paper.

4 Click **Cancel** to close the dialog box.

5 Repeat steps **2** to **4** for each item on the form.

in an instant

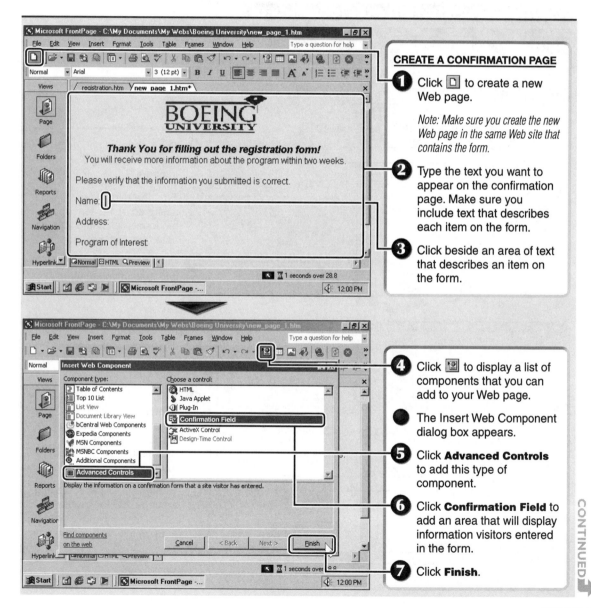

CREATE A CONFIRMATION PAGE

1. Click 🗋 to create a new Web page.

   Note: Make sure you create the new Web page in the same Web site that contains the form.

2. Type the text you want to appear on the confirmation page. Make sure you include text that describes each item on the form.

3. Click beside an area of text that describes an item on the form.

4. Click 🖼 to display a list of components that you can add to your Web page.

■ The Insert Web Component dialog box appears.

5. Click **Advanced Controls** to add this type of component.

6. Click **Confirmation Field** to add an area that will display information visitors entered in the form.

7. Click **Finish**.

CONTINUED

When creating a confirmation page, you need to enter the name you assigned to each item on the form. When visitors view the confirmation page, each name will be replaced with the information they entered in the form. After you finish creating the confirmation page, you need to assign the page to the form that you want to use the page.

CREATE A CONFIRMATION PAGE (CONTINUED)

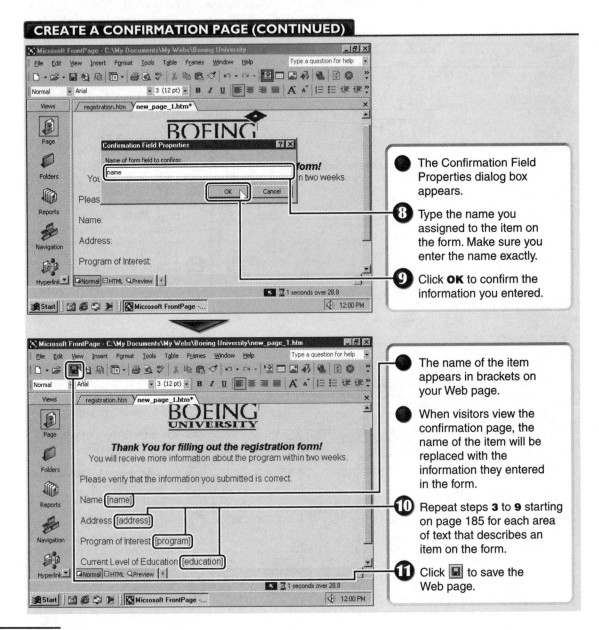

The Confirmation Field Properties dialog box appears.

8 Type the name you assigned to the item on the form. Make sure you enter the name exactly.

9 Click **OK** to confirm the information you entered.

The name of the item appears in brackets on your Web page.

When visitors view the confirmation page, the name of the item will be replaced with the information they entered in the form.

10 Repeat steps **3** to **9** starting on page 185 for each area of text that describes an item on the form.

11 Click 🖫 to save the Web page.

in an instant

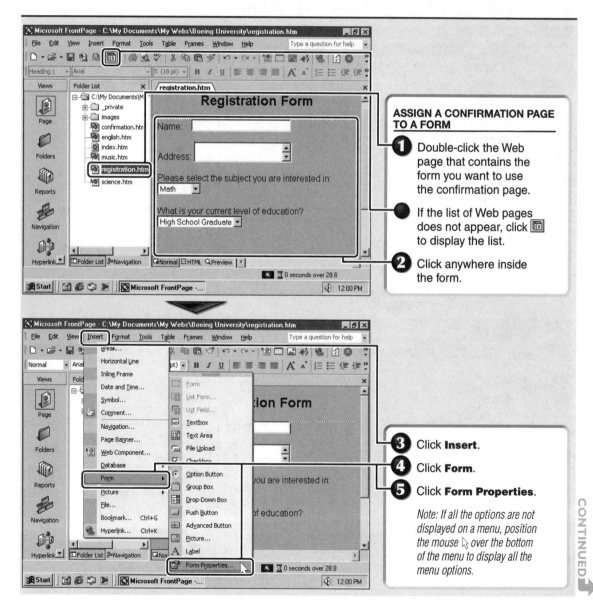

CONTINUED

ASSIGN A CONFIRMATION PAGE TO A FORM

1 Double-click the Web page that contains the form you want to use the confirmation page.

● If the list of Web pages does not appear, click 🔲 to display the list.

2 Click anywhere inside the form.

3 Click **Insert**.

4 Click **Form**.

5 Click **Form Properties**.

Note: If all the options are not displayed on a menu, position the mouse ⌖ over the bottom of the menu to display all the menu options.

After you assign a confirmation page to a form, the page will appear when visitors submit the form. Visitors will not be able to edit the information displayed on a confirmation page, however they can use the page to review the information they entered in the form.

CREATE A CONFIRMATION PAGE (CONTINUED)

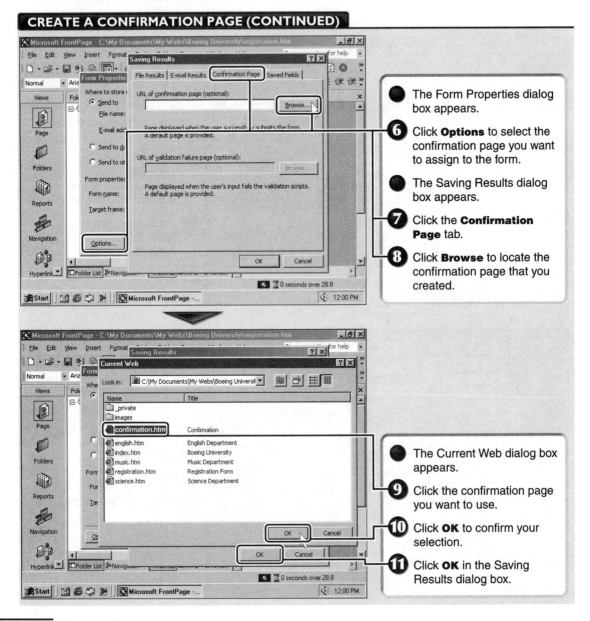

● The Form Properties dialog box appears.

⑥ Click **Options** to select the confirmation page you want to assign to the form.

● The Saving Results dialog box appears.

⑦ Click the **Confirmation Page** tab.

⑧ Click **Browse** to locate the confirmation page that you created.

● The Current Web dialog box appears.

⑨ Click the confirmation page you want to use.

⑩ Click **OK** to confirm your selection.

⑪ Click **OK** in the Saving Results dialog box.

in an **instant**

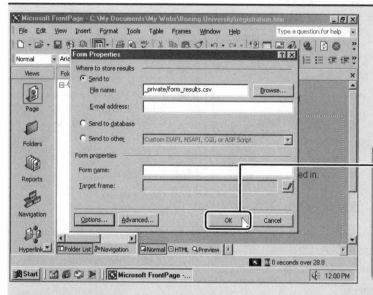

12 Click **OK** in the Form Properties dialog box.

● When visitors submit the form, the confirmation page you specified will appear.

Note: To test the confirmation page, you must publish your Web pages.

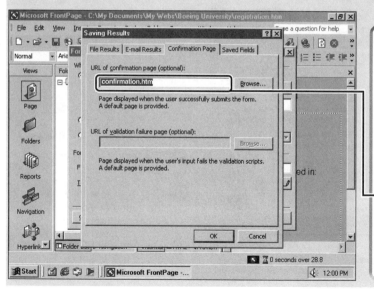

REMOVE A CONFIRMATION PAGE

● When you remove a conformation page you created from a form, the form will once again use the basic confirmation page FrontPage provides.

1 Perform steps **1** to **7** starting on page 187.

2 Press the Delete key to remove the information displayed in this area.

3 Press the Enter key twice to confirm your change.

You can create a link on a Web page that visitors can select to play a sound or video, such as a sound clip from a television show or a home movie. Many Web sites offer sounds and videos you can use. You can also obtain sounds and videos at computer stores or record your own sounds and videos.

CREATE A LINK TO A SOUND OR VIDEO

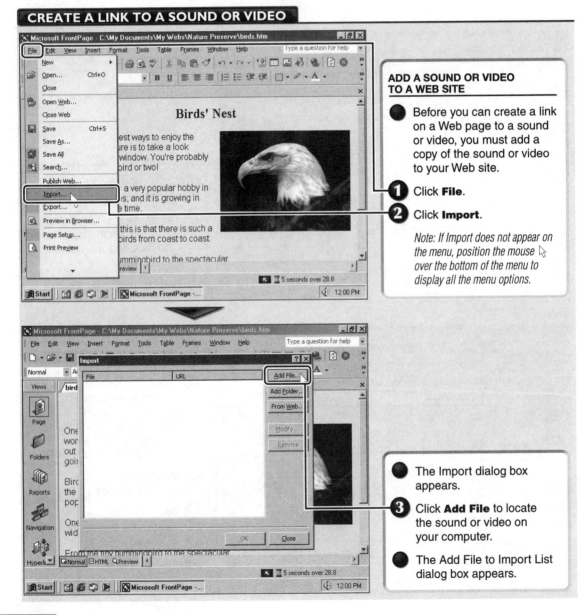

ADD A SOUND OR VIDEO TO A WEB SITE

● Before you can create a link on a Web page to a sound or video, you must add a copy of the sound or video to your Web site.

1 Click **File**.

2 Click **Import**.

Note: If Import does not appear on the menu, position the mouse over the bottom of the menu to display all the menu options.

● The Import dialog box appears.

3 Click **Add File** to locate the sound or video on your computer.

● The Add File to Import List dialog box appears.

in an *instant*

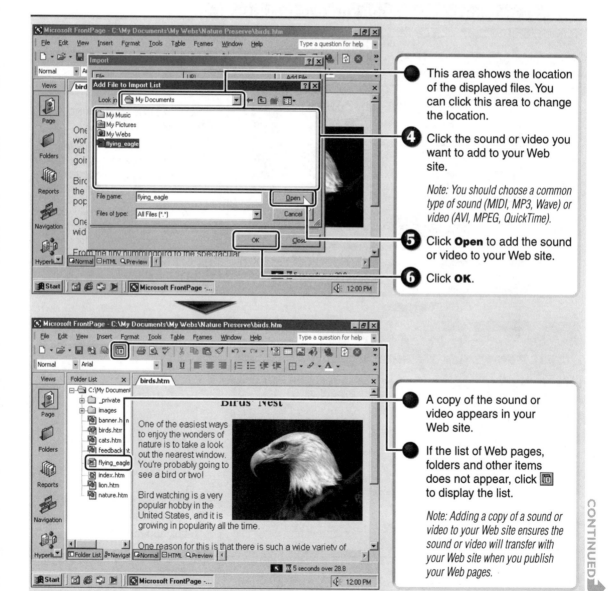

This area shows the location of the displayed files. You can click this area to change the location.

4 Click the sound or video you want to add to your Web site.

Note: You should choose a common type of sound (MIDI, MP3, Wave) or video (AVI, MPEG, QuickTime).

5 Click **Open** to add the sound or video to your Web site.

6 Click **OK**.

A copy of the sound or video appears in your Web site.

If the list of Web pages, folders and other items does not appear, click 📷 to display the list.

Note: Adding a copy of a sound or video to your Web site ensures the sound or video will transfer with your Web site when you publish your Web pages.

CONTINUED➡

Whenever possible, you should create a link to a sound or video with a small file size to ensure the sound or video quickly transfers and plays on a visitor's computer. Make sure you display on your Web page the file type, size and length of time the sound or video will play. Visitors can use this information to decide if they want to play the sound or video.

CREATE A LINK TO A SOUND OR VIDEO (CONTINUED)

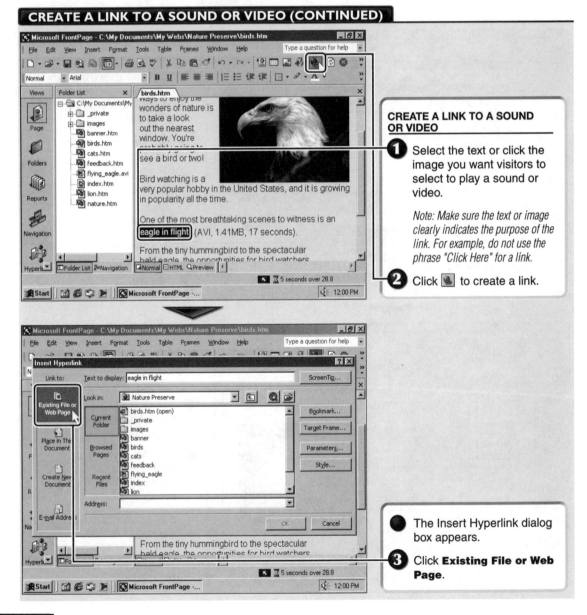

CREATE A LINK TO A SOUND OR VIDEO

1 Select the text or click the image you want visitors to select to play a sound or video.

Note: Make sure the text or image clearly indicates the purpose of the link. For example, do not use the phrase "Click Here" for a link.

2 Click 🖼 to create a link.

● The Insert Hyperlink dialog box appears.

3 Click **Existing File or Web Page**.

in an instant

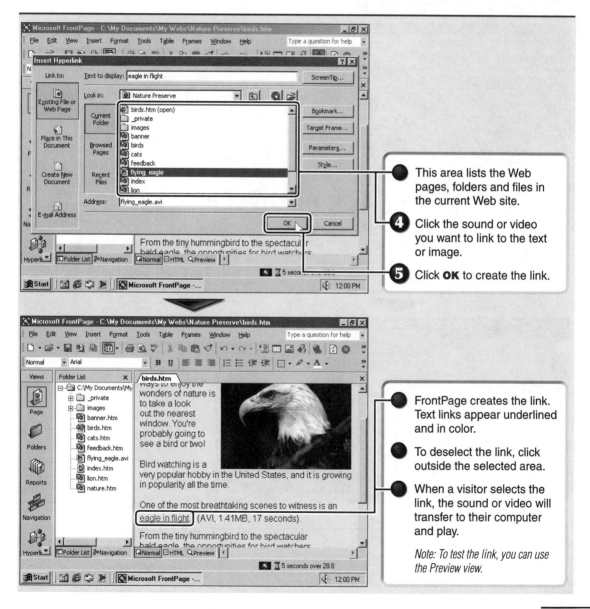

This area lists the Web pages, folders and files in the current Web site.

④ Click the sound or video you want to link to the text or image.

⑤ Click **OK** to create the link.

FrontPage creates the link. Text links appear underlined and in color.

To deselect the link, click outside the selected area.

When a visitor selects the link, the sound or video will transfer to their computer and play.

Note: To test the link, you can use the Preview view.

ADD A BACKGROUND SOUND

You can add a background sound to a Web page that will automatically play when visitors display the page. You should add a common type of sound, such as MIDI or Wave, to ensure that most Web browsers can play the sound. By default, the Netscape Navigator Web browser will not play a background sound that you add to a Web page.

ADD A BACKGROUND SOUND

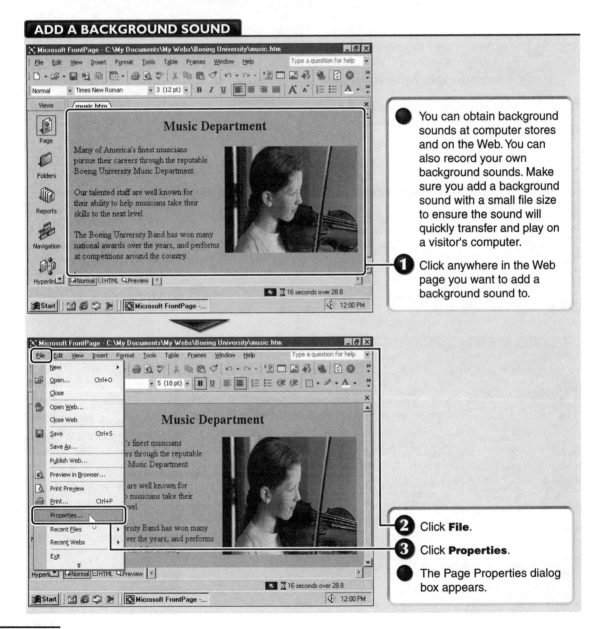

You can obtain background sounds at computer stores and on the Web. You can also record your own background sounds. Make sure you add a background sound with a small file size to ensure the sound will quickly transfer and play on a visitor's computer.

1 Click anywhere in the Web page you want to add a background sound to.

2 Click **File**.

3 Click **Properties**.

The Page Properties dialog box appears.

in an instant

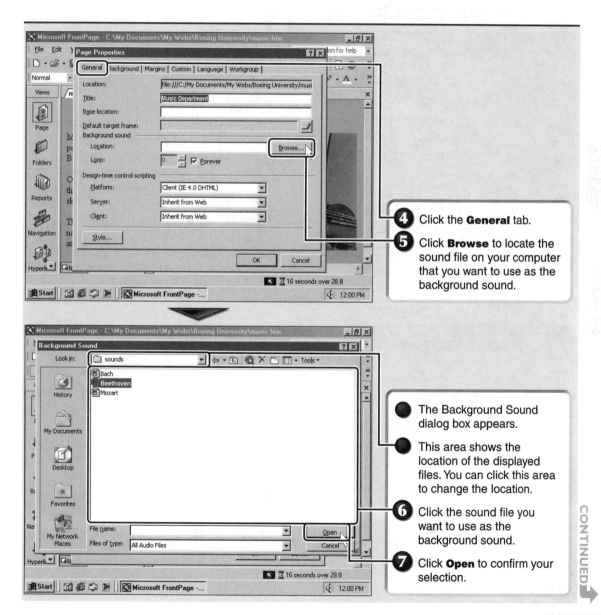

4 Click the **General** tab.

5 Click **Browse** to locate the sound file on your computer that you want to use as the background sound.

● The Background Sound dialog box appears.

● This area shows the location of the displayed files. You can click this area to change the location.

6 Click the sound file you want to use as the background sound.

7 Click **Open** to confirm your selection.

CONTINUED

ADD A BACKGROUND SOUND

You can choose to play a background sound continuously or only a specific number of times when a visitor displays your Web page. You may want to play a background sound only a specific number of times since playing the sound continuously may annoy some visitors. Visitors may turn off their speakers or leave your Web page.

ADD A BACKGROUND SOUND (CONTINUED)

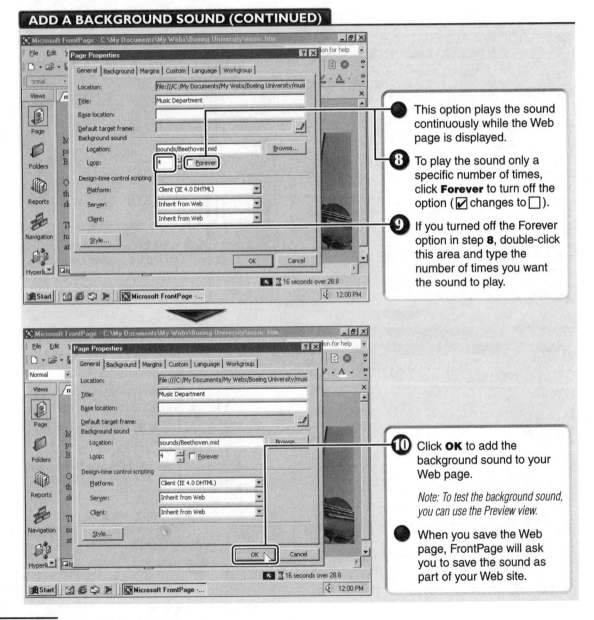

This option plays the sound continuously while the Web page is displayed.

⑧ To play the sound only a specific number of times, click **Forever** to turn off the option (☑ changes to ☐).

⑨ If you turned off the Forever option in step **8**, double-click this area and type the number of times you want the sound to play.

⑩ Click **OK** to add the background sound to your Web page.

Note: To test the background sound, you can use the Preview view.

● When you save the Web page, FrontPage will ask you to save the sound as part of your Web site.

in an *instant*

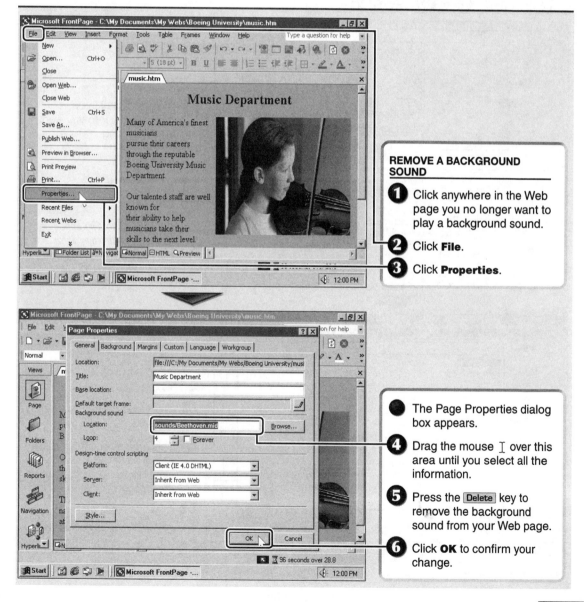

REMOVE A BACKGROUND SOUND

1 Click anywhere in the Web page you no longer want to play a background sound.

2 Click **File**.

3 Click **Properties**.

● The Page Properties dialog box appears.

4 Drag the mouse I over this area until you select all the information.

5 Press the Delete key to remove the background sound from your Web page.

6 Click **OK** to confirm your change.

ADD A VIDEO TO A WEB PAGE

You can add a video to a Web page that will play automatically when a visitor displays the page. You should use AVI videos since most Web browsers can play this type of video. By default, the Netscape Navigator Web browser will not display or play a video on a Web page.

ADD A VIDEO TO A WEB PAGE

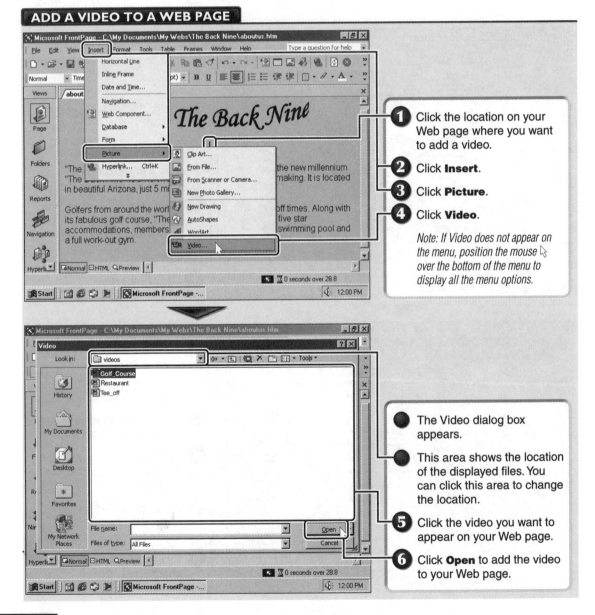

1 Click the location on your Web page where you want to add a video.

2 Click **Insert**.

3 Click **Picture**.

4 Click **Video**.

Note: If Video does not appear on the menu, position the mouse over the bottom of the menu to display all the menu options.

■ The Video dialog box appears.

■ This area shows the location of the displayed files. You can click this area to change the location.

5 Click the video you want to appear on your Web page.

6 Click **Open** to add the video to your Web page.

in an *instant*

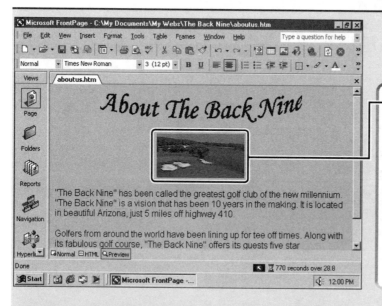

- The video appears on your Web page.

- You can resize a video as you would resize any image on a Web page.

  Note: To test the video, you can use the Preview view.

- When you save the Web page, FrontPage will ask you to save the video as part of your Web site.

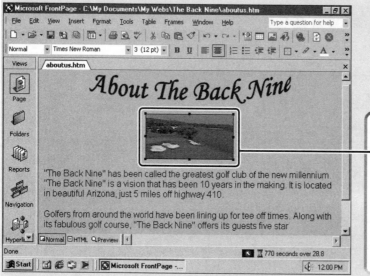

DELETE A VIDEO

1. Click the video you want to delete. Handles (■) appear around the video.

2. Press the Delete key to delete the video.

- The video disappears from your Web page.

CHANGE VIDEO PROPERTIES

You can change the properties of a video displayed on a Web page. For example, you can change the number of times a video will play and when a video will begin to play. You can also provide text that you want to appear on the Web page if a visitor's Web browser cannot play the video.

CHANGE VIDEO PROPERTIES

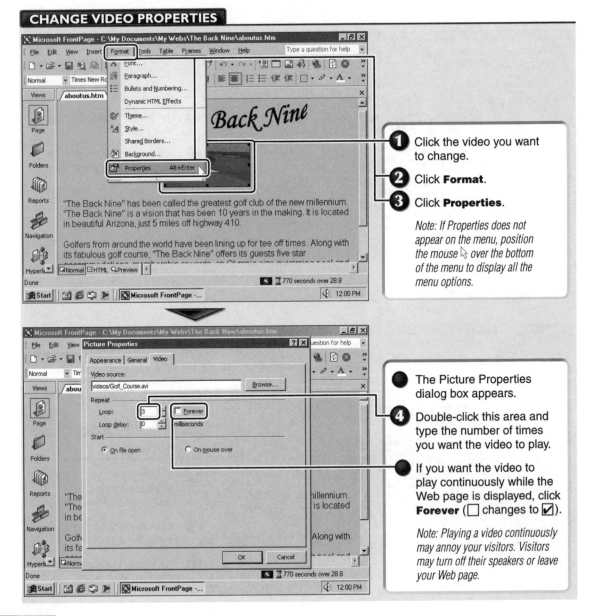

1 Click the video you want to change.

2 Click **Format**.

3 Click **Properties**.

Note: If Properties does not appear on the menu, position the mouse ⟍ over the bottom of the menu to display all the menu options.

■ The Picture Properties dialog box appears.

4 Double-click this area and type the number of times you want the video to play.

■ If you want the video to play continuously while the Web page is displayed, click **Forever** (☐ changes to ☑).

Note: Playing a video continuously may annoy your visitors. Visitors may turn off their speakers or leave your Web page.

in an instant

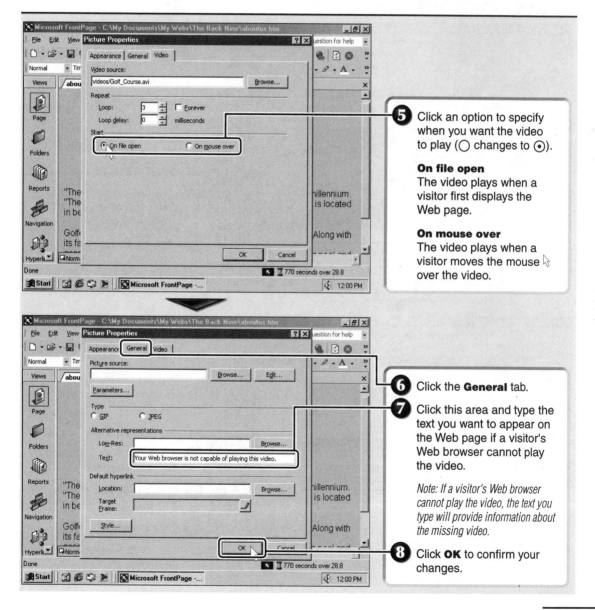

5 Click an option to specify when you want the video to play (○ changes to ⊙).

On file open
The video plays when a visitor first displays the Web page.

On mouse over
The video plays when a visitor moves the mouse over the video.

6 Click the **General** tab.

7 Click this area and type the text you want to appear on the Web page if a visitor's Web browser cannot play the video.

Note: If a visitor's Web browser cannot play the video, the text you type will provide information about the missing video.

8 Click **OK** to confirm your changes.

ADD A HIT COUNTER

You can add a hit counter to a Web page to keep track of the number of people who visit the page. A hit counter displays the number of times a Web page has been visited. For example, a hit counter will display "50" if one person visits the Web page 50 times or if 50 people visit the Web page once.

ADD A HIT COUNTER

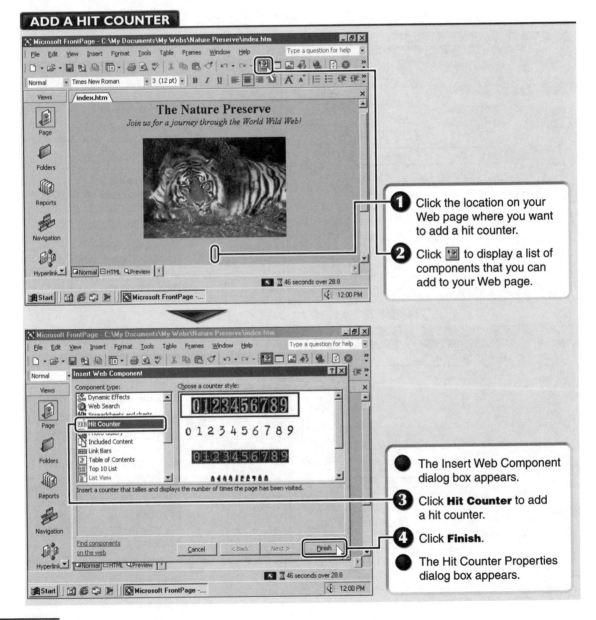

1 Click the location on your Web page where you want to add a hit counter.

2 Click 🔳 to display a list of components that you can add to your Web page.

■ The Insert Web Component dialog box appears.

3 Click **Hit Counter** to add a hit counter.

4 Click **Finish**.

■ The Hit Counter Properties dialog box appears.

in an instant

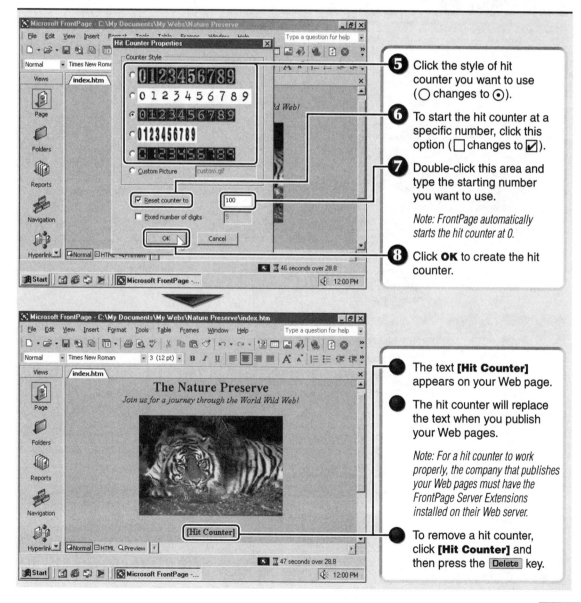

5 Click the style of hit counter you want to use (○ changes to ⊙).

6 To start the hit counter at a specific number, click this option (☐ changes to ☑).

7 Double-click this area and type the starting number you want to use.

Note: FrontPage automatically starts the hit counter at 0.

8 Click **OK** to create the hit counter.

● The text **[Hit Counter]** appears on your Web page.

● The hit counter will replace the text when you publish your Web pages.

Note: For a hit counter to work properly, the company that publishes your Web pages must have the FrontPage Server Extensions installed on their Web server.

● To remove a hit counter, click **[Hit Counter]** and then press the Delete key.

ADD A MARQUEE

You can add a marquee that displays text that moves across a Web page. The Netscape Navigator Web browser will not display a marquee properly. Netscape Navigator will display the marquee text, but the text will not move across the Web page.

ADD A MARQUEE

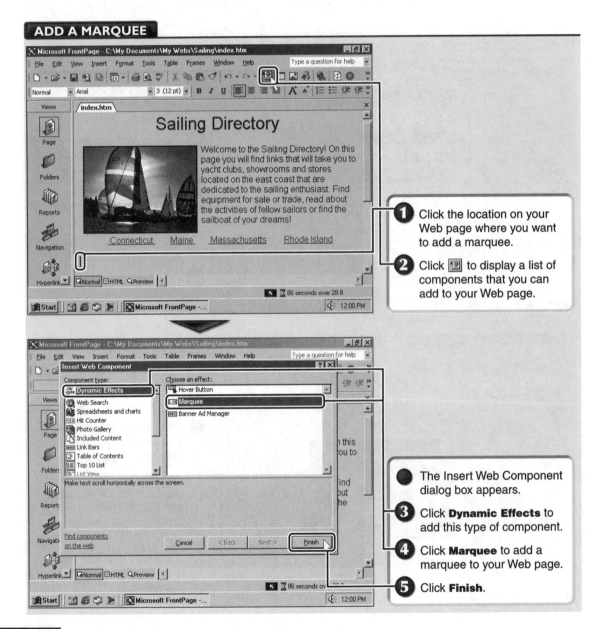

1 Click the location on your Web page where you want to add a marquee.

2 Click 🖼 to display a list of components that you can add to your Web page.

■ The Insert Web Component dialog box appears.

3 Click **Dynamic Effects** to add this type of component.

4 Click **Marquee** to add a marquee to your Web page.

5 Click **Finish**.

in an *instant*

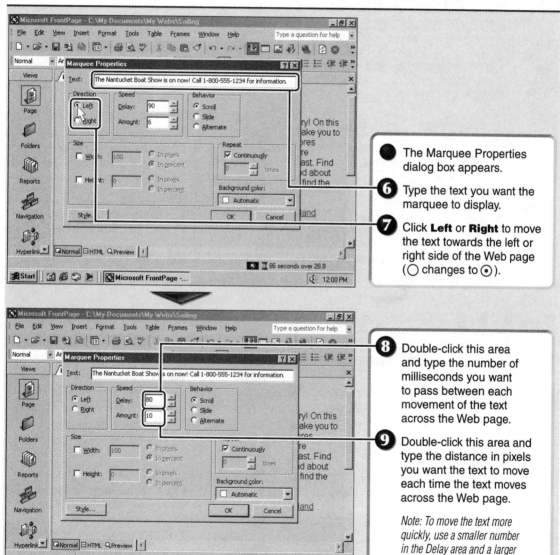

● The Marquee Properties dialog box appears.

6 Type the text you want the marquee to display.

7 Click **Left** or **Right** to move the text towards the left or right side of the Web page (○ changes to ⊙).

8 Double-click this area and type the number of milliseconds you want to pass between each movement of the text across the Web page.

9 Double-click this area and type the distance in pixels you want the text to move each time the text moves across the Web page.

Note: To move the text more quickly, use a smaller number in the Delay area and a larger number in the Amount area.

CONTINUED▶

FrontPage allows you to specify the way you want the text for a marquee to move across a Web page. You can have the text scroll across the screen and then disappear or slide across the screen and then stop at the other side of the Web page. You can also have the text alternate back and forth between the sides of the Web page.

ADD A MARQUEE (CONTINUED)

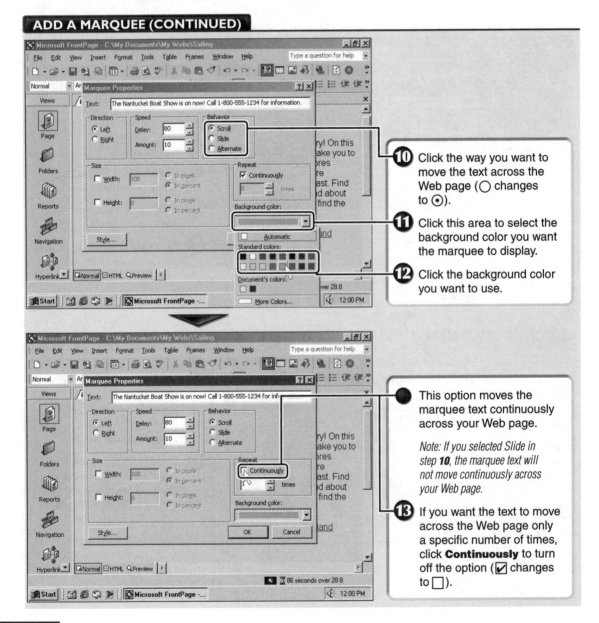

10 Click the way you want to move the text across the Web page (○ changes to ⊙).

11 Click this area to select the background color you want the marquee to display.

12 Click the background color you want to use.

This option moves the marquee text continuously across your Web page.

Note: If you selected Slide in step 10, the marquee text will not move continuously across your Web page.

13 If you want the text to move across the Web page only a specific number of times, click **Continuously** to turn off the option (☑ changes to ☐).

in an *Instant*

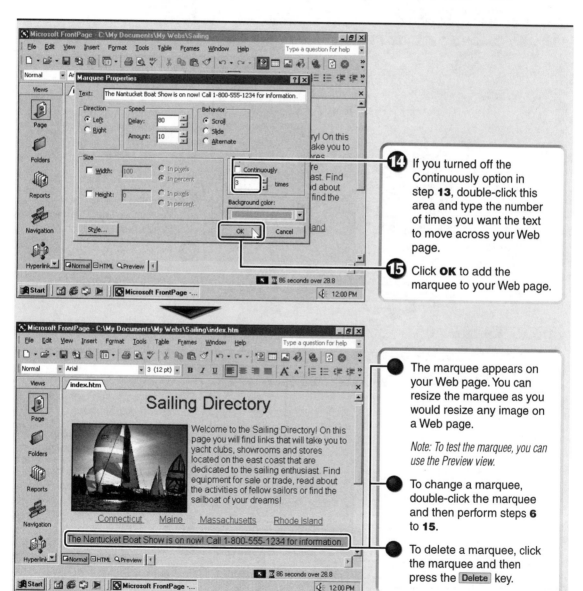

14 If you turned off the Continuously option in step **13**, double-click this area and type the number of times you want the text to move across your Web page.

15 Click **OK** to add the marquee to your Web page.

The marquee appears on your Web page. You can resize the marquee as you would resize any image on a Web page.

Note: To test the marquee, you can use the Preview view.

To change a marquee, double-click the marquee and then perform steps **6** to **15**.

To delete a marquee, click the marquee and then press the Delete key.

ADD A HOVER BUTTON

You can create a button that will change in appearance when a visitor moves the mouse over the button. This type of button is called a hover button. When creating a hover button, you can make the button a link that visitors can select to display another Web page.

ADD A HOVER BUTTON

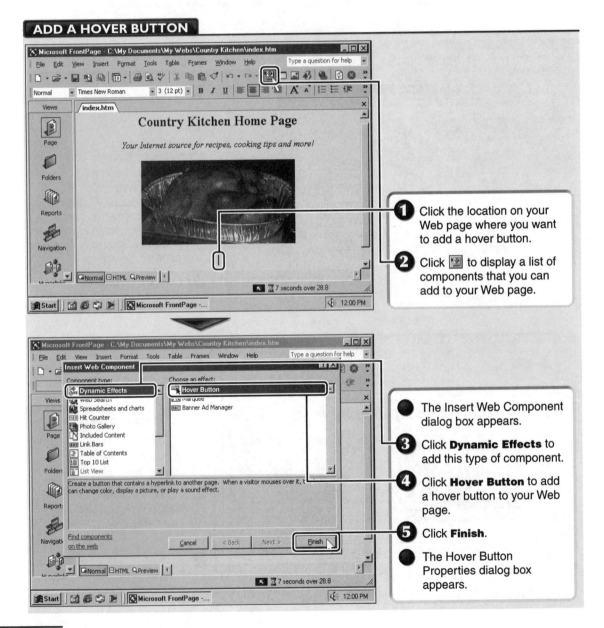

1 Click the location on your Web page where you want to add a hover button.

2 Click 🔳 to display a list of components that you can add to your Web page.

■ The Insert Web Component dialog box appears.

3 Click **Dynamic Effects** to add this type of component.

4 Click **Hover Button** to add a hover button to your Web page.

5 Click **Finish**.

■ The Hover Button Properties dialog box appears.

in an *instant*

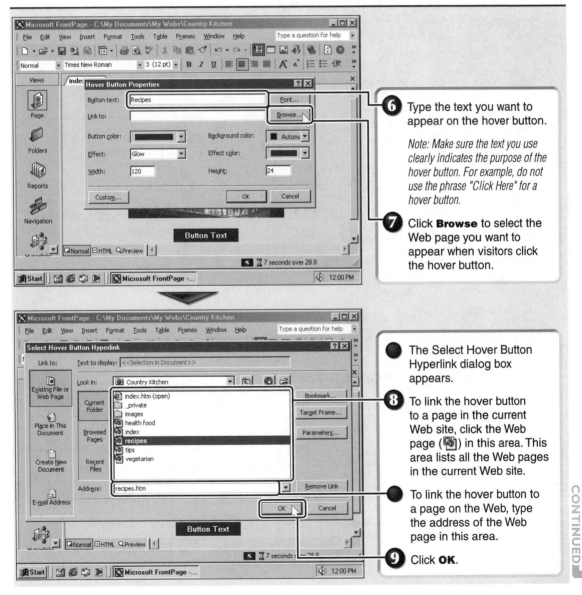

6 Type the text you want to
appear on the hover button.

*Note: Make sure the text you use
clearly indicates the purpose of the
hover button. For example, do not
use the phrase "Click Here" for a
hover button.*

7 Click **Browse** to select the
Web page you want to
appear when visitors click
the hover button.

■ The Select Hover Button
Hyperlink dialog box
appears.

8 To link the hover button
to a page in the current
Web site, click the Web
page (⬚) in this area. This
area lists all the Web pages
in the current Web site.

■ To link the hover button to
a page on the Web, type
the address of the Web
page in this area.

9 Click **OK**.

CONTINUED

ADD A HOVER BUTTON

When adding a hover button, you can select the color you want the button to initially display on a Web page. You can also choose from several effects that can occur when a visitor moves the mouse over the hover button, such as a glow or beveled edge.

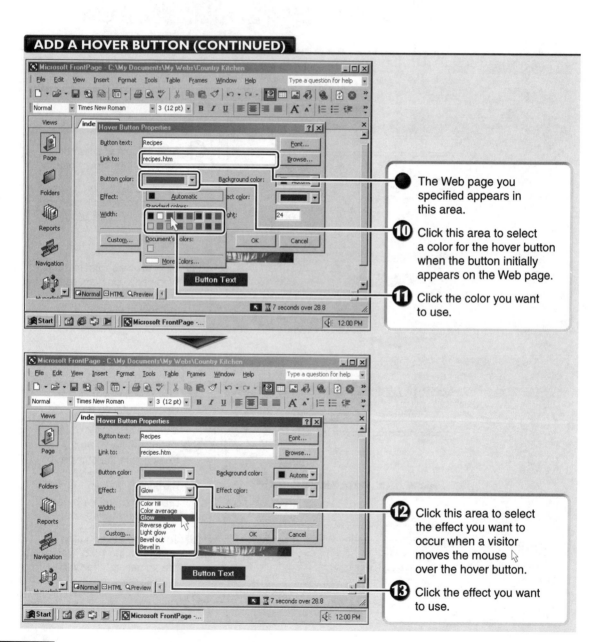

● The Web page you specified appears in this area.

⑩ Click this area to select a color for the hover button when the button initially appears on the Web page.

⑪ Click the color you want to use.

⑫ Click this area to select the effect you want to occur when a visitor moves the mouse over the hover button.

⑬ Click the effect you want to use.

in an *instant*

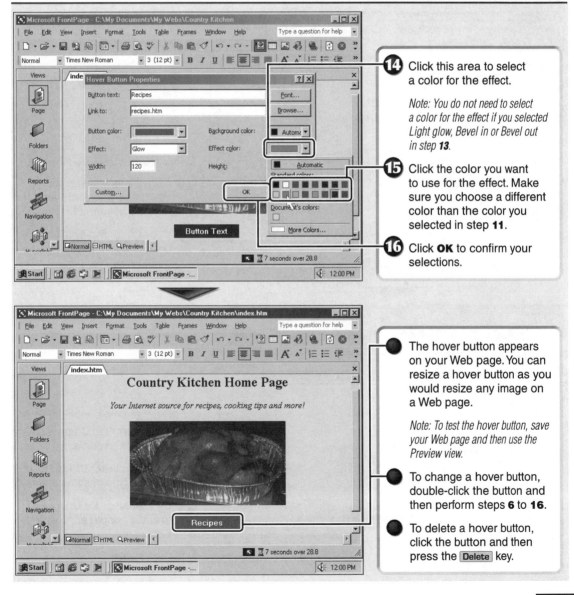

⑭ Click this area to select a color for the effect.

Note: You do not need to select a color for the effect if you selected Light glow, Bevel in or Bevel out in step 13.

⑮ Click the color you want to use for the effect. Make sure you choose a different color than the color you selected in step **11**.

⑯ Click **OK** to confirm your selections.

● The hover button appears on your Web page. You can resize a hover button as you would resize any image on a Web page.

Note: To test the hover button, save your Web page and then use the Preview view.

● To change a hover button, double-click the button and then perform steps **6** to **16**.

● To delete a hover button, click the button and then press the Delete key.

ADD A BANNER AD

You can add a banner ad that continuously rotates a series of images on a Web page. Banner ads are often used to display advertisements on Web pages. When adding a banner ad, you should use images that are approximately the same size.

ADD A BANNER AD

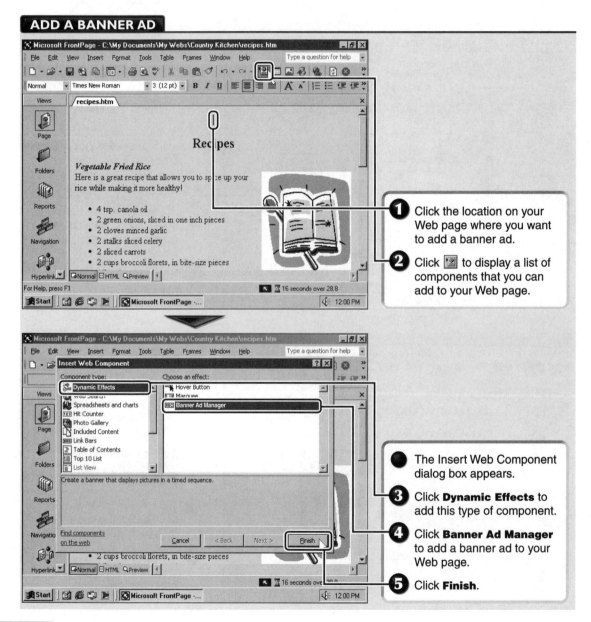

1 Click the location on your Web page where you want to add a banner ad.

2 Click 🖳 to display a list of components that you can add to your Web page.

■ The Insert Web Component dialog box appears.

3 Click **Dynamic Effects** to add this type of component.

4 Click **Banner Ad Manager** to add a banner ad to your Web page.

5 Click **Finish**.

in an *instant*

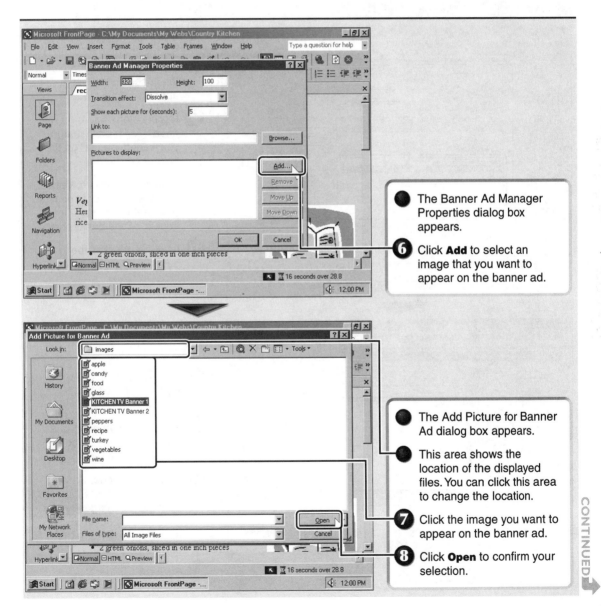

The Banner Ad Manager
Properties dialog box
appears.

6 Click **Add** to select an
image that you want to
appear on the banner ad.

The Add Picture for Banner
Ad dialog box appears.

This area shows the
location of the displayed
files. You can click this area
to change the location.

7 Click the image you want to
appear on the banner ad.

8 Click **Open** to confirm your
selection.

CONTINUED

You can link a banner ad to a Web page. When visitors click the banner ad, the Web page you specify will appear. All the images displayed on a banner ad will link to the same Web page. You cannot link each image on a banner ad to a different Web page.

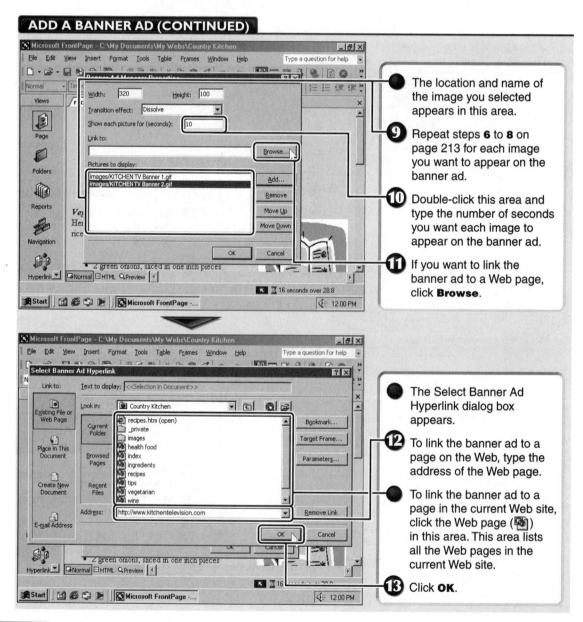

The location and name of the image you selected appears in this area.

9 Repeat steps **6** to **8** on page 213 for each image you want to appear on the banner ad.

10 Double-click this area and type the number of seconds you want each image to appear on the banner ad.

11 If you want to link the banner ad to a Web page, click **Browse**.

The Select Banner Ad Hyperlink dialog box appears.

12 To link the banner ad to a page on the Web, type the address of the Web page.

To link the banner ad to a page in the current Web site, click the Web page (🖳) in this area. This area lists all the Web pages in the current Web site.

13 Click **OK**.

in an *instant*

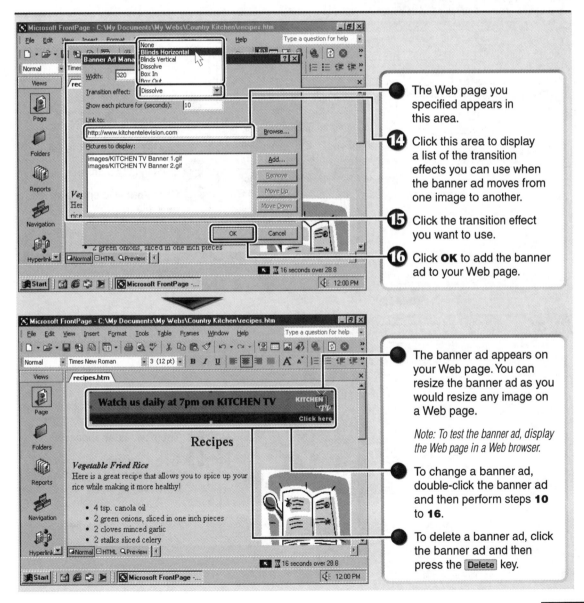

The Web page you specified appears in this area.

14 Click this area to display a list of the transition effects you can use when the banner ad moves from one image to another.

15 Click the transition effect you want to use.

16 Click **OK** to add the banner ad to your Web page.

The banner ad appears on your Web page. You can resize the banner ad as you would resize any image on a Web page.

Note: To test the banner ad, display the Web page in a Web browser.

To change a banner ad, double-click the banner ad and then perform steps **10** to **16**.

To delete a banner ad, click the banner ad and then press the Delete key.

CREATE A NEW FOLDER

You can create a new folder to help you organize the files in your Web site. For example, you can create a folder named multimedia to store sounds and videos. FrontPage automatically adds the _private folder to your Web site to store files you do not want visitors to access and the images folder to store images.

CREATE A NEW FOLDER

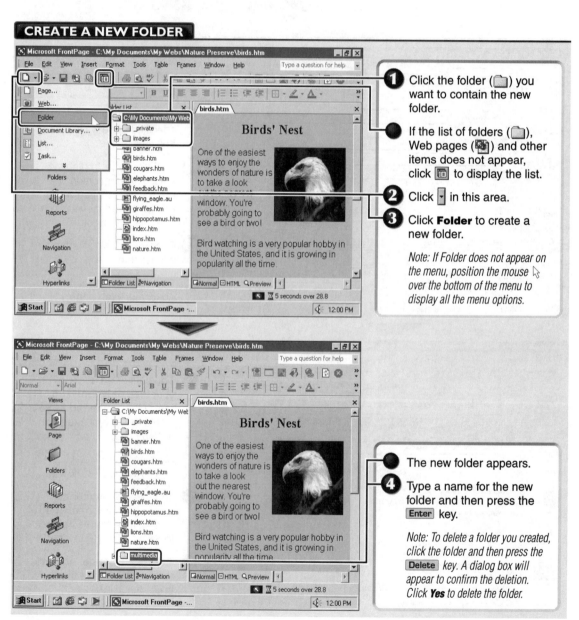

1. Click the folder (📁) you want to contain the new folder.

● If the list of folders (📁), Web pages (📄) and other items does not appear, click 🔲 to display the list.

2. Click ⏷ in this area.

3. Click **Folder** to create a new folder.

Note: If Folder does not appear on the menu, position the mouse ⬚ over the bottom of the menu to display all the menu options.

● The new folder appears.

4. Type a name for the new folder and then press the Enter key.

Note: To delete a folder you created, click the folder and then press the Delete key. A dialog box will appear to confirm the deletion. Click Yes to delete the folder.

You can move a file to a folder in your Web site. Moving files allows you to place related files in the same location. When you move a file to a folder, FrontPage will automatically update all links to the file.

MOVE A FILE TO A FOLDER

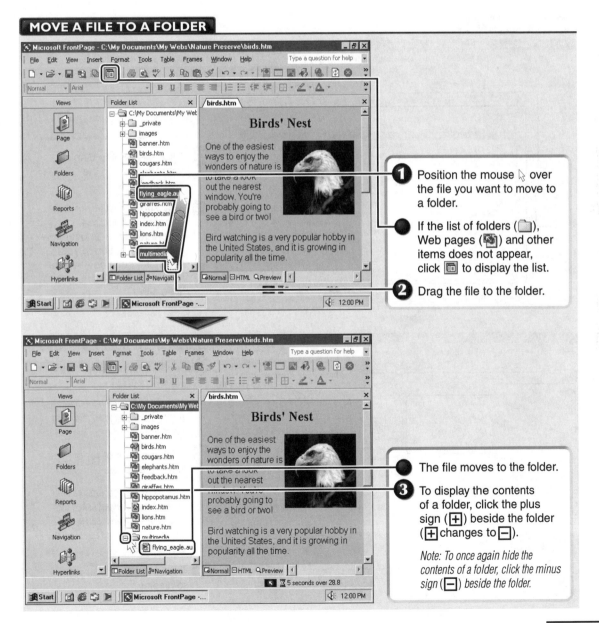

1 Position the mouse ⌖ over the file you want to move to a folder.

● If the list of folders (📁), Web pages (📄) and other items does not appear, click 📑 to display the list.

2 Drag the file to the folder.

● The file moves to the folder.

3 To display the contents of a folder, click the plus sign (➕) beside the folder (➕ changes to ➖).

Note: To once again hide the contents of a folder, click the minus sign (➖) beside the folder.

VIEW REPORTS

You can use the Reports view to display various reports that analyze and summarize information about your Web site. For example, you can display the All Files report to review information about each file in your Web site or the Unlinked Files report to list files you cannot access from your home page.

VIEW REPORTS

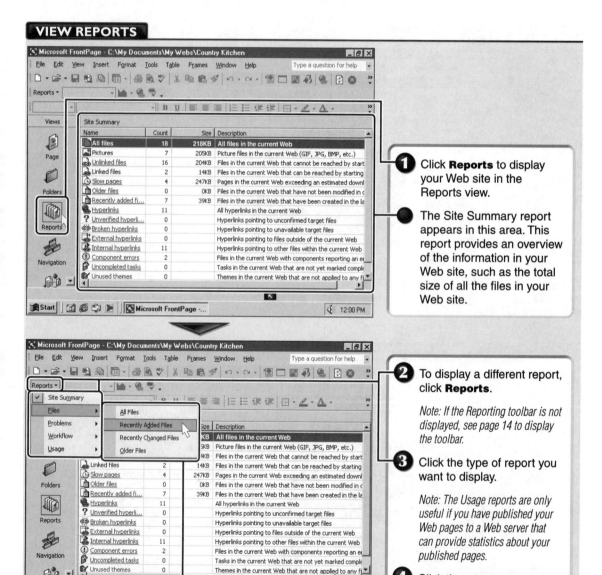

1 Click **Reports** to display your Web site in the Reports view.

● The Site Summary report appears in this area. This report provides an overview of the information in your Web site, such as the total size of all the files in your Web site.

2 To display a different report, click **Reports**.

Note: If the Reporting toolbar is not displayed, see page 14 to display the toolbar.

3 Click the type of report you want to display.

Note: The Usage reports are only useful if you have published your Web pages to a Web server that can provide statistics about your published pages.

4 Click the report you want to display.

in an *Instant*

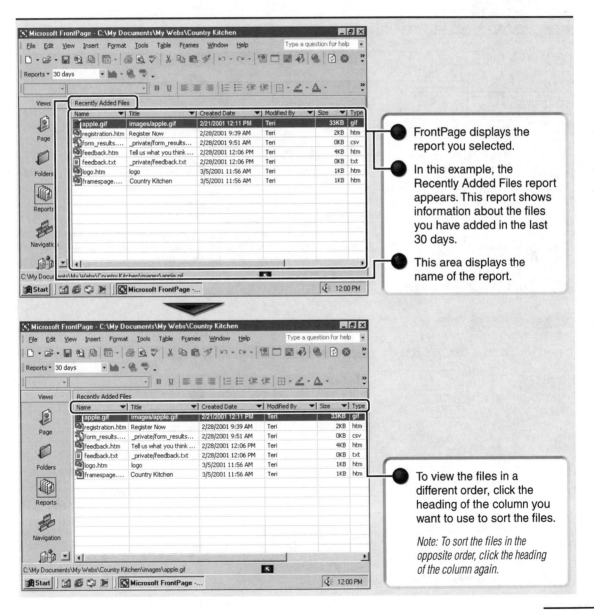

FrontPage displays the report you selected.

In this example, the Recently Added Files report appears. This report shows information about the files you have added in the last 30 days.

This area displays the name of the report.

To view the files in a different order, click the heading of the column you want to use to sort the files.

Note: To sort the files in the opposite order, click the heading of the column again.

ADD A TASK

You can add tasks to create a to-do list to keep track of Web pages you need to complete. Tasks can help remind you to add, update, review or confirm information on a Web page at a later time. You can associate each task you add with a specific Web page in your Web site.

ADD A TASK

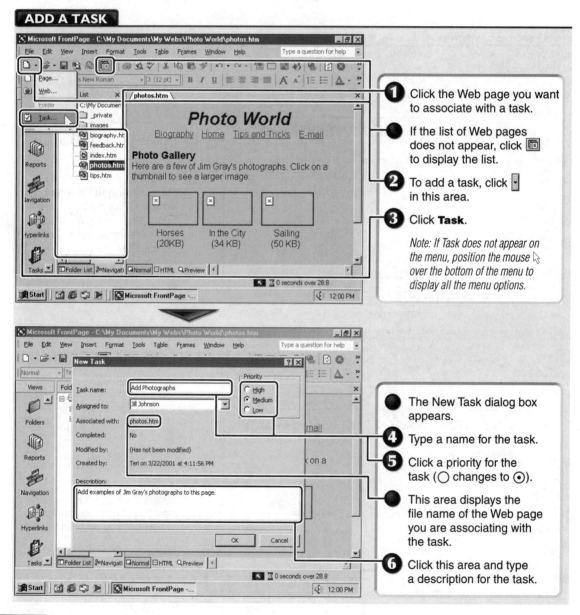

1. Click the Web page you want to associate with a task.

   If the list of Web pages does not appear, click 🔲 to display the list.

2. To add a task, click ▪ in this area.

3. Click **Task**.

   Note: If Task does not appear on the menu, position the mouse ⌖ over the bottom of the menu to display all the menu options.

■ The New Task dialog box appears.

4. Type a name for the task.

5. Click a priority for the task (○ changes to ⊙).

■ This area displays the file name of the Web page you are associating with the task.

6. Click this area and type a description for the task.

in an *instant*

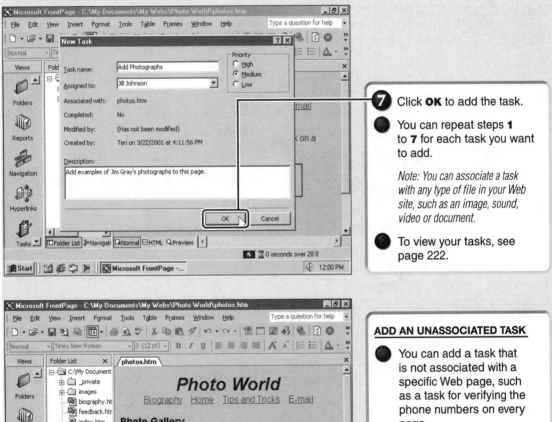

7 Click **OK** to add the task.

You can repeat steps **1** to **7** for each task you want to add.

Note: You can associate a task with any type of file in your Web site, such as an image, sound, video or document.

To view your tasks, see page 222.

ADD AN UNASSOCIATED TASK

You can add a task that is not associated with a specific Web page, such as a task for verifying the phone numbers on every page.

1 Click **Tasks**.

If the Tasks icon is not displayed, click ▼ to display the icon.

2 To add a task, perform steps **2** to **7** starting on page 220.

You can view a list of all the tasks you have added to your Web site. Tasks help you keep track of the Web pages you need to complete. When you view your list of tasks, FrontPage displays information about each task, such as the status and the priority of the tasks.

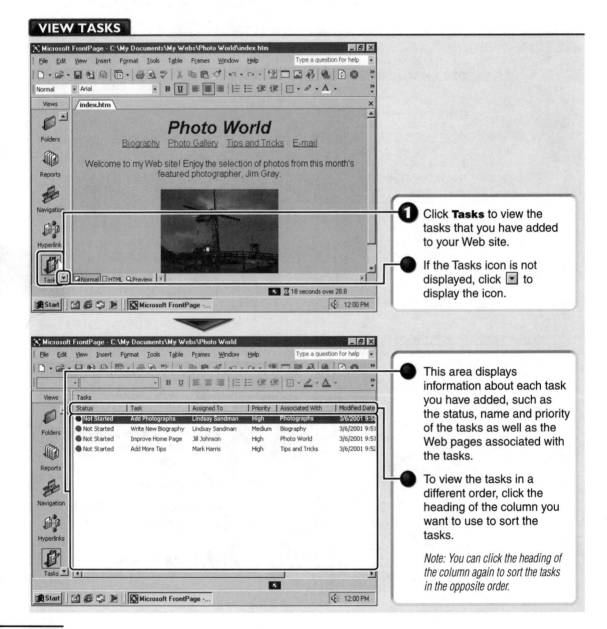

1 Click **Tasks** to view the tasks that you have added to your Web site.

If the Tasks icon is not displayed, click ▼ to display the icon.

This area displays information about each task you have added, such as the status, name and priority of the tasks as well as the Web pages associated with the tasks.

To view the tasks in a different order, click the heading of the column you want to use to sort the tasks.

Note: You can click the heading of the column again to sort the tasks in the opposite order.

FrontPage allows you to change the information you specified for a task. You can provide a more accurate name or a more detailed description for a task. You can also change the priority of a task to low, medium or high.

EDIT A TASK

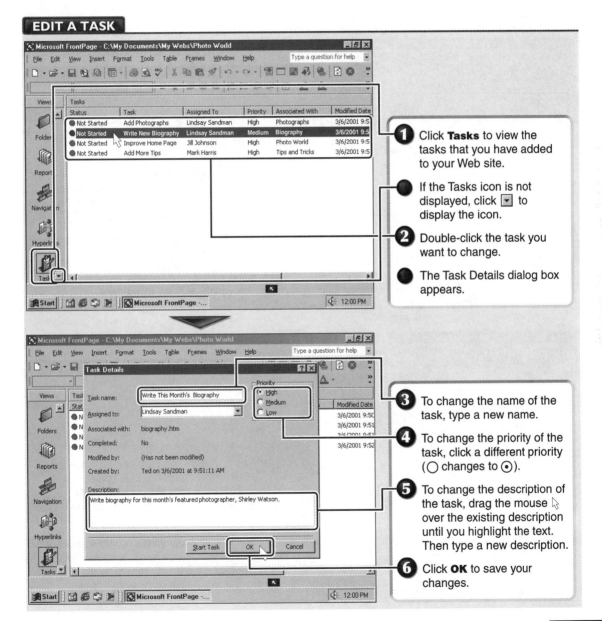

1. Click **Tasks** to view the tasks that you have added to your Web site.

● If the Tasks icon is not displayed, click ▾ to display the icon.

2. Double-click the task you want to change.

● The Task Details dialog box appears.

3. To change the name of the task, type a new name.

4. To change the priority of the task, click a different priority (○ changes to ⊙).

5. To change the description of the task, drag the mouse over the existing description until you highlight the text. Then type a new description.

6. Click **OK** to save your changes.

You can start a task that you associated with a specific Web page. When you start a task, FrontPage will open the associated Web page so you can finish reviewing, editing or formatting the Web page.

START A TASK

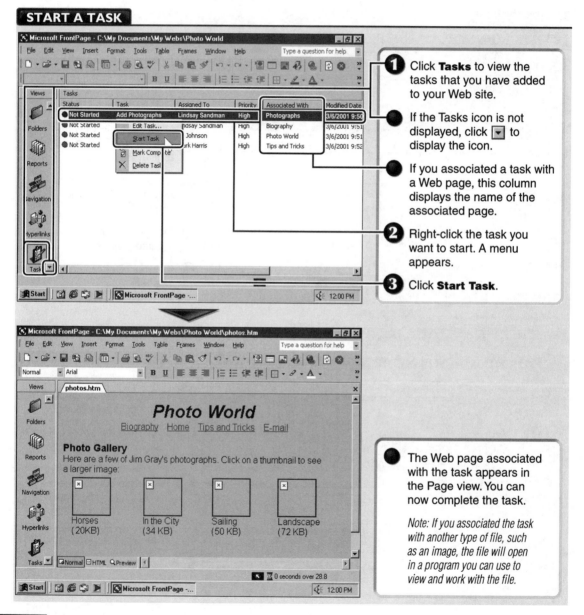

1 Click **Tasks** to view the tasks that you have added to your Web site.

● If the Tasks icon is not displayed, click ▼ to display the icon.

● If you associated a task with a Web page, this column displays the name of the associated page.

2 Right-click the task you want to start. A menu appears.

3 Click **Start Task**.

● The Web page associated with the task appears in the Page view. You can now complete the task.

Note: If you associated the task with another type of file, such as an image, the file will open in a program you can use to view and work with the file.

You can delete a task you have completed to keep your
list of tasks up to date and to reduce the clutter in your
task list. When you delete a task, a confirmation message
will appear to make sure that you want to delete the task.

DELETE A TASK

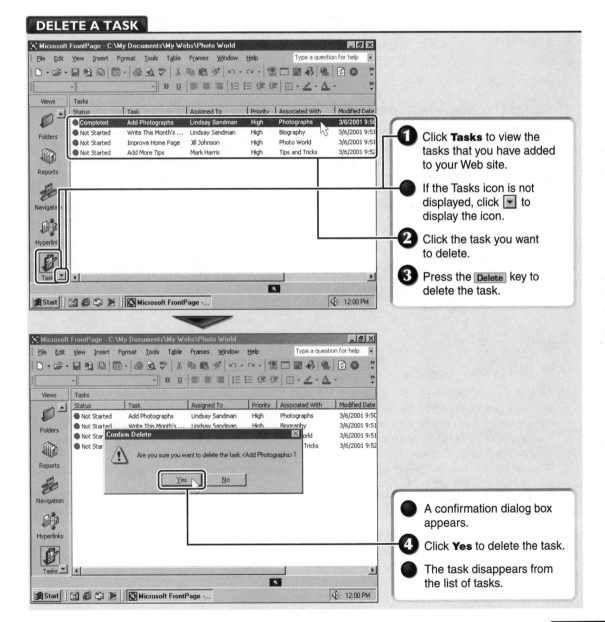

1 Click **Tasks** to view the
tasks that you have added
to your Web site.

■ If the Tasks icon is not
displayed, click ▼ to
display the icon.

2 Click the task you want
to delete.

3 Press the Delete key to
delete the task.

■ A confirmation dialog box
appears.

4 Click **Yes** to delete the task.

■ The task disappears from
the list of tasks.

CHOOSE A WEB HOSTING SERVICE

Web hosting services are companies that store Web pages and make them available on the Web for people to view. Web hosting services store Web pages on computers called Web servers. Web servers monitor and control access to Web pages.

TYPES OF WEB HOSTING SERVICES

DEDICATED WEB HOSTING SERVICES

Dedicated Web hosting services are companies that specialize in publishing Web pages. Dedicated Web hosting services are flexible and offer features that other Web hosting services do not offer. You can find dedicated Web hosting services at the following Web sites.

www.hostess.com

www.pair.com

You can search for a Web hosting service in your area at the www.microsoftwpp.com/wppsearch Web site.

INTERNET SERVICE PROVIDERS

Internet service providers are companies that offer people access to the Internet. Most Internet service providers offer space on their Web servers where customers can publish their Web pages. Although an Internet service provider offers the easiest way to publish Web pages, they may not provide all the features or technical support that you require.

FREE WEB HOSTING SERVICES

Some companies on the Web will publish your Web pages for free. These companies offer a limited amount of storage space and usually place advertisements on your Web pages. They also may not offer all the features you need. You can find companies that will publish your Web pages for free at the following Web sites.

geocities.yahoo.com

www.tripod.lycos.com

YOUR OWN WEB SERVER

Purchasing your own Web server is the most expensive way to publish Web pages and requires a full-time connection to the Internet. Setting up and maintaining your own Web server is difficult but will give you the greatest amount of control over your Web pages.

WEB HOSTING SERVICE CONSIDERATIONS

TRAFFIC LIMIT

When visitors view your Web pages, information transfers from the Web server to their computers. The amount of information that transfers from the Web server depends on the number of people that view your Web pages and the file size of your pages.

Most Web hosting services limit the amount of information that can transfer in one month. If more information transfers, you usually have to pay extra. Make sure you choose a Web hosting service that has a traffic limit that meets the needs of your Web site.

DOMAIN NAME REGISTRATION

A domain name is the address that people type to access your Web pages, such as www.maran.com. If you want your own personalized domain name, most Web hosting services can register a domain name for you. A personalized domain name is easy for people to remember and will not change if you switch to another Web hosting service. For information on registering your own domain name, visit the internic.net Web site.

TECHNICAL SUPPORT

A Web hosting service should have a technical support department to answer your questions. You should be able to contact a Web hosting service by telephone or e-mail and get a response to your questions within a day.

RELIABILITY

Make sure the Web hosting service you choose is reliable. A Web hosting service should be able to tell you how often their Web servers shut down. You may want to ask a Web hosting service for customer references. You should take into consideration that Web hosting services occasionally shut down their Web servers for maintenance and upgrades.

CONTINUED

CHOOSE A WEB HOSTING SERVICE

STORAGE SPACE

Most Web hosting services limit the amount of space you can use to store your Web site. If your Web site is larger than the space provided, you will have to pay extra. Choose a Web hosting service that provides enough space to store all the information for your Web site.

ACCESS LOGS

A good Web hosting service will supply you with statistics about your Web pages, such as which Web pages are the most popular and where your visitors are from. You should also be able to view any error messages visitors may see when viewing your Web pages, such as "Page Not Found." Access logs can help you determine if you need to make changes to your Web pages.

FRONTPAGE SERVER EXTENSIONS

Your Web hosting service must have the FrontPage Server Extensions installed on their Web server for some Web page features to work. For example, your Web server will need the FrontPage Server Extensions installed if you want to use forms and hit counters on your Web pages.

SECURE WEB SERVER

If you require visitors at your Web site to enter confidential information, such as credit card numbers, you should use a Web hosting service with a secure Web server. Secure Web servers encode the information that transfers over the Internet so that only the sending and receiving computers can read the information.

AVAILABLE BANDWIDTH

Bandwidth is the amount of data that can transfer over the Internet in a set amount of time. The speed and number of connections to the Internet determine a Web hosting service's bandwidth. A high bandwidth can decrease the amount of time visitors spend waiting to view your Web pages. Keep in mind that the available bandwidth is more important than the maximum bandwidth. You should ensure that a Web hosting service has enough available bandwidth to suit the needs of your Web site.

PUBLICIZE WEB PAGES

After you publish your Web pages, there are several ways you can let people know about the pages. Publicizing your Web pages is important if you want many people to view your pages. You can publicize your Web pages using traditional methods or by using the Internet.

EXCHANGE LINKS

If another Web site offers information, products or services related to your Web site, you can ask the individual or company to include a link to your Web pages if you will do the same. This allows people reading the other Web pages to easily visit your Web site.

E-MAIL MESSAGES

Most e-mail programs include a feature, called a signature, that allows you to add the same information to the end of every e-mail message you send. You can use a signature to include information about your Web pages in all your e-mail messages.

TRADITIONAL METHODS

You can mail an announcement about your Web pages to family, friends, colleagues and customers. You can also mail information about your Web pages to local newspapers and magazines that may be interested in your Web pages. If you created Web pages for your company, make sure you include your Web page address on business cards, letterhead and any print advertisements you produce.

WEB PAGE ADVERTISEMENTS

Many companies set aside areas on their Web pages where you can advertise your Web site for a fee. You can also use the bCentral Banner Network, which is a service that brings organizations together to exchange Web page advertisements. The bCentral Banner Network is located at the adnetwork.bcentral.com/services/bn Web site.

NEWSGROUPS

You can send an announcement about your Web pages to discussion groups on the Internet called newsgroups. Make sure you choose newsgroups that discuss topics related to your Web pages. You can also announce new or updated Web pages by using the comp.infosystems.www.announce newsgroup.

SEARCH TOOLS

Search tools help people quickly find information on the Web. Adding your Web pages to various search tools can help people easily find your Web pages. Some popular search tools include AltaVista (www.altavista.com) and Yahoo! (www.yahoo.com). The www.submit-it.com Web site allows you to add your Web pages to many search tools at once.

SPECIFY KEYWORDS FOR A WEB PAGE

You can specify keywords to help search tools index your Web pages. Search tools, such as AltaVista (www.altavista.com) and Yahoo! (www.yahoo.com), help people find information on the Web. When visitors enter words in a search tool that match your keywords, your Web page will more likely appear in the search results.

SPECIFY KEYWORDS FOR A WEB PAGE

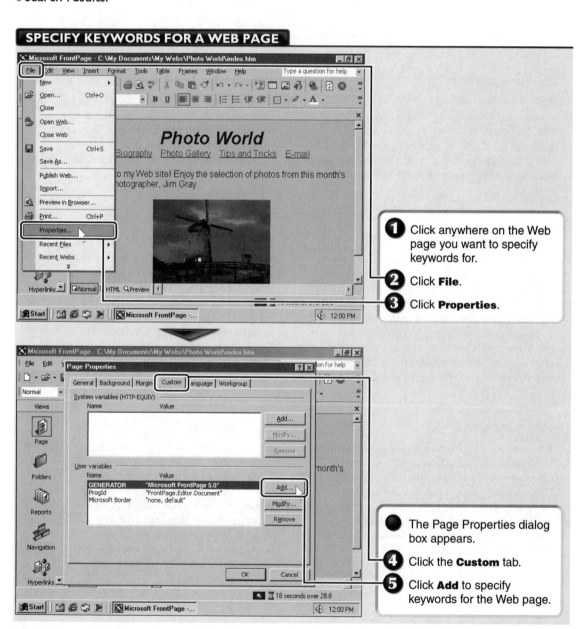

1 Click anywhere on the Web page you want to specify keywords for.

2 Click **File**.

3 Click **Properties**.

● The Page Properties dialog box appears.

4 Click the **Custom** tab.

5 Click **Add** to specify keywords for the Web page.

in an *instant*

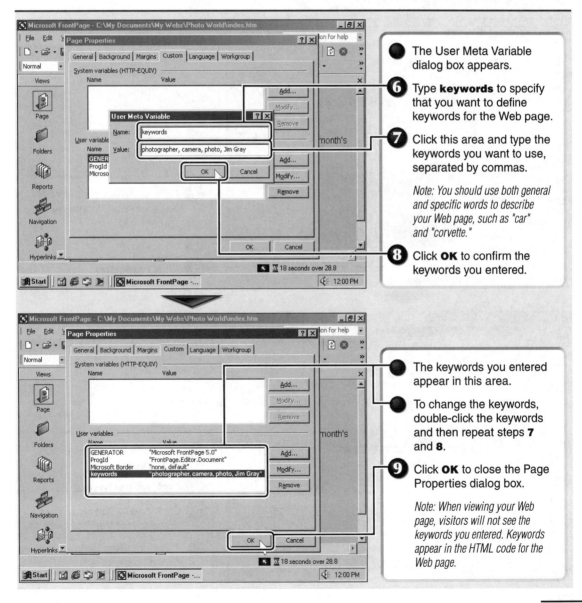

The User Meta Variable dialog box appears.

6 Type **keywords** to specify that you want to define keywords for the Web page.

7 Click this area and type the keywords you want to use, separated by commas.

Note: You should use both general and specific words to describe your Web page, such as "car" and "corvette."

8 Click **OK** to confirm the keywords you entered.

The keywords you entered appear in this area.

To change the keywords, double-click the keywords and then repeat steps **7** and **8**.

9 Click **OK** to close the Page Properties dialog box.

Note: When viewing your Web page, visitors will not see the keywords you entered. Keywords appear in the HTML code for the Web page.

You can specify a summary that search tools, such as AltaVista and Excite, will use to describe a Web page in your Web site. When visitors use a search tool to find information on the Web, the summary will appear if your Web page appears in the search results. If you do not specify a summary, the search results will display text from the top of your Web page for the summary.

SPECIFY A SUMMARY FOR A WEB PAGE

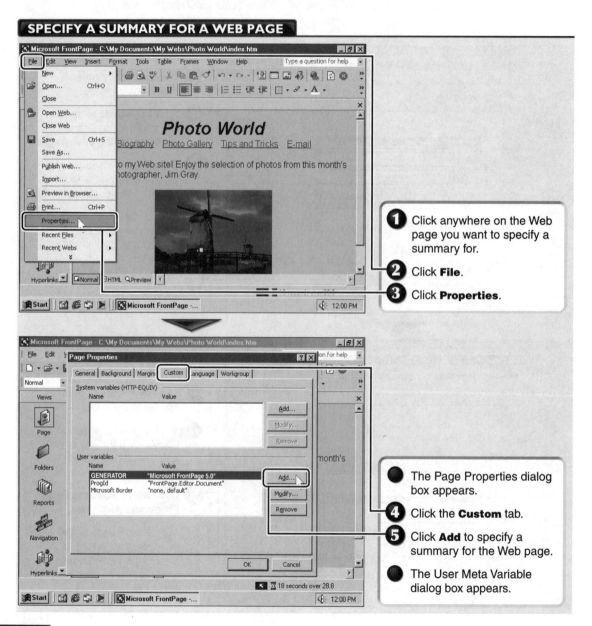

1 Click anywhere on the Web page you want to specify a summary for.

2 Click **File**.

3 Click **Properties**.

■ The Page Properties dialog box appears.

4 Click the **Custom** tab.

5 Click **Add** to specify a summary for the Web page.

■ The User Meta Variable dialog box appears.

in an *Instant*

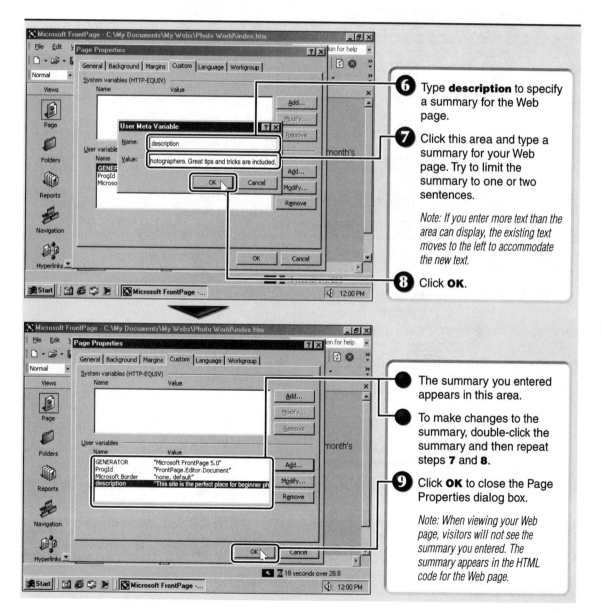

6 Type **description** to specify a summary for the Web page.

7 Click this area and type a summary for your Web page. Try to limit the summary to one or two sentences.

Note: If you enter more text than the area can display, the existing text moves to the left to accommodate the new text.

8 Click **OK**.

● The summary you entered appears in this area.

● To make changes to the summary, double-click the summary and then repeat steps **7** and **8**.

9 Click **OK** to close the Page Properties dialog box.

Note: When viewing your Web page, visitors will not see the summary you entered. The summary appears in the HTML code for the Web page.

You can specify the name of the author of your Web page. When specifying the name of the author, you may also want to include the names of any people who helped create the Web page. Only visitors who view the HTML code for your Web page will see the author information you specify.

SPECIFY AUTHOR INFORMATION

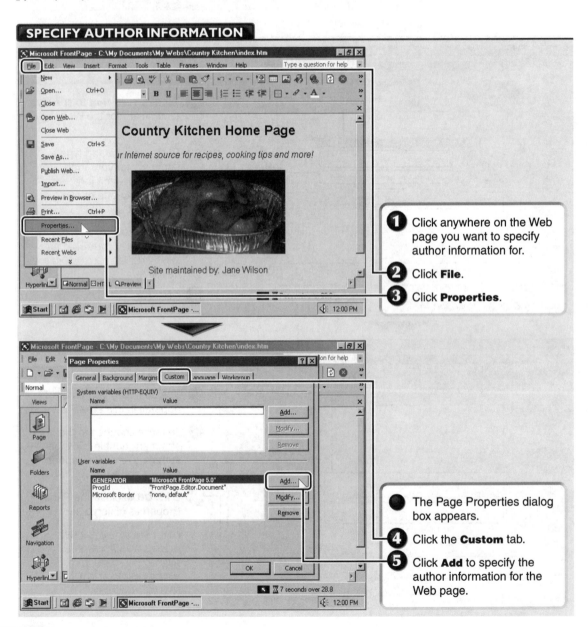

1 Click anywhere on the Web page you want to specify author information for.

2 Click **File**.

3 Click **Properties**.

■ The Page Properties dialog box appears.

4 Click the **Custom** tab.

5 Click **Add** to specify the author information for the Web page.

in an *instant*

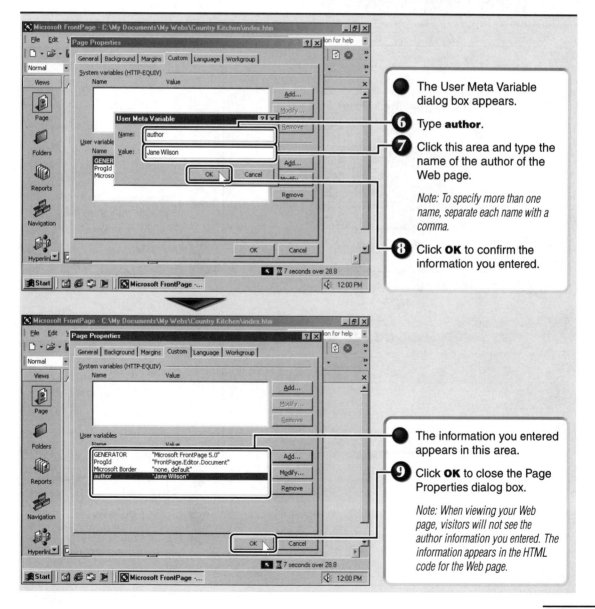

The User Meta Variable dialog box appears.

6 Type **author**.

7 Click this area and type the name of the author of the Web page.

Note: To specify more than one name, separate each name with a comma.

8 Click **OK** to confirm the information you entered.

The information you entered appears in this area.

9 Click **OK** to close the Page Properties dialog box.

Note: When viewing your Web page, visitors will not see the author information you entered. The information appears in the HTML code for the Web page.

SPECIFY COPYRIGHT INFORMATION

You can include a copyright statement for your Web page. Specifying copyright information lets you indicate that you do not want the information on your Web page copied without your permission. Only visitors who view the HTML code for your Web page will see the copyright information you specify.

SPECIFY COPYRIGHT INFORMATION

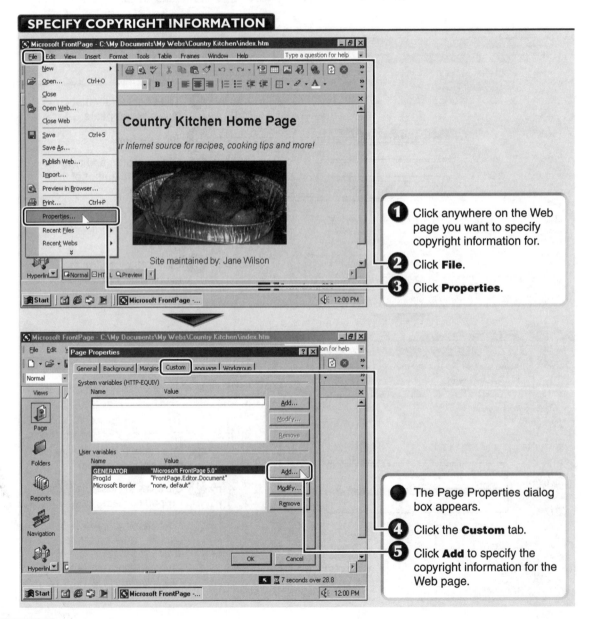

1 Click anywhere on the Web page you want to specify copyright information for.

2 Click **File**.

3 Click **Properties**.

■ The Page Properties dialog box appears.

4 Click the **Custom** tab.

5 Click **Add** to specify the copyright information for the Web page.

in an instant

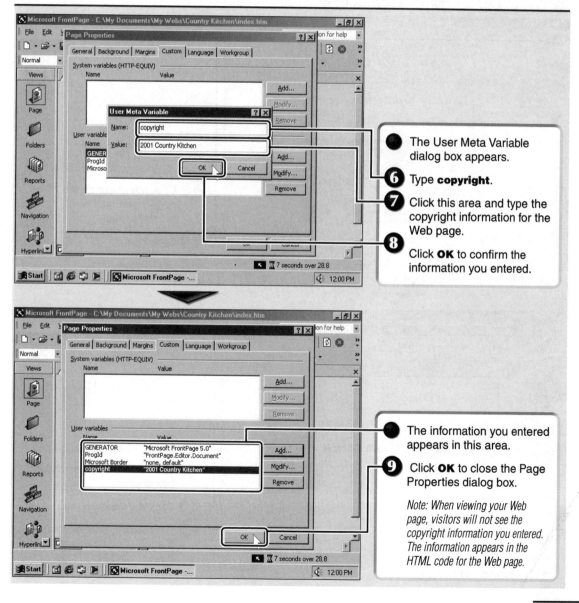

The User Meta Variable dialog box appears.

6 Type **copyright**.

7 Click this area and type the copyright information for the Web page.

8 Click **OK** to confirm the information you entered.

The information you entered appears in this area.

9 Click **OK** to close the Page Properties dialog box.

Note: When viewing your Web page, visitors will not see the copyright information you entered. The information appears in the HTML code for the Web page.

PREVENT ROBOTS FROM INDEXING

Many search tools use programs called robots to find new and updated pages on the Web. You can prevent most robots from indexing your Web page. This is useful when you have created a Web page for a specific audience, such as your family or company, and do not want other people to access the Web page.

PREVENT ROBOTS FROM INDEXING

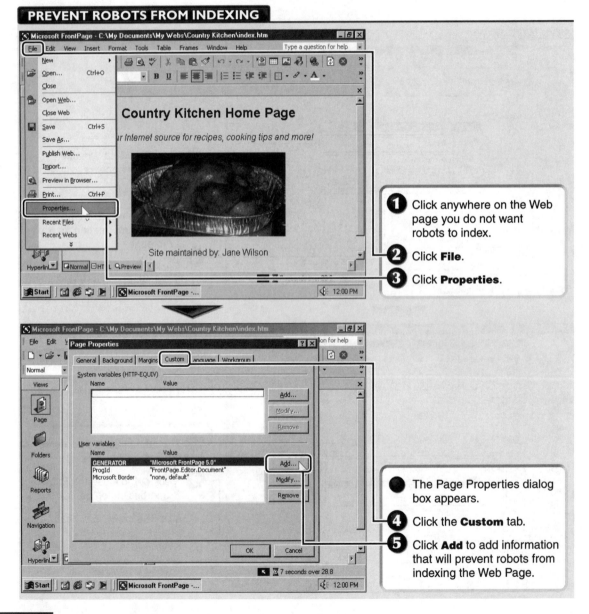

1 Click anywhere on the Web page you do not want robots to index.

2 Click **File**.

3 Click **Properties**.

The Page Properties dialog box appears.

4 Click the **Custom** tab.

5 Click **Add** to add information that will prevent robots from indexing the Web Page.

in an *Instant*

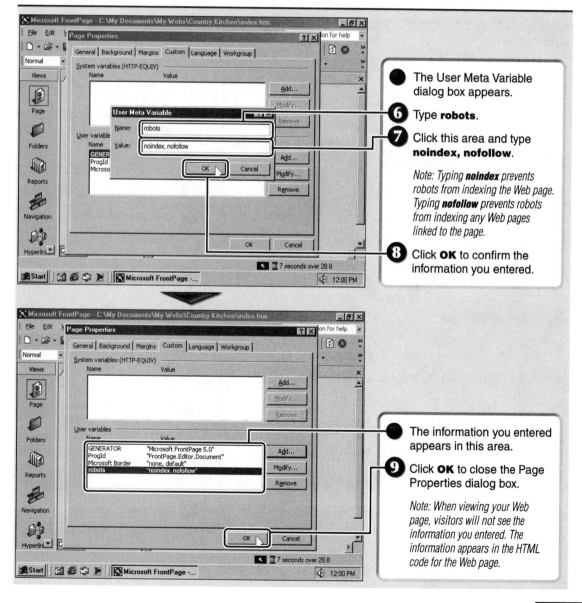

The User Meta Variable dialog box appears.

6 Type **robots**.

7 Click this area and type **noindex, nofollow**.

*Note: Typing **noindex** prevents robots from indexing the Web page. Typing **nofollow** prevents robots from indexing any Web pages linked to the page.*

8 Click **OK** to confirm the information you entered.

The information you entered appears in this area.

9 Click **OK** to close the Page Properties dialog box.

Note: When viewing your Web page, visitors will not see the information you entered. The information appears in the HTML code for the Web page.

TRANSFER WEB PAGES TO A WEB SERVER

When you finish creating your Web pages, you can transfer the pages to a Web server to make the pages available on the Web. Before transferring your Web pages, you must choose a Web hosting service to publish your pages. For information on Web hosting services, see pages 226 to 228.

TRANSFER WEB PAGES TO A WEB SERVER

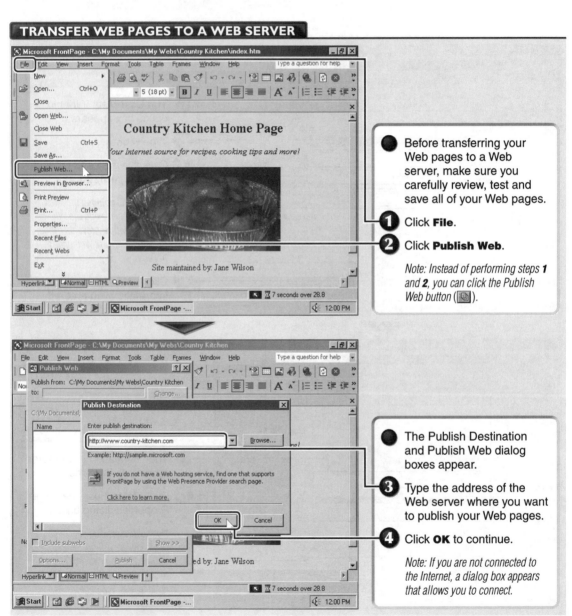

Before transferring your Web pages to a Web server, make sure you carefully review, test and save all of your Web pages.

1 Click **File**.

2 Click **Publish Web**.

Note: Instead of performing steps 1 and 2, you can click the Publish Web button (■).

The Publish Destination and Publish Web dialog boxes appear.

3 Type the address of the Web server where you want to publish your Web pages.

4 Click **OK** to continue.

Note: If you are not connected to the Internet, a dialog box appears that allows you to connect.

in an Instant

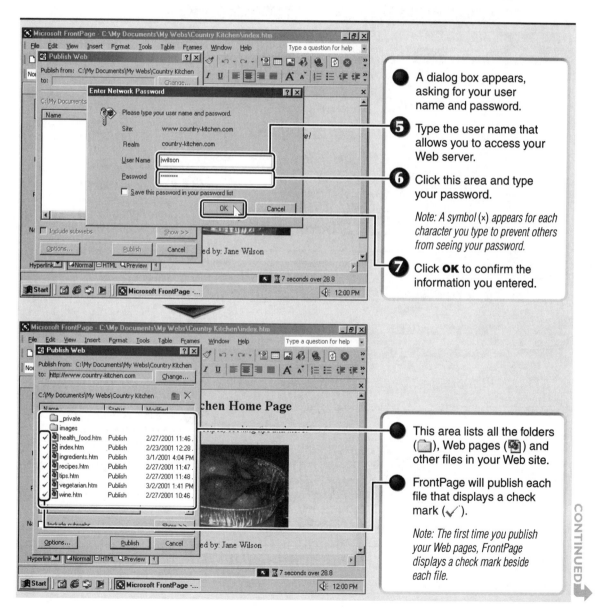

A dialog box appears, asking for your user name and password.

5 Type the user name that allows you to access your Web server.

6 Click this area and type your password.

Note: A symbol (×) appears for each character you type to prevent others from seeing your password.

7 Click **OK** to confirm the information you entered.

This area lists all the folders (📁), Web pages (📄) and other files in your Web site.

FrontPage will publish each file that displays a check mark (✓).

Note: The first time you publish your Web pages, FrontPage displays a check mark beside each file.

CONTINUED

You can choose not to publish a specific Web page in your Web site. This is useful if you have not yet completed a Web page, but you want to publish the rest of your pages.

TRANSFER WEB PAGES TO A WEB SERVER (CONTINUED)

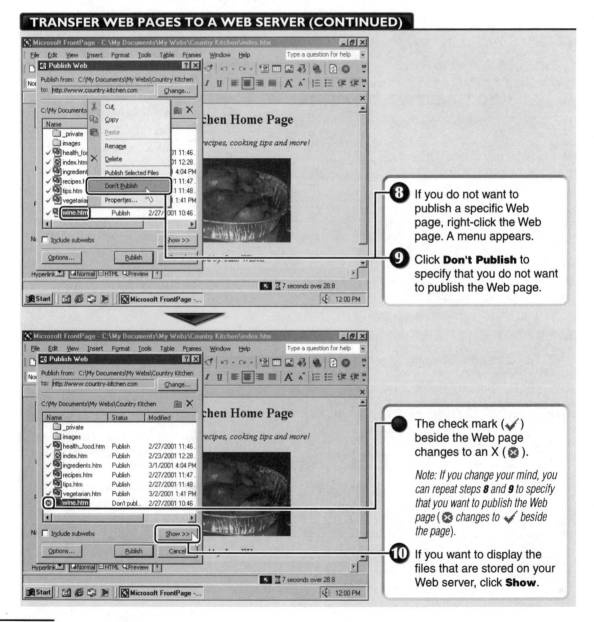

8 If you do not want to publish a specific Web page, right-click the Web page. A menu appears.

9 Click **Don't Publish** to specify that you do not want to publish the Web page.

The check mark (✔) beside the Web page changes to an X (✖).

Note: If you change your mind, you can repeat steps 8 and 9 to specify that you want to publish the Web page (✖ changes to ✔ beside the page).

10 If you want to display the files that are stored on your Web server, click **Show**.

in an instant

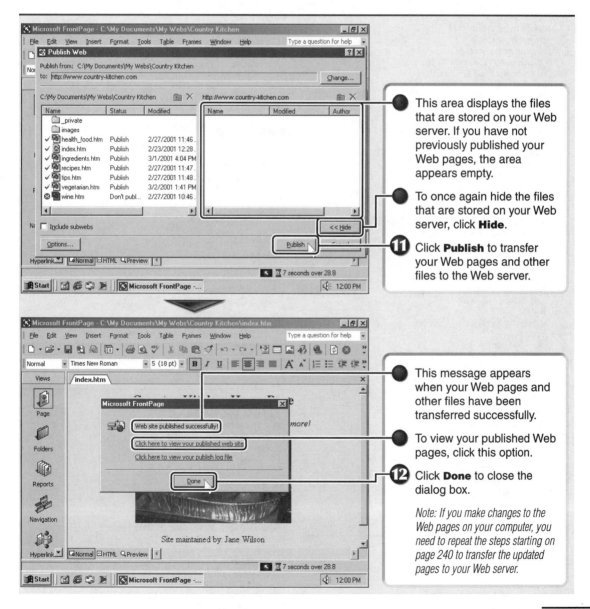

This area displays the files that are stored on your Web server. If you have not previously published your Web pages, the area appears empty.

To once again hide the files that are stored on your Web server, click **Hide**.

11 Click **Publish** to transfer your Web pages and other files to the Web server.

This message appears when your Web pages and other files have been transferred successfully.

To view your published Web pages, click this option.

12 Click **Done** to close the dialog box.

Note: If you make changes to the Web pages on your computer, you need to repeat the steps starting on page 240 to transfer the updated pages to your Web server.

INDEX

columns, in tables
add, 128-129
delete, 129
width, change, 130-131
to fit longest item, 131
combine cells, in tables, 132
confirmation pages
assign to forms, 187
create, 184-189
determine names of items on forms to, 184
remove, 189
connection speeds, view, 29
considerations, Web hosting services, 227-228
copy
formatting, 60
text, using
drag and drop, 42
toolbar buttons, 43
copyright information, specify, 236-237
correct one misspelled word, 47
create
blank Web pages, 15
confirmation pages, 184-189
folders, new, 216
frames, 148-149
image maps, 106-107
inline frames, 165
links
automatically, 109
e-mail, 114-115
automatically, 115
to frames, 156-157
to sounds or videos, 190-193
to Web pages, 108-109, 110-113
lists
bulleted or numbered, 64-65
definition, 63
with picture bullets, 66-67
photo gallery, 92-95
thumbnail images, 104
Web
pages, using templates, 16-17
sites, new, 8-9
crop images, 102-103
customize horizontal lines, 88-89

D

decrease indent, of text, 58
dedicated Web hosting services, 226
definition lists, create, 63
delete. *See also* **remove**
AutoShapes, 77
banner ads, 215
bookmarks, 111
captions, from tables, 133
check boxes, 173
clip art images, 82
columns, from tables, 129
drop-down boxes, 179
folders, 216
hover buttons, 211
images, 75
inline frames, 165

marquees, 207
option buttons, 175
photo gallery, 95
rows, from tables, 129
single characters, 27
tables, 127
tasks, 225
text, 27
text areas, 171
text boxes, 169
videos, from Web pages, 199
Web pages, 37
from navigational structure, 141
WordArt, 79
display. *See also* **view**
download time, for Web pages, 29
Folder List, 10
links, using Hyperlinks view, 118-119
Navigation Pane, 11
task panes, 20
different, 21
tasks, 222
toolbars, 14
Web pages
in Navigation view, 138-139
in Web browsers, 32-33
quickly, 33
domain name, registration, 227
download time
display, for Web pages, 29
estimated, as part of FrontPage window, 5
drag and drop, move or copy text using, 42
drop-down boxes, add, 176-179

E

edit and format, text, overview, 2
edit tasks, 223
effects, add
banner ads, 212-215
hit counters, 202-203
hover buttons, 208-211
change, 211
marquees, 204-207
change, 207
sounds
background, 194-197
links, create, 190-193
videos
change properties, 200-201
links, create, 190-193
to Web pages, 198-199
electronic mail. *See* **e-mail**
e-mail
links, create, 114-115
automatically, 115
publicize Web pages using, 229
use for form results, 180-183
enter text, 26
in tables, 127
estimated download time, as part of FrontPage window, 5
existing Web pages, add, to frames, 150-151

245

INDEX

INDEX

INDEX

Other Visual Series That Help You Read Less - Learn More™

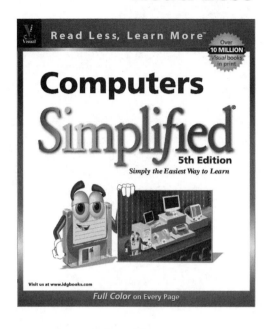

Simplified®

Teach Yourself VISUALLY™

Master VISUALLY™

Visual Blueprint

Available wherever books are sold

PC World—Winner of more editorial awards than any other PC publication!

Every issue is packed with the latest information to help you make the most of your PC — and it's yours risk-free!

Plus you will receive a FREE Hungry Minds/PC World CD wallet! It's perfect for transporting and protecting your favorite CDs.

Order Online Now!
www.pcworld.com/hungryminds

Send Today!

Here's how to order:

Cut and mail the coupon today to:
PC World, PO Box 37560, Boone, IA 50037-0560

- Call us at: (800) 825-7595

- Fax us at: (415) 882-0936

- Order online at: www.pcworld.com/hungryminds

YOURS FREE!